Christian Mission

 **McMaster Divinity College Press**
McMaster New Testament Studies Series

Patterns of Discipleship in the New Testament (1996)

The Road from Damascus: The Impact of Paul's Conversion on His Life, Thought, and Ministry (1997)

Life in the Face of Death: The Resurrection Message of the New Testament (1998)

The Challenge of Jesus' Parables (2000)

Into God's Presence: Prayer in the New Testament (2001)

Reading the Gospels Today (2004)

Contours of Christology in the New Testament (2005)

Hearing the Old Testament in the New Testament (2006)

The Messiah in the Old and New Testaments (2007)

Translating the New Testament: Text, Translation, Theology (2009)

Christian Mission

*Old Testament Foundations
and New Testament Developments*

edited by

STANLEY E. PORTER

and

CYNTHIA LONG WESTFALL

PICKWICK *Publications* · Eugene, Oregon

CHRISTIAN MISSION
Old Testament Foundations and New Testament Developments

McMaster New Testament Studies Series

Copyright © 2011 Wipf and Stock Publishers. All rights reserved. Except for brief quotations in critical publications or reviews, no part of this book may be reproduced in any manner without prior written permission from the publisher. Write: Permissions, Wipf and Stock Publishers, 199 W. 8th Ave., Suite 3, Eugene, OR 97401.

McMaster Divinity College Press
1280 Main Street West
Hamilton, Ontario, Canada
L8S 4K1

Pickwick Publications
An Imprint of Wipf and Stock Publishers
199 W. 8th Av.e, Suite 3
Eugene, OR 97401

www.wipfandstock.com

ISBN 13: 978-1-4982-5716-9

Cataloging-in-Publication data:

Christian mission : Old Testament foundations and New Testament developments / edited by Stanley E. Porter and Cynthia Long Westfall.

xii + 260 p. ; 23 cm. — Includes bibliographical references and indexes.

McMaster New Testament Studies Series

ISBN 13: 978-1-4982-5716-9

1. Missions—Biblical teaching. 2. Missions—History—Early church, cap. 30–600. 3. Mission of the church. I. Porter, Stanley E., 1956–. II. Westfall, Cynthia Long. III. Title. IV. Series.

BV2073 C5 2011

Manufactured in the U.S.A.

Scripture from the HOLY BIBLE, TODAY'S NEW INTERNATIONAL VERSION® TNIV® is copyright © 2001, 2005 by International Bible Society®. Used by permission of International Bible Society®. All rights reserved worldwide. "TNIV" and "TODAY'S NEW INTERNATIONAL VERSION" are trademarks registered in the United States Patent and Trademark Office by International Bible Society®.

Scripture from the REVISED STANDARD VERSION of the Bible, copyright © 1952 [2nd edition, 1971] And the NEW REVISED STANDARD VERSION of the Bible copyright © 1989 by the Division of Christian Education of the National Council of Churches of Christ in the United States of America. Used by permission. All rights reserved.

Contents

Preface / vii
Contributors / ix
Abbreviations / x

Introduction: Christian Mission: Old Testament Foundations and New Testament Developments—*Stanley E. Porter* and *Cynthia Long Westfall* / 1

1. "Declare His Glory among the Nations": The Psalter as Missional Collection—*Mark J. Boda* / 13
2. The Book of Daniel and the Roots of New Testament Mission—*Brian P. Irwin* / 42
3. Mark, Matthew, and Mission: Faith, Failure, and the Fidelity of Jesus—*Michael P. Knowles* / 64
4. A Light to the Nations: Isaiah and Mission in Luke —*Craig A. Evans* / 93
5. A Cord of Three Strands: Mission in Acts —*Stanley E. Porter* and *Cynthia Long Westfall* / 108
6. The Content and Message of Paul's Missionary Teaching —*Stanley E. Porter* / 135
7. Paul's Missionary Strategy: Goals, Methods, and Realities —*Eckhard J. Schnabel* / 155
8. The Hebrew Mission: Voices from the Margin? —*Cynthia Long Westfall* / 187
9. Bible and Mission: Missiology and Biblical Scholarship in Dialogue—*Michael W. Goheen* / 208

Modern Author Index / 237
Ancient Sources Index / 241

Preface

THE 2006 H. H. Bingham Colloquium in the New Testament at McMaster Divinity College in Hamilton, Ontario, Canada was entitled "Christian Mission: Old Testament Foundations and New Testament Developments." The Colloquium was the twelfth in a continuing series. At the Colloquium, scholars took the opportunity to exchange important perspectives on this contemporary but timeless New Testament theme. They presented the major issues in mission in the Bible, with a response from the perspective of contemporary missiology. An interested public attended, heard the papers, and responded with penetrating questions and comments. We hope that this volume will be of interest to general readers and serve as a useful textbook for the study of the biblical foundation and biblical theology of missions. We also trust that it makes a cogent contribution to the ongoing discussion of this important topic.

The Bingham Colloquium is named after Dr. Herbert Henry Bingham, who was a noted Baptist leader in Ontario, Canada. His leadership abilities were recognized by Baptists across Canada and around the world. His qualities included his genuine friendship, dedicated leadership, unswerving Christian faith, tireless devotion to duty, insightful service as a preacher and pastor, and visionary direction for congregation and denomination alike. These qualities endeared him both to his own church members and to believers in other denominations. The Colloquium has been endowed by his daughter as an act of appreciation for her father. We are pleased to be able to continue this tradition.

With this volume we continue publishing this series, now under the banner of McMaster Divinity College Press in conjunction with Wipf and Stock Publishers. Previous Colloquia published by Eerdmans in the McMaster New Testament Studies series include the following: *Patterns of Discipleship in the New Testament* (1996), *The Road from Damascus: The Impact of Paul's Conversion on His Life, Thought and Ministry* (1997), *Life in the Face of Death: The Resurrection Message of the New Testament*

(1998), *The Challenge of Jesus' Parables* (2000), *Into God's Presence: Prayer in the New Testament* (2001), *Reading the Gospels Today* (2004), *Contours of Christology in the New Testament* (2005), *Hearing the Old Testament in the New Testament* (2006), *The Messiah in the Old and New Testaments* (2007), and *Translating the New Testament: Text, Translation, Theology* (2009).

We would also like to thank a number of people for their particular contributions. First, we would like to thank the individual contributors for accepting the assignments, and for all their efforts in the preparation and presentation of papers that make a significant contribution of benefit to biblical scholars, missiologists, students of the Bible, and believers concerned about mission, all of whom should be engaged with this timely topic. We would also like to thank the staff and student helpers and volunteers at McMaster Divinity College, all of whom were integral in creating a pleasant environment and a supportive atmosphere. Thanks particularly go to Cathy Fraser and Virginia Wolfe, as well as Sean Adams, Matthew Lowe and Lois Fuller Dow. Finally, thanks to Cynthia Westfall's teaching assistant Beth Stovell, who put many hours into this project.

Both of us were co-chairs of the conference and edited this volume with the hope that it will bring important issues to light concerning Christian mission from its roots in the Old Testament to its beginnings and propagation recorded in the New Testament, and that the dialogue may flourish between biblical studies and missiology.

Stanley E. Porter
Cynthia Long Westfall
McMaster Divinity College
Hamilton, Ontario, Canada

Contributors

MARK J. BODA, Professor of Old Testament, McMaster Divinity College, Hamilton, Ontario, Canada.

CRAIG A. EVANS, Payzant Distinguished Professor of Biblical Studies, Acadia Divinity College, Wolfville, Nova Scotia, Canada.

MICHAEL W. GOHEEN, Geneva Professor of Worldview and Religious Studies, Trinity Western University, Langley, British Columbia, Canada, and Teaching Fellow in Mission Studies, Regent College, Vancouver, British Columbia, Canada.

BRIAN P. IRWIN, Assistant Professor of Old Testament and Hebrew Scripture, Knox College, Toronto, Ontario, Canada.

MICHAEL P. KNOWLES, George Hurlburt Professor of Preaching, McMaster Divinity College, Hamilton, Ontario, Canada.

STANLEY E. PORTER, President and Dean, and Professor of New Testament, McMaster Divinity College, Hamilton, Ontario, Canada.

ECKHARD J. SCHNABEL, Professor of New Testament, Trinity Evangelical Divinity School, Deerfield, Illinois, USA.

CYNTHIA LONG WESTFALL, Assistant Professor of New Testament, McMaster Divinity College, Hamilton, Ontario, Canada.

Abbreviations

AB	Anchor Bible
ABD	David Noel Freedman, ed. *The Anchor Bible Dictionary*. New York: Doubleday, 1992.
AGJU	Arbeiten zur Geschichte des antiken Judentums und des Urchristentums
ANE	Ancient Near East
ANET	James B. Pritchard, ed. *Ancient Near Eastern Texts Relating to the Old Testament*. Princeton: Princeton University Press, 1950.
ANRW	Hildegard Temporini and Wolfgang Haase, eds. *Aufstieg und Niedergang der römischen Welt: Geschichte und Kultur Roms im Spiegel der neueren Forschung*. Berlin: de Gruyter, 1972–.
BA	*Biblical Archaeologist*
BBR	*Bulletin for Biblical Research*
BECNT	Baker Exegetical Commentary on the New Testament
Bib	*Biblica*
BibSac	*Bibliotheca Sacra*
BIS	Biblical Interpretation Series
BNTC	Black's New Testament Commentaries
BZAW	Beihefte zur *ZAW*
BZNW	Beihefte zur *ZNW*
CBC	Cambridge Biblical Commentary
EBC	Expositor's Bible Commentary
EKK	Evangelisch-Katholischer Kommentar zum Neuen Testament
EQ	*Evangelical Quarterly*
ET	English Translation
FRLANT	Forschungen zur Religion und Literatur des Alten und Neuen Testaments

HSM	Harvard Semitic Monograph
HTKNT	Herders theologischer Kommentar zum Neuen Testament
HUCA	Hebrew Union College Annual
HNTC	Harper's New Testament Commentaries
ICC	International Critical Commentary
Int	*Interpretation*
JBL	*Journal of Biblical Literature*
JGRChJ	*Journal of Greco-Roman Christianity and Judaism*
JSNT	*Journal for the Study of the New Testament*
JSNTSup	Journal for the Study of the New Testament, Supplement Series
JSOT	*Journal for the Study of the Old Testament*
JSOTSup	Journal for the Study of the Old Testament, Supplement Series
JTS	*Journal of Theological Studies*
MAMA	*Monumenta Asiae Minoris Antiqua*. Manchester and London, 1928–1993.
mg.	margin
MNTS	McMaster New Testament Studies
NICNT	New International Commentary on the New Testament
NIGTC	The New International Greek Testament Commentary
NIV	New International Version of the Bible
NovT	*Novum Testamentum*
NovTSup	Novum Testamentum Supplements
NRSV	New Revised Standard Version of the Bible
NSBT	New Studies in Biblical Theology
NTD	Das Neue Testament Deutsch
NTS	*New Testament Studies*
NTSup	New Testament Supplement
OTL	Old Testament Library
PAST	Pauline Studies
PBM	Paternoster Biblical Monographs
RAC	*Reallexikon für Antike und Christentum*. Edited by T. Kluser et al. Stuttgart, 1950-.
RB	*Revue Biblique*
RHPR	*Revue d'histoire et de philosophie religieuses*

RSV	Revised Standard Version of the Bible
SBG	Studies in Biblical Greek
SBLDS	SBL Dissertation Series
SBS	Stuttgarter Bibelstudien
SBT	Studies in Biblical Theology
SJT	*Scottish Journal of Theology*
SNTSMS	Society for New Testament Studies Monograph Series
SP	Sacra Pagina Series
TCGNT4	Metzger, Bruce M. *A Textual Commentary on the Greek New Testament. A Companion Volume to the United Bible Societies' Greek New Testament 4th Revised Edition*. Second Edition. Stuttgart: Deutsche Bibelgesellschaft, 1994.
TJT	*Toronto Journal of Theology*
TNTSI	The New Testament and the Scriptures of Israel
TOTC	Tyndale Old Testament Commentary
VT	*Vetus Testamentum*
WBC	Word Biblical Commentary
WTJ	*Westminster Theological Journal*
WW	*Word and World*
WUNT	Wissenschaftliche Untersuchungen zum Neuen Testament
ZAW	*Zeitschrift für die alttestamentliche Wissenschaft*

Introduction

Christian Mission

*Old Testament Foundations
and New Testament Developments*

Stanley E. Porter *and* Cynthia Long Westfall

The colloquium topic of "Christian Mission" focused on answering the question: "How did a first-generation Jewish messianic movement develop the momentum to become a dominant religious force in the Western world?" It was answered by investigating the roots of the mission in the Old Testament and Second Temple Judaism, by finding the core and the call in the mission of Jesus to the Jews and Gentiles, and by documenting the spread of mission in the apostolic missionary activity in Acts, Paul's ministry to the Gentiles documented in his epistles, and the Hebrew mission reflected in the Johannine literature, Hebrews, and the General Epistles. This perspective was also seen as the foundation of the continuing missiological work of the Christian church. As a result, this conference was able to reach back into the background of what was to become the Christian mission, and reach forward through the New Testament to the continuing Christian mission.

The first two chapters, by Mark Boda and Brian Irwin, focus on the Old Testament roots of mission. These essays have a definite correlation with the fourth chapter, by Craig Evans, which explicitly explores the Old Testament in the New Testament in Luke–Acts. Boda's chapter investigates the mission of God in Psalms in relation to the nations of the world. He notes that key mission passages in the New Testament cite Psalms as a "key source for the early church's understanding of the gospel of Christ (the Messiah will suffer and rise from the dead on the third day), but also for the early church's understanding of mission." Boda is primarily interested in the inclusive vision in Psalms for all nations on earth. He first looks at the theology of the nations in the Psalms and then examines the relevant structure of Psalms, or what he calls "the thematic and linear context of the book." He finds God's rule over all the earth to be fundamental to the theology of the nations in Psalms. God rules the nations, and the nations' acts of rebellion against God and his people challenge his rule. The response of praise is a particular sign of the inclusive vision of mission in both Israel's proclamation to the nations and the praise of the nations themselves. Boda then takes a canonical approach to analyze the treatment of the nations by those who gave the canon its final shape. Examining the doxologies of the five books of Psalms, he concludes that "everlasting praise to Yahweh is the *telos* of this book," but, even more, he asserts that one can detect a development of the theme of Yahweh, king, people, and the nations in the rhetorical structure of the book. The role of the messiah figure is developed as key to God's rule, but this figure also functions as a priest and servant. The book ends with the focus shifting between the privilege of Zion and the praise of the nations. Boda concludes by offering several key implications for Christian missiology that he draws from the Psalms, where he reformulates his argument into a call and a challenge to those who follow the Servant in mission.

In the second chapter, Brian Irwin explores the model of the kingdom in the book of Daniel and its implications for what it means to be a church in relationship with culture. He asserts that the arrival of the kingdom of God (which is wherever God rules) was the defining message of Jesus' ministry. He suggests that the idea of the kingdom of God in the Gospels is imbedded in the Old Testament, and offers Daniel as "an often-overlooked illustration of what it means to live in the world as members of the kingdom." He looks at narratives of engagement with culture in the first six chapters of Daniel, and finds a cycle of interaction between God, the faithful, and the alien culture: *crisis>vindication>royal acknowledgment of God>promotion*. Five repetitions of the cycle reveal an unseen kingdom where God is the omnipotent ruler who visibly and invisibly rescues his people who are striving to live faithfully in a foreign world. After a transition in Daniel 7, which shows a series of four kingdoms with the final kingdom destroyed and replaced by the kingdom of God, the three visions in the second half of the book convey the era of persecution without immediate vindication that is characteristic of the condition of God's people during the first three kingdoms. Irwin concludes that Daniel portrays no single way to live as members of the kingdom of God in relationship to an alien and hostile culture. Instead, sometimes engagement is possible, but at other times, engagement is impossible because the kingdoms of the earth are hostile and unreceptive. Irwin then finds correspondences between Daniel's images of the kingdom and the images of the kingdom in the New Testament, which sometimes are actually drawn from the book of Daniel. He notes the New Testament use of Daniel's portrayal of the kingdom in times of persecution in Revelation and Matthew. He finds remarkable consistency between Daniel's portrayal of the kingdom in times of engagement and the parables that portray the hidden reality and the growth of the kingdom. Engagement is also demonstrated in actions and teaching. Irwin concludes with a caution against applying the wrong model inappropriately. Instead, God's people should be "appropriately reflective regarding themselves and society and careful in thinking about how best they should act out their identity as members of God's kingdom."

In the third chapter, Michael Knowles examines missiology in Mark and Matthew in terms of religious identity. The question that Jesus asks his disciples, "Who do people say that I am?" (Mark 8:27), finds its counterpart in the question: "Who do the Gospels say that *we* are?" Knowles finds a series of meaningful theological linkages in key passages that answer this question. After Mark's programmatic opening statement, "The beginning of the gospel of Jesus Christ, son of God" (Mark 1:1), Mark reports Jesus' mission as a direct expression and re-assertion of the divine reign. It constitutes a call into being a new community with a new identity (Mark 1:14–15). It is therefore clear from the beginning that God initiates and sustains the kingdom and the disciples' mission. The call of the first four disciples (Mark 1:16–20) is immediate, specific, and individual, rather than being generic or nationalistic, and is the product of Jesus' mission and initiative (the mission, therefore, can never be the cause of the kingdom). The conditions of discipleship are revealed in the choosing of the Twelve (3:13–19); they are a renewed Israel chosen to be with Jesus and sent out to imitate Jesus in proclamation, exorcism, and healing. In the commissioning of the Twelve (6:7–13), the instructions about what they should take when they go out shows that God may be relied on to furnish their needs. There are parallels to the conditions of Israel's wilderness journeying. In Mark, after the initial success of the disciples, they are more noted for their failures, depicted in a three-fold cycle that represents the failure of Jesus' word and preaching in them in terms of mission, ministry, and discipleship. Their condition is depicted in the three failed sowings in the Parable of the Sower, and this is confirmed by features of thematic content and specific wording. Mark, therefore, relativizes human or ecclesiastical agency in the foundation and growth of the mission and kingdom—"only the authority of Jesus makes mission possible in the face of human inadequacy and hardhearted or uncomprehending discipleship."

Knowles's study of Matthew concentrates on points of departure from Mark, where Matthew's missiology is most evident at his conclusion instead of at the beginning, as in Mark. In addition, instead of emphasizing the disciples' presence with Jesus, Matthew emphasizes his presence with *them*, which emerges in the naming of the infant Jesus, Jesus' instructions to the church, and his departing words of commissioning for ministry. The disciples are charged with the imitation and continuation of Jesus' ministry, but the disciples' attempts to do this end in abject failure, so that the actual fulfillment of the responsibility appears to lie in the life of the community to and for which the evangelist writes, which Knowles places in the post-70 "dark shadow of abortive revolt and the catastrophic destruction to which it led." Matthew's emphasis on the enabling presence of Christ is relevant for today's resource-rich church and the implicit cultural imperialism of much of Western missiology, while Mark provides a timely message for a contemporary church with triumphalist tendencies.

Craig Evans demonstrates in chapter 4 that the global Christian missionary movement in Luke–Acts is rooted in the prophetic Scriptures of Israel, particularly Isaiah. He shows that important words and phrases from Isaiah appear in the song of Mary (the Magnificat), the song of Zechariah (the Benedictus), the song of Simeon (the Nunc Dimittis), and the account about Anna. Furthermore, the infancy narratives provide a rough foundation for the scriptural themes in the inaugural proclamations of John and Jesus, the missionary commissions, and the proclamation of the apostles. The John the Baptist narrative is reminiscent of temporal notices in the prophets, and extends Mark's quotation of Isaiah 40 to include a passage that foreshadows salvation for the Gentiles. In

Jesus' proclamation in the Nazareth synagogue, we are given an edited text from Isaiah 61 and a sermon. The editing of Isaiah and the interpretative illustrations from the ministries of Elijah and Elisha make it clear that Luke understands Isaiah 61 as proclaiming good news for the Gentiles as much as for ethnic Israel. In the missionary commissions, there is an allusion to two passages in Isaiah that say that forgiveness of sins is to be preached "to all nations" or "all Gentiles," and the goal of the witness and mission "to the end of the earth" repeats a phrase from Isa 49:6. Additionally, Isa 49:6 predicts "I will give you a light to the nations," and provides a theme that runs through the book of Acts, particularly in the accounts of Paul's conversion and the Jerusalem Council. Paul's application of the passage to the mission to the Gentiles is explicit at points and confirmed along the way. Evans concludes with an epilogue concerning two fourth-century inscriptions on the so-called Tomb of Absalom about Zechariah and Simeon that refer to Isa. 49:6. Evans has demonstrated that the prophecy of Isaiah, and particularly that of Isa 49:6, plays a foundational role from beginning to end in Luke–Acts.

Chapter 5, on mission in Acts, by Stanley Porter and Cynthia Westfall, focuses on the particular contribution of Acts to the understanding of mission in the New Testament.[1] While Evans shows the connection between Old Testament prophecy and the global mission in Luke–Acts, Porter and Westfall show how Luke demonstrates the continuity between Jesus' mission, the Jewish mission of the apostles, and the mission of Paul in Luke–Acts. In Acts, Luke places the focus of the two-volume work on the legitimacy of Paul's mission. The conclusion of Luke and the beginning of Acts firmly establish the continuity between Jesus' mission and the Jewish mission of the twelve disciples, which underscores their appointment to function as witnesses to Jesus' suffering and resurrection and his mission. This is then picked up in Paul's conversion. The paper begins by showing that the continuity between Paul's mission and the Jewish mission (composed of the Palestinian Jews and the Hellenistic Jewish Christians from the Diaspora) is created by certain parallels, including similar appointments to witness, the baptism of the Holy Spirit, the lives of the disciples who were transformed by encounters with the resurrected Jesus, the extension of the gospel to Gentiles, and revivals that began to intentionally target Gentiles for conversion. According to

---

1. This paper was not read at the colloquium, but has been added in order to include a commensurate and necessary focus on the contribution of Acts to Christian mission.

Luke in Acts, before Paul and Barnabas were ever sent out, the features of the Pauline mission were already present in the Jewish mission, resulting from direct divine guidance, and having historic precedence, apostolic approval, and the confirmation of signs and wonders. Luke then shows that Paul grasped the special significance of what it meant to be the apostle to the Gentiles in a way that pressed the church's boundaries into new and challenging areas. In terms of strategy, Paul is depicted as bringing a sense of system and order to the spread of the gospel to both Jews and Gentiles. His strategy invariably involved first establishing contact in the synagogues with the Jews who had similar religious and ethnic backgrounds to his own, before moving to the Gentiles. "To the Jew first and then to the Greek" (Rom 1:16; 2:9, 10) was his slogan. Three missionary speeches in Acts show how he fashioned the content appropriately for his audiences, speaking as a Jew to the Jews or as one born and reared in the Hellenist world to the Greeks, laying an appropriate foundation, positively utilizing the audience's background, and establishing common ground to bridge who they were and the message he wanted to bring. Luke effectively validates Paul's mission by showing its continuity with Jesus' mission and the Jewish mission, and further demonstrates how Paul effectively built upon the other two foundations.

In chapter 6, Stanley Porter examines the content and message of Paul's missionary teaching in the epistles. He offers an overview of the various approaches and recent proposals concerning Paul's expectations for his churches' engagement in mission, and concludes that we still have some distance to go in the journey of discovering Paul's missionary content. He finds one foundational passage that indicates the substance of Paul's missionary preaching, 2 Cor 5:20. This verse is in the conclusion of 2 Cor 5:11–21, one of Paul's four major reconciliation passages. Thus, the notion of God's reconciling actions provides the context for Paul's discussion of himself and his followers as persuaders for the gospel. Porter finds exegetical support for his interpretation of 2 Cor 5:20 in a closer analysis of the text. Rather than portraying himself as an ambassador to the Corinthians, Paul calls them all ambassadors on behalf of Christ. The exhortation is addressed to those to whom the Corinthian believers are ambassadors. The content of the message is: "We are pleading on behalf of Christ that you be reconciled to God." This is a call to the still unconverted world. The implications involve the substance of the teaching and how it encapsulates Paul's missionary message for others. As far as substance, reconciliation is at the heart of Paul's gospel, and there is a transfer of responsibility to the Corinthians to become ambassadors on behalf of the cause of God's reconciling activity. Reconciliation encapsulates Paul's message by addressing the human predicament as sinners deserving God's wrath, through the language of sacrifice for the forgiveness of sins, and in the reconciliation of Jews and Gentiles. Therefore, in its very formulation, 2 Cor 5:20 is central to the content of Paul's missionary teaching.

In chapter 7, Eckhard Schnabel explores the goals, methods, and realities of Paul's missionary strategy in the epistles. He breaks out the most pertinent aspects of Paul's missionary strategies in great detail by close exegesis of a number of key passages. Paul's missionary work targeted audiences on a number of fronts. His geographic strategies can be summarized as traveling the major and minor Roman roads from city to city, and preaching in a variety of milieus to reach areas in which the gospel had never been proclaimed. As far as claims about Paul's urban strategies, Schnabel stops short of claiming an exclusively "metropolitan mission" for Paul, asserting that, while Paul targeted cities, he reached smaller towns and villages as well. His social strategies included contacts with members of the ruling class and elite, some of whom were converted. However, in both his ethnic and social strategies, he deliberately disregarded the traditional social and cultural categories and classifications, because the gospel concerned everyone without regard to any human classifications. Schnabel also describes a "local strategy" where the early Christian mission was closely connected to private houses for a number of pragmatic reasons.

In addition to strategy, Schnabel discusses the communication of the gospel. Paul entered the local synagogue as an experienced interpreter of Scripture, but deliberately dispensed with the behavior and rhetoric expected of "orators" by the educated Gentiles, so that the hearers' faith would rest on the power of God rather than on human wisdom. The preaching of a crucified Savior made it impossible to employ the traditional rhetorical methods in Paul's strategy of persuasion. Furthermore, Paul regarded God as the primary communicator, while he himself and other apostles were messengers or ambassadors. Paul's message and subject matter were determined by his focus on Jesus. His topics included: turning from idols to serve the true and living God, the death and resurrection of Jesus, the identity of Jesus as Messiah, *Kyrios*, and Savior, the coming day of judgment, and the return of Jesus. Paul was aware that as a messenger, his personal credibility was important and his credentials included rabbinic training, Roman citizenship, his behavior, his ministry, and his personal relationships with the people who had come to faith through him. Paul's Jewish and Gentile audiences would have found certain aspects of his teaching extraordinary. The teaching had a variety of responses, ranging from conversion to overt persecution. Though some elements of the message were attractive to both groups, the primary obstacles to communication included Paul's central emphasis on a crucified Savior as well as the resurrection. With his Jewish audience, there was also an acceptance break-down over the incorporation of Gentiles into God's people without circumcision. Of course, the goal of missionary proclamation is the conversion of Jews and pagans to faith in Jesus Messiah, Savior, and Lord.

Cynthia Westfall examines the Jewish Christian mission to the Jews in chapter 8. She analyzes the Hebrew mission through the lenses of the terminology of contemporary mission statements: identity, vision, values, and strategy. The earliest Christians did not see themselves as distinct from Judaism, and at first showed limited concern for a mission to the Gentiles, though by the time the Pauline mission began the Hebrew mission had been actively reaching Gentiles. The Hebrew mission was centered in Jerusalem, which was the home base for the apostles' mission trips and where the Jerusalem Council set policy for missions. The Hebrew Christian corpus consists of Matthew, Hebrews, the Johannine literature (including Revelation) and the rest of the general epistles, all of which traditionally and textually have apostolic associations, with the exception of Hebrews, which is anonymous. The circumstances in which the Hebrew mission operated were conflict and opposition due to the "parting of the ways" with Judaism and conflict with the Roman government. This led to a tighter self-definition and shaped the corpus. The Hebrew mission proclaimed a gospel contextualized for the Jews and/or primarily informed by and oriented to Judaism, though it continued to convert Gentiles as well as Jews. The message(s) of the Hebrew mission included the universal need for Christ and the identification of Jesus as the Messiah and its implications. The development of Christology is the greatest theological contribution of the Hebrew corpus and Christology defined the circle of membership. Furthermore, the Hebrew corpus brought forward powerful statements and terminology that applied

Israel's Old Testament identity to the church. Hebrews, 2 Peter, and Revelation are particularly concerned with the vision of mission—they are concerned with the future and inspiring believers to move forward. The corpus is united in stressing that the values of holiness and reverence are integral to the proclamation of the mission. The mission strategies include other approaches besides explicit and direct proclamation, and there is an overriding conviction that God is responsible for the conversion of the Gentiles. Suffering, proclaiming a sense of identity in the face of adversity, and experiencing martyrdom have a crucial role in witness—participating in the sufferings of Christ is a normal experience. Sometimes it is claimed that Jewish Christianity failed, but that is to misunderstand its significant contributions forged under great adversity, as well as its goals and vision.

In chapter 9, Michael Goheen takes up the challenge of responding to the colloquium papers by setting up a dialogue between the participants and key themes that are current in mission studies. Goheen suggests that older understandings of the biblical material on mission are inadequate and that there is a growing awareness of our missionary calling in our own culture as well as abroad. The dramatic rise of the Majority World church and the marginalization of the church in the West have reframed our understanding and opened up new interpretive categories that allow us to see new things in the text. To address this, Goheen employs a number of key themes. The first theme is the meaning of mission as participating in the *missio Dei*. He affirms Westfall's application of "mission statements" that speak of purpose and identity as a helpful interpretive category for identity and purpose, asserts that Knowles has built his paper on the notion of *missio Dei*, and flags a number of insights that contribute to important themes concerning God's mission.

The second theme is missionary dimension and intention. Goheen attempts to resolve a potential tension between Porter and Westfall's narrow and broader definitions of mission by suggesting that we affirm the validity of evangelism and intentional missionary activities as essential and yet distinctive activities within the total mission of the church.

The third theme is mission and evangelism, which are often distinguished from each other in mission studies. Goheen accepts evangelism as a central and indispensable dimension of the church's larger mission, with which he frames Porter's primary concern for evangelism, yet questions if reconciliation in 2 Cor 5:20 is the only image or whether we can find other fresh and powerful images in the twenty-first century to interpret the fullness of salvation.

A fourth theme is the contemporary distinction between mission, which is sometimes applied to the entire task of the church, and missions, as the specific task of making Christ known where he is not yet known. By detailed interaction with Paul's mission in Schnabel, Porter, and Westfall, as well as the references to global mission in the Old Testament highlighted by Boda and Evans, Goheen agrees that missions is not just another part of mission that stands alongside of others, but is the ultimate horizon of the whole missionary task of the church. However, Goheen challenges biblical scholars to work through how we can appropriate and continue the New Testament's missionary concern in imaginative and creative ways in new contexts and cultural settings. Goheen concludes by summarizing the centrality of mission to the biblical story, and the importance of that story as a model for missionary encounter with culture. Goheen traces the centrality of mission in the Old Testament through Boda's chapter on Psalms and Evans's chapter on Luke's use of Isaiah, and adds it to the three-fold connection between Jesus' mission, the Jewish mission, and Paul's mission in Porter and Westfall. He argues that this overarching missional purpose of God must be grasped for a consistent missional hermeneutic.

Finally, in discussing the importance of a model for missionary encounter with culture, Goheen interacts with the theme of suffering in Westfall's chapter on the Hebrew mission and the theme of resistance of idolatrous power in Irwin's paper on Daniel, and affirms Irwin's concern about the church's application of the wrong model in the relationship of church and culture—different contexts call for different responses. Goheen concludes with a call to a two-way dialogue between biblical scholarship and mission studies rather than a relay-race where the biblical scholar determines what the text means and then passes along the complete package to the missiologist who, in turn, transposes those meanings into the contemporary situation, making them relevant. Rather, biblical scholars need to bring to the text an awareness of, and have a concern for, the key issues of mission studies.

As in previous years, all of the papers (except for Porter and Westfall's on Acts) were presented in their oral form at the colloquium,[2]

---

2. Porter and Westfall's "A Cord of Three Strands" was presented by Porter and

where they generated questions, comments, and dialogue among the contributors and with the general audience at the conclusion of each paper. The colloquium then concluded with a panel discussion that invited a more extensive interaction between the contributors and the audience. As became clear in the ensuing dialogue, Goheen's significant and developed contribution, cautions, and call to dialogue between missiology and biblical studies has been heard, so that perhaps we have made progress together in that area.

Westfall at McMaster Divinity College's Theological Research Seminar (31 October 2006), where there was even more opportunity for interaction with the audience. We are grateful that Michael Goheen so graciously adjusted his response to interact with this additional paper.

1

"Declare His Glory among the Nations"

The Psalter as Missional Collection[1]

Mark J. Boda

INTRODUCTION

MISSION IS NOT IMMEDIATELY what comes to mind when most Christians think of the worship of Israel. Instead, most have images of exclusive access to the tabernacle (later temple) precincts, with admission open to the priestly-levitical personnel and closed to the rest of Israel, let alone the Gentiles. The multitude of ritual instructions and laws suggest a liturgical system that repels rather than invites worshippers.

For the early church, however, the Psalms were filled with evidence of the mission of God through Christ. This is highlighted in the closing pericope of the Gospel of Luke in which Christ reminds his disciples of his teaching: "Everything must be fulfilled that is written about me in the Law of Moses, the Prophets and the Psalms" (Luke 24:44).[2] What "must be fulfilled" and "is written about me" is then rehearsed: "The Messiah

---

1. My interest in studying the Old Testament in earnest was sparked in a missiology course I took with the late Professor Harvey Conn at Westminster Theological Seminary. He was the first to show me the potential of the Old Testament for exploring a Christian biblical theology of mission. This paper is dedicated to his memory with thanks to God for the opportunity to hear such teaching of the mission of God in redemptive-history.

2. Biblical citations in this paper usually will be from the TNIV, although at times I will use my own translation. The verse numbers will follow the English versification.

will suffer and rise from the dead on the third day, and repentance for the forgiveness of sins will be preached in his name to all nations, beginning at Jerusalem" (Luke 24:46–47). Here the Psalms are highlighted not only as a key source for the early church's understanding of the gospel of Christ (the Messiah will suffer and rise from the dead on the third day), but also for the early church's understanding of mission (repentance for the forgiveness of sins will be preached in his name to all nations, beginning at Jerusalem).[3] Here, at the end of the Gospel of Luke, the role envisioned for the Psalms is played out in the rest of the New Testament. It is, as Moyise has written, "together with Isaiah—the most extensively used Old Testament book."[4]

The purpose of this chapter is to investigate afresh the book of Psalms in order to present its treatment of the mission of God, especially in relation to the nations of the world. This presentation will look to both the thematic and linear context of the book. That is, it will present a theological synthesis of this theme in the book, but also trace the linear development of this theme in the final rhetorical structure of the book as a whole. It will be discovered that the worship of the Psalter is emphatically international in its scope.

SYNTHESIS

The Reign of Yahweh over the World

The vast majority of references to the nations in the book of Psalms are found in psalms focused on the reign of Yahweh in this world. Thus, the belief that Yahweh rules over all the earth is foundational to the theology of the nations in the Psalms and, as a result, all the nations must submit to him. The declaration in Ps 22:27 that "All the ends of the earth will remember and turn to the LORD, and all the families of the nations

---

3. Earlier in Luke 24, Jesus talks with two disciples on the road to Emmaus. The Gospel writer tells us that "beginning with Moses and all the Prophets, he explained to them what was said in all the Scriptures concerning himself" (Luke 24:27). This explanation is in response to Jesus' question: "Did not the Messiah have to suffer these things and then enter his glory?" (24:26). The focus there appears to be on the gospel of Christ (his death, resurrection, ascension) with no mention of the mission of his followers. In Luke 24:44–49, however, when the topic broadens to include the mission to "all nations," the source now expands from "Moses and all the Prophets" (24:27) to "the Law of Moses, the Prophets and the Psalms" (24:44).

4. Moyise and Menken, eds., *Psalms in the New Testament*, 2.

will bow down before him" is based on the fundamental belief articulated in 22:28 that "dominion belongs to the LORD and he rules over the nations."

1. Sphere of God's Rule over the World

According to the psalmists, God's rule cannot be limited to the land promised to Abraham, but rather extends over all the earth. Psalm 47 calls him "the great king over all the earth" (v. 2) and "the King of all the earth" (v. 7), while Psalm 97 proclaims him as "the LORD of all the earth" (v. 5). This is why "his kingdom rules over all" (Ps 103:19), why he is "exalted over all the nations" (Ps 113:4), and why he "makes war cease to the ends of the earth" (Ps 46:9). The Davidic king who, as we will soon see in detail, rules as vice-regent of the divine King (Ps 2), has been granted a dominion that extends "from sea to sea ... from the River to the ends of the earth" (Ps 72:8), an extent that is described in the same psalm as encompassing "all kings" and "all nations" (Ps 72:11). Furthermore, Yahweh's claim is that he not only owns the world (Ps 50:12: "for the world is mine, and all that is in it"), but also claims the nations as his inheritance (Ps 82:8: "for all the nations are your inheritance").

2. Centre of God's Rule over the World

This "Mighty One, God, the LORD," who "speaks and summons the earth from the rising of the sun to where it sets," does so "From Zion, perfect in beauty," as we are told in Ps 50:1–2. Zion is Yahweh's holy mountain and is identified with his sanctuary through which there is access to his heavenly royal throne room.[5] Psalm 2 makes it clear that from there his rule extends to the nations. As Ps 99:1–3 declares:

> The LORD reigns,
>   let the nations tremble;
> He sits enthroned between the cherubim,
>   let the earth shake.
> Great is the LORD in Zion;
>   he is exalted over all the nations.
> Let them praise your great and awesome name—
>   he is holy.

It is from his sanctuary that he declares his royal battle plans to defeat the nations (Ps 108:7).

---

5. Cf. Kraus, *Theology of the Psalms*, 76.

It is also to Zion that all the nations will come to express their submission to Yahweh the king. This submission is demonstrated in the assembling of the nations to worship the Lord in Zion (Ps 102:21–22; cf. 7:7–8). It is to the temple that Ps 68:29 tells us "kings" and Ps 76:11 tells us "all the neighboring lands" will bring their tribute to the Lord. To Zion will come the envoys of Egypt and Cush to express their submission to God (Ps 68:30–31), expressed in imperial imagery that resonates with the descriptions of the ancient empires.[6]

3. Signs of God's Rule over the World

Yahweh's divine rule over this world is displayed in four ways. First, his rule is seen in his ability to subdue the nations in battle. In the ancient Near East in general and Israel in particular, the one who is the warrior is the one who is king.[7] Psalms related to the Zion tradition are filled with confident declarations that God's reign is expressed in his ability to subdue the nations in battle, especially when the nations attack Jerusalem (Pss 2; 46; 48). So also in Ps 10:16, the declaration that "The Lord is King for ever and ever" is the basis for the confident hope that follows: "the nations will perish from his land." This section of Psalm 10 introduces a second sign of Yahweh's rule and that is his exercise of justice in this world,[8] affirming in vv. 17–18 that: "You, Lord, hear the desire of the afflicted; you encourage them, and you listen to their cry, defending the fatherless and the oppressed." This link between kingship and justice is

---

6. With this theology in mind, one can understand the pain that Israelite captives felt at singing the songs of Zion in exile in a foreign land subjugated by the nations (Ps 137). Such songs celebrated Zion as the place of God's rule over the nations with Israel by his side.

7. This theology is made explicit in that ancient hymn of Exod 15, which begins with the praise of God as warrior: "The Lord is a warrior; the Lord is his name" (15:3) and ends with the praise of God as king: "The Lord reigns for ever and ever" (15:18).

8. The link between kingship and justice is seen elsewhere in the ANE. For example, Hammurabi calls himself the "protecting king," declaring in the conclusion to his great ancient legal code: " . . . I am the salvation-bearing shepherd, whose staff is straight, the good shadow that is spread over my city; on my breast I cherish the inhabitants of the land of Sumer and Akkad; in my shelter I have let them repose in peace; in my deep wisdom have I enclosed them. That the strong might not injure the weak, in order to protect the widows and orphans . . . in order to declare justice in the land, to settle all disputes, and heal all injuries . . . " *ANET,* 164. The same emphasis can be seen in the role expected of the king in Israel (2 Sam 8:15; 12:5–6; 14:4–20; 1 Kgs 3:28; Isa 9:7; 11:1–5; 16:5; 32:1; Jer 23:5; 33:15; cf. Isa 42:1–7; 61:1–3).

also highlighted in Ps 146:7–9, which provides an extensive list of the kinds of actions expected of the just Divine King:

> He upholds the cause of the oppressed
>   and gives food to the hungry.
> The LORD sets prisoners free,
>   The LORD gives sight to the blind,
> The LORD lifts up those who are bowed down,
>   The LORD loves the righteous.
> The LORD watches over the foreigner
>   and sustains the fatherless and the widow,
>   but he frustrates the ways of the wicked.

The list is followed immediately by the declaration: "The LORD reigns forever, your God, O Zion, for all generations" (146:10).[9] Yahweh's rule is thus not only signaled by his success in battle (divine Warrior), but also by his administration of justice (divine Judge). This emphasis on God's role as judge of the nations is ubiquitous in the Psalms. His people cry out to him to "Rise up, O God, judge the earth, for all the nations are your inheritance" (Ps 82:8; cf. Pss 7:6–11; 9:19–20; 94:2; 96:13; 97:9). "The assembled peoples gather" around the one "enthroned on high," so that Yahweh may judge the peoples (Ps 7:7–8).[10] God's judgment is to be seen as an exercise of his justice as Ps 98:9 makes clear: "Let them sing before the LORD, for he comes to judge the earth. He will judge the world with righteousness and the peoples with equity." This emphasis on justice is a hallmark of the kingship psalms in Psalms 93–100, as Zenger has noted: "In all of them the universal reign of Yahweh is in view, which consists

---

9. Clearly this psalm is focused on divine kingship as it contrasts the human royals who are ephemeral and incompetent (Ps 146:3–4) with the divine royal who is eternal and faithful.

10. In Ps 82:1 "God presides in the great assembly; he gives judgment among the 'gods.'" This appears to be drawn from a depiction of God in his divine council where the other divine beings in the court are being judged. It is possible that these divine beings are being demoted to ephemeral status because of disobedience and that this is related to the nations in that these were deities over particular nations. It may also be that the metaphor of the divine council is being used to speak about the rulers of nations over whom Yahweh declares his authority. See further Morgenstern, "Mythological Background," 32–34; Mullen, *Divine Council*, 230; Tate, *Psalms 51–100*, 334; VanGemeren, "Psalms," 533; with thanks to my former student Andrew McGinn and his thesis, "Divine Council and Israelite Monotheism."

primarily in the realization of justice (מִשְׁפָּט) in the sense of a just and life-affirming world order."[11]

Yahweh's kingship is displayed in his acts of war and his decisions of justice, but also in the third sign: his handiwork in creation. Psalm 8 is typical of this theme when the psalmist declares: "LORD, our Lord, how majestic is your name in all the earth" (Ps 8:1, 9). This majesty appears to be linked not only to the created order, but more particularly to the vice-regency of humanity on earth (v. 6).

The final sign of Yahweh's rule on earth is his vice-regent in Zion, that is, the rule of the Davidic king. By placing Yahweh and his anointed king regularly in parallel lines throughout Psalm 2, the psalmist makes it clear that Yahweh has designated his anointed one as his vice-regent on earth. Thus, to rise up and band together against Yahweh is to do so against "his anointed" (v. 2). These nations are bound by "their chains" and "their shackles" according to v. 3, as "their" is a reference to Yahweh and his anointed. The only way for the nations to respond is to submit to both Yahweh and his anointed, that is, to "Serve the LORD with fear" and to "Kiss his son" (vv. 11–12). The king attains this status because of the declaration of Yahweh: "You are my son; today I have become your father" (2:7), a declaration that is echoed in Ps 89:27 ("I will appoint him to be my firstborn, the most exalted of the kings of the earth"). In Psalm 110 the status is linked to the appointment of the royal figure to priesthood: "You are a priest forever, in the order of Melchizedek" (110:4), an appointment that ensures that Yahweh "will extend your mighty scepter from Zion, saying, 'Rule in the midst of your enemies'" (110:2). These psalms lay the foundation for the consistent portrayal throughout the Psalter of the submission of the nations to the human king in Zion (Pss 18:43–44, 47–49; 45:5, 17; 72:8–11, 17; 144:2).

4. Basis for Yahweh's Rule

Yahweh's rule over the world is based on several of his qualifications. His status as Creator and Sustainer of the cosmos is foundational to his rule. This is seen clearly in Psalm 33 in which the submission of the nations to Yahweh (v. 8), Yahweh's control over the plans of the nations (v. 10), and his omniscient rule over all humankind (vv. 13–15) are all based on his role as Creator of the entire cosmos (vv. 6–7, 9) and each human being

---

11. Zenger, "Psalm 87," 169.

(v. 15). Psalm 86:9 reminded the ancient Israelites that Yahweh had made even "all the nations" and this is why they would worship him.[12]

In the kingship psalms (Pss 93–100) Yahweh as Creator is closely linked to his kingship (Pss 93; 96:5, 9–10). In Psalm 93 the claim that "the LORD reigns" is based on the establishment of the world (93:1). This language of establishment is echoed in 93:2 in the phrase "Your throne was established long ago." Special reference is made in 93:3–4 to the "lifting up" of the seas and "the thunder of the great waters," but these are no match for the might of Yahweh on high (93:4). The connection between the creation of the world and his control over the nations is forged by what appears to be an allusion to the imagery of God's control over the unruly forces of chaos. As God's rule over creation was established by his control over the chaos forces of the waters, so his rule endures through his control over the chaos forces of the nations.[13] Thus in Ps 96:9–10 the declaration among the nations that "The LORD reigns" is immediately linked to the fact that "The world is firmly established, it cannot be moved" and that "he will judge the peoples with equity."

Yahweh's creative act, however, is not the only basis for his universal rule over the nations. It is also his enduring omniscient superintendence of all creation from the vantage point of the heavenly court that qualifies him for kingship. It is because his throne is established in heaven that the psalmist can claim "his kingdom rules over all" (Ps 103:19). From such a height Yahweh "looks down and sees all humankind . . . watches all who live on earth . . . considers everything they do" (Ps 33:13–15; cf. 113:4). From there he looks for those among the nations who might be faithful to his reign (Ps 53:2), but also for those who might rebel (Ps 66:7).

5. SUMMARY

The reign of God is fundamental to the Psalter's theology of the nations. Yahweh's reign extends over the entire world from his capital in Zion and to his throne the nations come to submit to his rule. His rule over the nations can be discerned in his victorious battles, gracious justice,

---

12. See Deut 32:8, which speaks of Yahweh apportioning territory for the nations.

13. See especially Ps 65:7 where Yahweh is depicted as the one "who stilled the roaring of the seas, the roaring of their waves, and the turmoil of the nations," and Ps 144:7 where the psalmist creates a parallel between "from the mighty waters" and "from the hands of foreigners"; cf. Booij, "Psalm 87," 24, who confirms the link between the "traditional motif" of "the raging of nations and kings against Zion" and "the mythical theme of the sea raging against Yahweh" (citing Pss 46:4; 65:8).

creative handiwork, and Davidic vice-regent and is based on his status as Creator and Sustainer of the cosmos.

Challenges to the Reign of God

Often psalms dealing with Yahweh and the nations appeal to the "wrath" of God. This is most often linked to acts of rebellion by the nations against God and his people. His anger in Ps 7:6–8 is to "rise up against the rage of my enemies" and his wrath in Ps 79:6 is directed against "the nations that do not acknowledge you, on the kingdoms that do not call on your name." As "righteous judge" of the world, God "displays his wrath every day" (Ps 7:11). In the two key Zion Psalms, 2 and 110, it is the wrath of the divine and human king in Zion that is aroused by the rebellious challenge of the nations (Pss 2:12; 110:5).

This rebellion is often depicted as political insurrection against Yahweh and sometimes also against his anointed king in Zion (Pss 2; 46; 48; 66:7; 68:12, 14; 144:7, 10). In these psalms God is depicted as or called upon to defeat and exact devastating judgment upon the rebellious nations. He is one who will "bring down" (Ps 56:7), "punish" (59:5), "discipline" (94:10), "judge" (110:5–6) and even "scoff at" (59:8) the nations and their kings. At times the punishment of the nations is carried out by human agents. It is before the Davidic king that "foreigners cower" (18:43–44), beneath his feet that "nations fall" (45:5) and under him that Yahweh subdues nations (144:2). In Psalm 149 this extends to "the people of Zion" (v. 2; "all his faithful people," in v. 9) who "inflict vengeance on the nations and punishment on the peoples" with the praise of God "in their mouths and a double-edged sword in their hands" (vv. 6–7).[14]

The point of conflict is identified in certain psalms as the contrast between the "plans of the nations" and the "purposes of the peoples," and the "plans of the LORD" and the "purposes of his heart" (Ps 33:10–11; cf. Psalm 2). The psalmists regularly identify the "nations" as the "enemy," the "adversary," and the "wicked" (Pss 7; 9; 10; 18; 56; 59; 83; 110).[15] They are those who attack the people of God and in doing so arouse the Lord's wrath. The nations are also recipients of the Lord's discipline because

---

14. So also in Ps 118:10–12, the psalmist declares that he cut down all the nations who surrounded him. It is unclear whether this is declared by a royal figure or not.

15. Kraus, *Theology of the Psalms*, 125–36, distinguishes between the enemy of the nation and the enemy of the individual, but one must be careful since the psalms in this list refer to the enemy of an individual as the nations.

they are those "who do not acknowledge ... do not call on" him (Ps 79:6) or who "forget God" (Ps 9:17).

Such a depiction of the nations' challenge to the reign of God formed a fixed component in the foundational narrative of Israel. The defeat of the nations (Egypt) is essential to the salvation of Israel from Egypt and the gift of a land in Canaan (Pss 77:14–15; 78:43, 55; 80:8; 81:10; 89:10; 105:38, 44; 111:6; 135:8–12; 136:10–22). Yahweh is celebrated as the God who "performs miracles" and displays his power "among the peoples" (77:14). Such displays of power among the nations are seen as promoters of the exaltation of God on earth. Psalm 46 declares that the nations are in uproar and the kingdoms fall as God brings an end to war through his powerful reign. This leads in v. 10 to the call: "Be still and know that I am God; I will be exalted among the nations, I will be exalted in the earth."

It is this declaration that offers the first glimpse of a positive vision for the nations in the Psalter. The goal of God's punishment and discipline of the nations is that he might be exalted among the nations.

Signs of the Exaltation of God among the Nations

1. THE PRAISE OF THE PEOPLE OF GOD AMONG THE NATIONS

Not surprising for a book that is entitled "Praises" (*Tehillim*), the Psalter identifies oral praise as the key sign of the exaltation of God among the nations. In the first place, the people of God are to consider the nations as the context of their expressions of praise. In Psalm 9, the psalmist encourages the people to "Sing the praises of the LORD, enthroned in Zion; proclaim among the nations what he has done" (9:11). In Psalm 18, after the Davidic king exalts the "God who avenges me, who subdues nations under me, who saves me from my enemies," he says: "Therefore, I will praise you, LORD, among the nations; I will sing the praises of your name" (vv. 47–49). Israel's response to God's salvation, especially rescue from its enemies, is to praise God "among the nations" (Pss 57:9; 105:1; 108:3–4).[16]

---

16. See Eaton, *Kingship*, 182–85. Eaton has an interesting section entitled: "The king as God's witness to the world." Whether one agrees with his view that the individual in the Psalter is most often a royal figure, he has identified the importance of witness in the psalms: "From the uniquely rich experience that the king has of God, he must bear witness for him before the congregation and in principle before all the world" (183). He does note that this role for the king is evident in the broader ancient Near Eastern world: "In Mesopotamia also there is stress on the king's task as proclaimer of his deity's

2. Praise, Revelation, and Proclamation of the People of God

At times in the Psalter the vocabulary of praise is linked to the vocabulary of knowledge and proclamation. Thus to "sing the praises of the LORD" in 9:11 is parallel to "proclaim among the nations what he has done." After expressing hope in God's salvation of Israel and punishment of the nations, the psalmist declares in Ps 59:13: "Then it will be known to the ends of the earth that God rules over Jacob." Praise is linked to making known God's ways and salvation on earth among all nations in 67:2. Psalm 96 probably expresses this best. It begins with the call to "sing to the LORD, all the earth" (96:1), but then transitions to "Proclaim his salvation day after day. Declare his glory among the nations, his marvelous deeds among all peoples" (96:2–3). The praise of God is thus a form of revelation and even proclamation to and among the nations. The content of that proclamation is the reign, glory, and mighty acts of God (cf. Pss 79:10; 96:9–10; 98:2; 102:21–22; 105:1).

3. The Praise of the Nations

This call to praise and proclaim God among the nations, however, is not limited to the people of God, but rather in many cases is directed towards the nations themselves. The call to "Clap your hands, all you nations; shout to God with cries of joy" in Ps 47:1 is linked in v. 2 to God's kingship over all the earth and his subduing of nations under Israel's feet. This becomes a dominant theme in the kingship psalms (Pss 93–100) with their calls to "Sing to the LORD, all the earth" (96:1), "Ascribe to the LORD, all you families of nations, ascribe to the LORD glory and strength" (96:7–8), "Shout for joy to the LORD, all the earth . . . shout before the LORD, the king" (98:4–6; 100:1; cf. 96:1, 9–10; 97:1; 99:1–3). The psalmists thus regularly envision the nations and their rulers declaring the praise of God, often as a sign of their submission to his rule (Pss 66:1–2, 4; 67:3–5; 68:32; 86:9; 117; 138:4–5; 148:11; 150:6).

This praise of the nations is often linked to the salvation and blessing of Israel, and it is such praise that is to be a motivation for God to redeem and bless his people. This is expressed strongly in Psalm 67, at the heart of which is the depiction of universal praise of God among the nations (vv. 3–5):

---

glory to all the peoples, among the gods, and for ever" (185, noting the words of the Hittite king Hattussilis III).

> May the peoples praise you, God;
>> may all the peoples praise you.
> May the nations be glad and sing for you,
>> For you rule the peoples with equity
>> and guide the nations of the earth.
> May the peoples praise you, God;
>> may all the peoples praise you.

Surrounding this central image, however, is the prayer for God's blessing, clearly leveraging language from the Aaronic blessing of Num 6:24–26 (vv. 1, 6):[17]

> May God be gracious to us and bless us
>> and make his face shine on us—
>> so that your ways may be known on earth,
> Your salvation among all nations.
> ...
> The land yields its harvest;
>> God, our God, blesses us.
> May God bless us still,
>> so that all the ends of the earth will fear him.

Similarly, in Psalm 48, God's rescue of Zion against the onslaught of its enemies extends God's praise "to the ends of the earth," and in Psalm 117 God's great love and faithfulness toward Israel is the foundation for the call to the nations to praise the Lord. At times concern is expressed that when God fails to act there is danger that God's reputation will be maligned among the nations, highlighted by the apostrophic statement: "Where is their God?" (Pss 79:10; 115:2). The blessing and redemption of Israel, therefore, is a catalyst for the praise of the nations, both as they observe this salvation (Ps 98:2) and hear of it through the praises of Israel (cf. Pss 46; 102:15; 126:1–3).

There is, however, one other catalyst for the praise of the nations, and it is the evidence of God's character in creation itself. This is expressed most succinctly in Ps 97:6 which reads: "The heavens proclaim his righteousness, and all peoples see his glory."

---

17. See Kaiser, *Mission*, 60–63. However, I disagree with Kaiser's claim that here "the psalmist has directly applied what the high priest Aaron and his fellow priests bestowed on the nation Israel to all the peoples and nations on earth" (31). Rather, God's blessing of Israel is to prompt the praise of the nations.

4. Praise and Submission among the Nations

While the response of the nations is dominantly praise in the Psalter, there are other types of responses registered as well. Wise nations and their rulers will "Serve the LORD with fear and celebrate his rule with trembling" (Ps 2:10–12) and it is this "fear" and "reverence" that can be traced regularly throughout the Psalter (Pss 33:8; 67:7; 102:15). Psalm 22 envisions "all the ends of the earth . . . all the families of the nations" remembering, turning to, and bowing down before the LORD (22:27–29). This is the vocabulary not only of submission (bowing down), but also of covenant (remembering, turning to). This evidence reminds us that the psalmists envision a response to Yahweh that is more than just lip service.

These indications of a deeper connection between the nations and Yahweh help us to make sense of several passages in the Psalter in which the nations are given identities that one would expect were reserved exclusively for Israel. For instance, Ps 47:8–9 declares "God reigns over the nations; God is seated on his holy throne. The nobles of the nations assemble as the people of the God of Abraham, for the kings of the earth belong to God; he is greatly exalted." In a psalm that has celebrated God's subjugation of nations under Israel's feet (47:3), the nations are first of all given access to God's royal assembly. This theme of the pilgrimage of the nations is seen elsewhere in the Psalter (Pss 86:9; 96:7–9; 102:22),[18] but a surprising feature of Psalm 47 is that here they are afforded the same status "as the people of the God of Abraham" (v. 9).

A similar privilege is afforded the nations in Ps 72:17. In this psalm, which prays for and celebrates Israel's human king, the psalmist ends with the universal impact of his reign: "all nations will be blessed through him, and they will call him blessed." Here one can discern an echo of the fulfillment of the Abrahamic blessing in Gen 12:1–3, but the king of Israel is identified as the one through whom this blessing will be finally realized.

The third example of this close connection between the nations and Yahweh is Psalm 87.[19] The psalmist begins by celebrating Zion, which is

---

18. Booij, "Psalm 87," 24.

19. See Zenger, "Psalm 87," 123–60, for a superb summary of the various views on the referents in this psalm: whether Diaspora Jews, individual proselytes, or the nations. Zenger argues superbly for the last view; cf. Booij, "Psalm 87," 16–25, here 23–24: "In Ps. lxxxvii we certainly meet a remarkable view of the relationship of nations to the 'holy

identified clearly as Yahweh's city, the holy mountain, a city that he loves more than any other in Israel. What follows, however, is the declaration that Rahab (Egypt), Babylon, Philistia, Tyre, and Cush all not only "acknowledge" Zion (or Yahweh), but also are given the status of having been born in Zion (what one author calls: "theological citizenship").[20] The significance of the mention of Rahab and Babylon at the outset is highlighted by Zenger:

> Rahab and Babylon are plainly mythical figures of violence and war. That they are now named in first position is connected with the symbolism, as well as with the fact that they were the two great forces of destruction for Zion. With their "conversion" to Yahweh, which Yahweh personally "decides" and announces (Ps 87:4), the renewal of all the nations of the world begins.[21]

Although there is considerable debate over the identity of the first person voice of v. 4, v. 6 declares clearly that "the LORD will write in the register of the peoples: 'This one was born in Zion.'" There could be no greater identity than the place of one's birth. Here Zion is the place of identity for the nations.

5. Nations and the Punishment of Israel

Interestingly, at times the nations are actually used by God as agents and locations for the discipline of his people. Thus, rather than being the object of his wrath, they are the purveyors of his wrath. The bitterness of the psalmist's cry of Ps 79:1 that "the nations have invaded your inheritance" is heightened by the fact that he links the disaster to God's wrath in v. 5: "How long, LORD? Will you be angry forever?" This anger is clearly traced to the sin of Israel: "Do not hold against us the sins of past generations; may your mercy come quickly to meet us" (v. 8).[22] The great penitential prayer of Psalm 106 clearly outlines the role of the nations as locations for God's disciplinary program: "He gave them into the hands

---

city.' No doubt, in other psalms too the nations have a strong orientation towards Zion; but this orientation is ambivalent . . . more often than not the nations figure as strangers and adversaries."

20. Zenger, "Psalm 87," 126.

21. Ibid., 156.

22. Contrast this with Ps 44:11, which sees the scattering among the nations (v. 11) as unrelated to the sin of Israel (v. 17).

of the nations, and their foes ruled over them. Their enemies oppressed them and subjected them to their power" (106:41, cf. 106:26–27, 47).

Summary

What the psalmists grant us is a vision of God's universal rule over the cosmos. Yahweh is not the localized god of Canaan, but rather the God of all nations. Commenting on Psalm 117, McCann summarizes this universal emphasis when he writes:

> What is particularly noteworthy is that the invitation is extended to "all you nations" and "all you peoples," not just to Israel or to Judah or to some group of the faithful. Praise inevitably pushes toward universality, toward the transcendence of barriers. It is the "mode of existence" God desires for *everybody!* [23]

His rule is to be recognized among the nations and obeisance is expressed usually through the nations' praise. While the nations are the objects of the judgment of God, especially as they challenge God's rule, the nations are also invited to find their identity in this universal God of Israel. The way this identity is expressed makes it clear that the nations are invited to participate in Israel's identity, rather than find their own avenues for connection to Yahweh. This challenges the conclusion of Martin-Achard, who sees the call to the nations to glorify God as based on the realm of creation, rather than a sharing in Israel's faith.[24]

The people of Israel are consistently called to the proclamation of Yahweh through their praise and adoration among the nations. As Kraus has written: "Israel has the task of telling Yahweh's deeds and miracles among the peoples and of bearing witness to them . . . Israel calls the peoples to praise Yahweh . . . for the God of Israel is the Lord and king of the peoples."[25] The created order itself also universally bears witness to Creator Yahweh.

The theme of the nations is thus ubiquitous in the Psalter and, through it, we catch a glimpse of an inclusive vision for all nations on earth. We also catch a glimpse of the mission of Israel as those who proclaim Yahweh's rule among the nations through their praise. Thus,

---

23. McCann and McCann, *Theological Introduction*, 56.
24. Martin-Achard, *Light to the Nations*, 58; with thanks to Kaiser, *Mission*, 29.
25. Kraus, *Theology of the Psalms*, 59.

for Kraus, the Psalter clearly identifies the mission of Israel among the nations:

> The Psalms are witness to the reality of Israel, even there where individual voices are raised Israel is Yahweh's first partner, a people chosen, caught up in and enclosed in community and in faithfulness to the covenant. It is the first answer, the first witness. None other than the God of this people is the king of all peoples. The "meaning" of Israel's existence is the mission to the peoples.[26]

STRUCTURE

To this point we have investigated the theme of the nations in a synthetic way, seeking to penetrate the ideological viewpoint of the Psalter as a whole. Now, however, we turn to analyze the final rhetorical structure of the Psalter as a whole to discern how the nations are treated by those responsible for taking up the Psalms, permeated by this theology of the nations, and creating its final canonical shape.[27]

Redactional Doxologies

It has long been noted that the book of Psalms is divided up into five sections called "books."[28]

Book I	Psalms 1–41
Book II	Psalms 42–72
Book III	Psalms 73–89
Book IV	Psalms 90–106
Book V	Psalms 107–150

---

26. Ibid.

27. It will become obvious that my views here are heavily dependent on the extensive work undertaken by several key interpreters over the past two decades, especially Wilson: Wilson, *Editing*; Wilson, "Use of Royal Psalms"; Wilson, "Shaping the Psalter"; Wilson, "Understanding the Purposeful Arrangement"; McCann, *Shape and Shaping*; McCann, "Books I–III"; McCann and McCann, *Theological Introduction*; Mays, "Torah-Psalms"; Smith, "Theology of the Redaction of the Psalter"; Miller, "Beginning of the Psalter"; Anderson, "Division and Order"; Mays, *The Lord Reigns*; Lohfink and Zenger, *Der Gott Israels*; Lohfink and Zenger, *God of Israel*; deClaissé-Walford, *Reading*; deClaissé-Walford, *Introduction*; cf. review of scholarship in Howard, "Editorial Activity," and critiques in Nasuti, *Defining the Sacred Songs*; Whybray, *Reading*.

28. For the earliest testimony to the fivefold division of the Psalter in both Jewish and Christian writings see especially Gese, "Entstehung," and Jacquet, *Psaumes*, 1:72–73.

A perusal of the final verses of the psalms at the ends of Books I–IV in the Psalter reveals striking similarities:

> Ps 41:13
> Blessed be Yahweh, the God of Israel,
> 　from everlasting to everlasting.
> Amen and Amen.

> Ps 72:18–19
> Blessed be Yahweh God, the God of Israel,
> 　who alone does marvelous deeds.
> Blessed be his glorious name forever;
> 　may the whole earth be filled with his glory.
> Amen and Amen.

> Ps 89:52
> Blessed be Yahweh forever.
> Amen and Amen.

> Ps 106:48
> Blessed be Yahweh, the God of Israel,
> 　from everlasting to everlasting.
> Let all the people say, "Amen!"

Common features include:

1. "Blessed be" (ברך): Pss 41:13; 72:18, 19; 89:52; 106:48
2. "Yahweh, God of Israel" (יהוה אלהי ישראל): Pss 41:13; 72:18; 106:48
3. "Forever/everlasting" (עולם): Pss 41:13; 72:19; 89:52; 106:48
4. "Amen" (אמן): Pss 41:13; 72:19; 89:52; 106:48

For the majority of the past century, scholars generally have treated these four passages as doxologies placed at the end of each book of the Psalter, claiming either that the doxologies were later redactional insertions,[29] or that because there was a doxology in each of these psalms, they were candidates for the final position in each book.[30] That they

---

29. Riedel, "Redaktion"; Kissane, *Psalms*, 1:ix, 2:173; Dahood, *Psalms 1–50*, xxx–xxxii, 253; Dahood, *Psalms 51–100*, 185, 320; Dahood, *Psalms 101–150*, 77; Anderson, *Psalms*, 1:27; Kidner, *Psalms 1–72*, 4; Rogerson and McKay, *Psalms*, 1:3; Kraus, *Psalms 1–59*, 1:16–21.

30. Weiser, *Psalms*, 21, 99–101, 345, 504, 683; Mowinckel, *Psalms*, 2:193–94, 197, 199; Westermann, *Praise and Lament*, 250–58. Briggs and Briggs, *Psalms*, 1:83, suggests that

represent redactional activity is suggested by evidence of disconnection between the doxologies and their respective psalms. For instance, Psalm 72 is a prayer to God for the king, focusing on the potential of the human royal through a series of jussives. The doxology, however, switches the verbal form to the passive participle and makes no mention of the king. There is greater dissonance in Psalm 89, which ends with deep and bitter lament over God's abandonment of the "anointed one" (89:50–51) before the abrupt transition to the pithy and positive doxology of praise. The doxology in Psalm 106 also does not match the concluding cry for help in v. 47.[31] Assuredly that cry is for God to "save us . . . and gather us from the nations . . . that we may give thanks (ידה) . . . and glory (שׁבח) in your praise (תהלה)," but the terms used do not match the root ברך that is a consistent feature in the doxologies. The only doxology that may be related to its respective psalm is Ps 41:13, which appears at the end of a psalm that looks to God for mercy. In this one case, however, it is not necessary to the psalm. The evidence favors the view that the doxologies are later redactional insertions. The diversity in the forms of the doxologies, however, suggests that these doxologies were not created all at once, but rather represent common doxologies used at various stages in the development of the Psalter as a written collection.

The absence of a doxology at the end of the final book of the Psalter has been variously explained. Long ago Riedel argued that in an earlier phase the Psalter concluded at Psalm 135, with 135:19–21 serving as the final doxology and Psalms 136–150 representing a later appendix to the Psalter.[32] This potential final doxology in Ps 135:19–21 does use the verbal root ברך ("blessed") as in the other doxologies, and comes at the end of a psalm that uses the root הלל ("praise") at the outset (135:1–3). Notwithstanding this evidence, most scholars have argued that Psalm 150 serves as the concluding doxology.[33] Wilson, however, has challenged this consensus by identifying Psalms 146–150 as a grand finale and finds its motivating force in the final verse of Psalm 145, v. 21,

---

the theory that doxologies were used at the end of every psalm was not accepted by scholars because of the lack of evidence.

31. See Zenger, "Psalms 90–106," 165 n. 7, for a superb response to Gese's denial of Ps 106 as the conclusion to Book IV; cf. Gese, "Entstehung," 159–64.

32. Riedel, "Redaktion," argued that 135:19–21 represented the final doxology. Psalms 136–150 formed an appendix to the Psalter.

33. Nearly all cited above see this point, e.g., Mowinckel, *Psalms*, 2:196.

where David "calls forth this great paean of praise with his exhortation."[34] A close look at Psalm 145:21 reveals that it not only employs the verbal root ברך ("blessed"), but also the term עוֹלָם ("everlasting"), which is common to the doxologies. In addition, it makes reference to the name יהוה (Yahweh) and to שֵׁם קָדְשׁוֹ ("his holy name"), the latter reminiscent of the שֵׁם כְּבוֹדוֹ ("his glorious name") in the doxology of Psalm 72:19. The lack of the phrase אֱלֹהֵי יִשְׂרָאֵל ("the God of Israel") is not unusual since it is missing in the doxology of Psalm 89 and the absence of the term אָמֵן ("Amen") is not odd since Psalm 145 is technically not the end of the final book, but rather an introduction to the collection in Psalms 146–150. Thus, although Ps 135:19–21 may have been an earlier concluding doxology to the Psalter, Ps 145:21 is most likely the "missing" doxology, functioning now as an introduction to the finale of praise in Psalms 146–150.[35]

The Doxologies and the Nations

The doxologies are important to the theological message of the Psalter as a whole. The consistent use of the verbal root ברך ("blessed"), the term עוֹלָם ("everlasting") and the covenant name Yahweh in each of the doxologies sets the tone for the theme of this book called *Tehillim* (Praises) in Hebrew. The doxologies are a constant reminder that the ultimate *telos* of the book is the enduring and everlasting praise of Yahweh. Even as the reading community and individual encounter the darkest of the laments within this book, there is the constant reminder that it is praise that is the expected outcome. Westermann noted this long ago in his analysis of the forms of the Psalter, when he suggested that the two fundamental forms of expression to God in the Psalter were lament and praise. For Westermann, the pendulum was always swinging back towards praise, that is, even in the darkest of the psalms, there is an element of praise.[36] Brueggemann expressed this with his Ricoeurian cycle of worship that

---

34. Ibid., 189.

35. The suggestion of Riedel, "Redaktion," is much less probable, as the formula at the end of Ps 135 reveals little similarity with that of the other doxologies.

36. Westermann, *Praise and Lament*, 75: "in the Psalms of the O.T. there is no, or almost no, such thing as 'mere' lament and petition . . . By nature it cannot be *mere* petition or lament, but is always underway from supplication to praise."

always circles around past Disorientation to New Orientation in order to return to Orientation.[37]

While these elements of similarity set the tone for the book as a whole, one should not overlook the points of dissimilarity. On the one side, in three of the doxologies Yahweh is identified explicitly as the "God of Israel," giving pride of place to Israel as a nation through whom God is revealed to the world. This Yahweh is known as the particular God of Israel. On the other side, in two cases there is a universal tone to the doxologies: Ps 72:19 expresses the hope that the whole earth may be filled with his glory and Ps 145:21 that every creature may bless his holy name.

Thus, as one moves through the Psalter at regular intervals, there is the reminder that everlasting praise to Yahweh is the *telos* of this book, that the character of this God deserving of this praise is made known through Israel, and that this praise is to involve every nation and all creation.

Redactional Seam Psalms

As noted earlier, Psalm 145 plays a key role at the end of the Psalter. This observation is accentuated further by Wilson's argument that Psalm 145 forms a bracket with Psalm 1 around the Psalter as a whole. The wisdom Psalm 1 introduces the reader to the Psalter with both a blessing and a warning, differentiating between the "wicked" and the "righteous." Psalm 145 concludes the Psalter and also reveals close affinities with the wisdom tradition with its careful acrostic pattern. As Psalm 1 opens the Psalter with blessing to the righteous and curse to the wicked, so Psalm 145 ends on the same note in v. 20, reminding the readers that "The LORD watches over all who love him, but all the wicked he will destroy." Wilson also notes affinities between Psalm 144 and Psalm 2, creating an inner bracket to reinforce the Psalms 1/145 inclusio around the collection as a whole. In both Psalms 2 and 144 there is emphasis on a royal figure who is not only rescued from the attacks of foreigners (2:1–6, 9; 144:7, 10–11), but also given authority over the nations (2:8, 10–12; 144:2). Both end with the declaration of "blessing" (אשרי) of those connected to Yahweh (2:12b; 144:15). This evidence suggests that the Psalter begins and ends with double psalm units.

---

37. Brueggemann, *Message of the Psalms*, 15–23; Brueggemann and Miller, *Psalms*.

That Psalms 1–2 function as a united introduction to the Psalter is suggested by several pieces of evidence.[38] First, the lack of superscriptions on these two psalms distinguishes them among the psalms of Book One (MT). The two other instances where a superscription is missing in Book One are Psalms 10 and 33. In both cases there is clear evidence that the Psalm without the superscription was originally joined to the previous psalm, with Psalm 10 completing the acrostic begun in Psalm 9 (see LXX where Psalms 9–10 are one psalm) and with Psalm 33 functioning as a response to Psalm 32 (compare the final verse of Psalm 32 with the opening verse of Psalm 33). The lack of superscription on Psalm 2 suggests its cohesion with Psalm 1, while the lack of superscription on Psalm 1 suggests the role of this unified complex as introduction to the Psalter as a whole. Secondly, the two psalms are closely related lexically יָשַׁב (sit//dwell; 1:1//2:4), הָגָה (meditate//conspire; 1:2//2:1), דֶּרֶךְ (path; 1:6//2:12), אָבַד (destroy; 1:6//2:12), and especially אַשְׁרֵי (blessed; 1:1//2:12), the last creating a bracket around the two-psalm complex.[39]

Recent scholars have highlighted as well the final rhetorical character of the Psalms that are placed at the end of each of the books of the Psalter and that conclude with the doxologies, that is, Psalms 41, 72, 89, 106. If we were to take these psalms then that comprise the rhetorical skeleton of the Psalter (1–2, 41, 72, 89, 106, 144–145, 146–150), what would it have to say about the theme of the nations?

Seam Psalms and the Nations

A close look at this rhetorical skeleton provides a snapshot of the structural message of the Psalter as a whole that highlights the relationship between Yahweh, the king, the people of Israel, and the nations.[40]

---

38. See Wilson, *Editing*; Creach, *Yahweh as Refuge*, 77–80; Sheppard, *Wisdom*, 139–40; Mays, "Torah-Psalms," 3–12. However, Creach's treatment of this issue subverts the emphasis of Ps 2 to that of Ps 1, rather than see the theme of Ps 1 as foundational to the presentation of the royal house in Ps 2 as, for instance, Brownlee, "Psalms 1–2."

39. For this list, see Creach, *Yahweh as Refuge*, 78, and Sheppard, *Wisdom*, 139–40. In some early manuscripts of the book of Acts, the citation of Ps 2:7 in Acts 13:33 is considered to be from the "first psalm" and in some Hebrew manuscripts Ps 1, though present and initial, is unnumbered and the enumeration begins with our Ps 2. For this see Wilson, *Editing*, 204 and Willis, "Psalm 1."

40. For this I largely agree with Wilson, *Editing*, and McCann and McCann, *Theological Introduction*, 41–50, but find that they limit the role of the monarchy a bit too much in the latter section of the Psalter, transferring the prerogatives of the royal house to the people of Israel as a whole. The development of the theme of kingship

Psalm 1 is a wisdom psalm encouraging the way of righteousness, which is the way of Torah, while condemning the way of wickedness. Psalm 2, on the other hand, is a royal Zion psalm, often traced to a coronation liturgy. In light of the evidence that we have seen elsewhere in the Psalter (see above), that is, that the "wicked" and "enemy" are often linked together and also are regularly identified as the nations, it is very likely that Psalm 1 encourages the royal figure of Psalm 2 to walk in the way of Torah, that is, the way of the righteous, confident that the way of the wicked will be destroyed.[41] Psalm 2 then completes this picture with the actual coronation ceremony.[42] As a double-psalm complex, Psalms 1–2 picture the messianic figure as one who is deeply rooted in the Torah and who will endure even in the midst of the nations. The messianic figure will be "blessed" for delighting in the Torah of Yahweh (1:1). So also "all who take refuge in him" will be blessed (2:12b). It may be that the reference to "all who take refuge" is to the people of Zion or God, but it is interesting that the immediate antecedent appears to be "you kings . . . you rulers of the earth" in v. 10. Furthermore, although there is a strong warning about the destruction of the "wicked" at the end of Psalm 1 (אבד), by the end of Psalm 2 such destruction (אבד) can be averted by submission to the king.

At the end of Book One in the Psalter is the "Davidic" Psalm 41. The psalm does not particularly refer to the royal house beyond the superscription, but does focus on "those who have regard for the weak," a role that was connected with the royal house in ancient Israel and the ancient Near East (see above).

Psalm 72, at the end of Book Two, however, is clearly a royal psalm, praying that the king would be endowed with God's justice and righteousness. This psalm, connected with Solomon (in the superscription),

---

suggests that the royal house needed to understand that their reign found significance only in and through the reign of God. Zenger appears to retain a larger role for the king than Wilson, but still distinguishes between the "messianic program" of Pss 2–89 and the "theocratic program" of Pss 90–150 (Zenger, "Psalms 90–106," 161).

41. Many have suggested that the final stanza of Ps 2 (vv. 10–12) was added when Pss 1–2 were combined; Creach, *Yahweh as Refuge*, 78; Zenger, "Psalms 90–106," 161 n. 2. If this is sustained, then it would support the view that the foreign nations are identified as the "wicked."

42. Brownlee, "Psalms 1–2," 321–36, sees Pss 1–2 as originally a coronation liturgy, using Deut 17:14–20 and the call to read the law by the king; cf. Bardtke, "Erwängungen"; Lipiński, "Macarismes"; Wilson, *Editing* ; contra Willis, "Psalm 1."

envisions the king ruling throughout the world and then in the end bringing blessing to the nations.

With Psalm 89 it is clear that the great hopes expressed in Psalm 72 have been dashed. Clearly the hope of the Davidic covenant is the exaltation of the Davidic scion over all the kings of the earth, but instead of this, the nations taunt the royal figure now in exile. The psalm ends with an emphasis on the mockery of the "anointed one." This appearance of the term מְשִׁיחֶךָ ("your anointed one") to close Psalm 89 creates an inclusion with the opening Psalm complex of Psalms 1–2 and is the reason that Psalms 1–89 have been referred to as the "Messianic Psalter."[43]

Many have noted a radical shift of emphasis in Book Four in the Psalter. The book opens with the cry of "Moses" at the outset before the focus shifts clearly on to the divine kingship of Yahweh (without reference to David) in the Kingship Psalms of Psalms 93–100. These psalms continue to emphasize Zion (97:8; 99:2), reminding the readers that the "holy mountain" (99:9) is still the center of God's dominion. In Psalms 101–103, David's voice re-emerges, confessing his commitment to "be careful to lead a blameless life" (101:2) and "to silence all the wicked in the land" (101:8). The cry is for God to have compassion on Zion (102:13), which will lead to the submission of the nations (102:15–17, 21–22). David even leverages the time of Moses (103:7–12) as the basis for present grace, declaring in the end that "the Lord has established his throne in heaven, and his kingdom rules over all" (103:19). Book Four finishes with the recital of the pre-monarchic history of Israel in Psalms 104–106, ending with the cry of Israel among the nations in exile in the "seam" at Psalm 106. In Book Four, thus, there is a shift away from the role of the messianic figure and onto the role of Yahweh as king as the people long for a return from the discipline of the exile among the nations. Neither Zion nor David is lost in this book, but Moses and his era are given first and last word, with David confessing the failures of his line and expressing the hope for a new era of grace akin to the Mosaic period.[44]

With Psalm 107, we move into Book Five and listen in on the people celebrating their escape from exile (Psalm 107). Early on there is a reappearance of hope in the Davidic covenant, not only in the re-

---

43. Zenger, "Psalm 87," 159–60. I do not agree with Zenger's view that Ps 106 democratizes the Davidic covenant (cf. textual reading "your servants" in Ps 89:50 [51]). This does not explain the singular "anointed one" in v. 51 [52].

44. For this see Zenger, "Psalms 90–106," 190.

appearance of "Davidic psalms," but more importantly the placement of the key Royal Zion Psalm, Psalm 110. Here the themes of Psalm 2 are reiterated, but the emphasis shifts to the Davidic king as a priest: "You are a priest forever, in the order of Melchizedek." This new role is demonstrated in the inclusion of a long Davidic collection in Psalms 138–145, a collection that ends with those two key psalms, Psalms 144 and 145, identified earlier as the final bracket of the Psalter because of their links to Psalms 1–2. In Psalm 144, David is depicted as the great warrior trained by Yahweh who "subdues peoples under" him (144:2). It is clear throughout that Yahweh is the one who must act on David's behalf; David is powerless without Yahweh coming down to "scatter the enemy" (144:5–6). In Psalm 145, David truly fulfils the role set out in Psalm 110: he is now the priestly prompter of praise. The prompting is not just directed at Israel, but also at the nations of the earth: "Let *every* creature praise his holy name" (145:21). As DeClaissé-Walford has put it: "David, then, announces and leads the praise of Yahweh that takes place in the last five psalms of the Psalter."[45] Psalms 144–145 thus affirm that David is to fill a priestly role in praise, but also regain his role as warrior empowered by Yahweh.

As mentioned earlier, Psalm 145 opens the way for the grand finale in Psalms 146–150. Psalm 146 challenges the people to put their trust in Yahweh rather than human rulers. Any temptation for the people to shift their trust to the human royal warrior is squelched. Psalm 147 calls for praise to Yahweh who gathers the exiles, with emphasis on special revelation to Israel alone ("He has revealed his word to Jacob, his laws and decrees to Israel. He has done this for no other nation; they do not know his laws," 147:20). In contrast, Psalm 148 expands the praise to encompass the entire earth.

deClaissé-Walford has noted the progression in Psalms 146–148:

> First David, then the people of Zion, and now all of creation is called upon to praise Yahweh. Psalms 146, 147, and 148 are purposely placed by the shaping community to "widen the scope" of praise, from the heavens (vv. 1–6) to the earth (vv. 7–13), until it includes even the
>
> Kings of the earth and all peoples;
>   Princes and all judges of the earth;
> Both young men and virgins;
>   Old men and children (148:11–12).[46]

---

45. deClaissé-Walford, *Reading*, 99.
46. Ibid., 101.

In all of this, however, there is some uncertainty over the future of the Davidic house. Psalm 146 keeps the people's trust focused on the divine king. Psalm 148:14, however, refers to the "horn" he has raised up for his people. It is unclear whether this "horn" in Ps 148:14 refers to the Davidic house as it does elsewhere in the Psalter (Pss 89:17; 132:17), or whether it is being used more generally for the power of the people (Pss 75:4–5; 92:10; 112:9).[47] It is true that Psalm 149 appears to give to the people of Zion as a whole the prerogatives once given to the Davidic house, that is, martial punishment on the nations, but Psalm 144 does picture David reassuming his role as the warrior under whom God subdues the peoples. Even though there appears to be a future hope for the restoration of the Davidic line, Psalm 149 brings the people of Zion more clearly into focus. In this psalm, the people of Zion are called to exact vengeance on the nations; there is no room for the rebellion of the nations. While Psalm 149 echoes Psalm 147, Psalm 150 echoes Psalm 148, by calling all creation to praise the Lord.

Summary

One can discern in the rhetorical structure of the Psalter a development of the theme of Yahweh, king, people, and the nations. The introduction to the Psalter in Psalms 1–2 identifies the key role that the Messiah will play in the exercise of Yahweh's dominion on earth over all nations. The nations are invited to submit to and find refuge in God and his Messiah. The role of this Messiah figure is developed throughout the Psalter, especially in Psalms 41, 72, and 89. Psalm 72 represents the height of this development as the royal figure is to exercise rule over the nations and bring the Abrahamic blessing to the entire earth. With Psalm 89, however, the nations are depicted as defeating the messianic figure. The hope of Psalms 1–2, 41, and 72 has been shattered. With hope lost, the focus shifts to the divine king who must now lead and rescue the people and human king scattered in exile (Pss 90–106). But there is still hope for the royal figure, now called to be a royal priest (Ps 110) who not only prompts the praise of the people of God (Pss 138–143) and the nations (Ps 145), but also regains his warrior status. The Psalter ends with an emphasis on the kingship of Yahweh at Zion (Ps 146) with the focus

---

47. For horn as reference to royal house, see Ryken, Wilhoit, and Longman, eds., "Horn," 400 (cf. Ezek 29:21).

vacillating between the privilege of Zion (Pss 147, 149) and the praise of the nations (Pss 148, 150).

CONCLUSION

This review of the nations in the Psalter has identified the importance of this theme to both the theology and structure of the book. This theme reminds us that for Israel the mission of God was related to the establishment of his rule over all the nations of the earth. This view of God's mission was shaped in their verbal worship. So ubiquitous is this theme that Israel could never escape this fundamental international perspective. In their praise they were consistently reminded that their destiny was not for themselves alone but for the world. Their salvation was to be a testimony to the nations of the earth; their praise was to reverberate and spread throughout the globe. Both king and people were to act as vice-regents of God; their purpose lay beyond their own salvation and prosperity, that is, to express the reign of God on earth. As Bavinck once wrote: "in such frequently recurring testimonies, Israel reminded itself that it lived before the entire world, and that God's dealings with Israel also included those who still dwelled in the fatal enchantment of heathenism."[48]

Although the Psalms may contain the greatest concentration of the theology of the nations in the Old Testament, this theme is not somehow unique to the Psalms. It is exemplified in the fact that the world story prefaces the Torah (Gen 1–11), that the Abrahamic covenant introduces the redemptive story (Gen 12:1–3), that the Sinai Covenant identified Israel as a "kingdom of priests" (Exod 19:4–6), that the genealogies of Chronicles begin with "Adam" (1 Chron 1:1), that Jonah and Ruth were included in the canon, that Daniel highlights the submission and worship of foreign kings, and that the prophets envisioned both judgment and salvation for the nations.

It was the great Old Testament scholar Hans-Joachim Kraus who saw in the Psalms the theological foundation for the theology of the nations in the New Testament:

> The themes that are so frequent in the Psalms, "judgment on the nations" and "salvation for the nations," appear in the kerygma of the Acts of the Apostles: the theme of judgment in Acts 17:31 (cf.

---

48. Bavinck, *Science of Missions*, 16.

Ps. 9:8; 96:13; 98:9); the theme of salvation in Acts 28:28 (cf. Ps. 67:2; 98:3).[49]

Furthermore, Kraus notes how important the Psalms were for the theology in Romans of the "universal, cosmic character of the preaching of the gospel," citing especially Rom 10:18 (Ps 19:4); Rom 15:9, 11 (Pss 18:49; 117:1); Rom 3:10–18 (Pss 59:9; 14:1ff.; 140:3); and Rom 3:18 (Ps 36:1).[50]

The Psalter, then, is truly a missional collection and was instrumental for shaping the early mission of the church that "repentance for the forgiveness of sins will be preached in his name to all nations, beginning at Jerusalem" (Luke 24:46–47).

IMPLICATIONS

There are several key implications that can be drawn from this study for a Christian missiology. First and foremost, this study has shown the depth of theological resources available in the Psalter for developing a biblical theology of mission. The Psalms, representing the theological reflection of the Old Testament community throughout its history, reveal the antiquity and ubiquity of a missional vision for the nations among the people of God. Second, the Psalter reveals that the roots of Christian proclamation can be found in the command to Israel to give praise to God by testifying to his gracious and powerful intervention in their history (cf. Rom 10:15). Third, the Psalter reminds us that God's purpose for his people as well as the nations is universal praise as an expression of their submission to the reign of God. Mission has as its goal, then, the establishment of the worship of Yahweh among all the peoples of the world. Fourth, the Psalter reveals the power of the praise of the community as the avenue through which missional theology is formed. The hymnody of the past was filled with a theology for the nations and the same should be encouraged from those who are shaping the praise of the present. Fifth, the Psalter never compromises the exclusivity of Yahweh's universal claim to kingship. Although his reign is proclaimed through the universal praise of creation and the global proclamation of his redeemed, the demand of the divine king is submission to him at

---

49. Kraus, *Theology of the Psalms*, 199. He also notes the impact of Ps 2 on Acts 4:25–26 (pp. 183–84).

50. Ibid., 200.

Zion, the seat of his rule and that of his anointed one(s). Sixth, if the evidence of God's rule is seen in his exercise of justice, it is imperative that this be evident in the missional enterprise. Any mission worthy of God is one that seeks for the establishment of the justice of God alongside the proclamation of his reign. This means that where the gospel of the kingdom is proclaimed, the vulnerable and powerless will be protected and defended. Finally, the reign of God is also evidenced in Yahweh's victory in battle, but in Christ we see a redefinition of the method of this victory. The second part of the book of Isaiah echoes the Psalter's anticipation of the inbreaking of the reign of God, expecting this to be instituted by a great display of the "arm of Yahweh" (Isa 49:9–11; 50:2; 51:5; 51:9). In Isa 52:7–10 this reaches a climax as runners in the mountains are commanded to bring the good news ("Your God reigns!" 52:7) of the victory of God, a victory wrought by "his holy arm in the sight of all the nations" (52:10). The irony, however, comes in the section that follows. It is the revelation of a suffering servant (52:13—53:12), who is identified as "the arm of the Lord" (53:1). The "arm of the Lord," that image for the military prowess of Yahweh, is nothing short of Yahweh's suffering servant. In the end then it is the "arm of the Lord" that brings God's victorious reign on earth, through the suffering of the Messiah and through the victorious suffering of the community that bears his name. This has been the pattern from the outset of the Christian mission in the book of Acts, and nothing less will be required of those who follow the Servant in mission.

BIBLIOGRAPHY

Anderson, A. A. *The Book of Psalms*. I. *Introduction and Psalms 1–72*. London: Oliphants, 1972.

Anderson, R. D. "The Division and Order of the Psalms." *WTJ* 56 (1994) 219–41.

Bardtke, H. "Erwängungen zu Psalm 1 und Psalm 2." In *Symbolae Biblicae et Mesopotamicae: Francisco Mario Theodoro de Liagre Böhl dedicatae*, edited by M. A. Beek, 1–18. Studia Francisci Scholten Memoriae Dicata. Leiden: Brill, 1973.

Bavinck, J. H. *An Introduction to the Science of Missions*. Translated by David H. Freeman. Phillipsburg, NJ: Presbyterian and Reformed, 1960.

Booij, T. "Some Observations on Psalm 87." *VT* 37 (1987) 16–25.

Briggs. C. A., and E. G. Briggs. *A Critical and Exegetical Commentary on the Book of Psalms*. ICC. Edinburgh: T. & T. Clark, 1910.

Brownlee, W. H. "Psalms 1–2 as a Coronation Liturgy." *Bib* 52 (1971) 321–36.

Brueggemann, W. *The Message of the Psalms: A Theological Commentary*. Augsburg Old Testament Studies. Minneapolis: Augsburg, 1984.

Brueggemann, W., and P. D. Miller. *The Psalms and the Life of Faith*. Minneapolis: Fortress, 1995.

Creach, J. F. D. *Yahweh as Refuge and the Editing of the Hebrew Psalter*. JSOTSup 217. Sheffield: Sheffield Academic, 1996.

Dahood, M. J. *Psalms 1–50*. AB 16. Garden City, NY: Doubleday, 1965.

———. *Psalms 51–100*. AB 17. Garden City, NY: Doubleday, 1968.

———. *Psalms 101–150*. AB 17A. Garden City, NY: Doubleday, 1970.

deClaissé-Walford, N. L. *Introduction to the Psalms: A Song from Ancient Israel*. St. Louis: Chalice, 2004.

———. *Reading from the Beginning: The Shaping of the Hebrew Psalter*. Macon, GA: Mercer University Press, 1997.

Eaton, J. H. *Kingship and the Psalms*. SBT 32. London: SCM, 1976.

Gese, H. "Die Entstehung der Büchereinteilung des Psalters." In *Wort, Lied, und Gottespruch. II. Beiträge zu Psalmen und Propheten. Festschrift für Joseph Ziegler*, edited by J. Schreiner, 159–64. Forschung zur Bibel. Würzburg: Echter, 1972.

Howard, J. David M. "Editorial Activity in the Psalter: A State of the Field Survey." *WW* 9 (1989) 274–85.

Jacquet, L. *Les Psaumes et le coeur de l'homme*. 3 vols. Gembloux, Belgium: Duculot, 1975.

Kaiser, Walter C. *Mission in the Old Testament: Israel as a Light to the Nations*. Grand Rapids: Baker, 2000.

Kidner, D. *Psalms 1–72*. TOTC. London: Inter-Varsity, 1973.

Kissane, E. J. *The Book of Psalms*. 2 vols. Dublin: Browne-Nolan, 1953–1954.

Kraus, H. J. *Psalms 1–59: A Commentary*. Continental Commentaries. Minneapolis: Augsburg, 1988.

———. *Theology of the Psalms*. Translated by K. R. Crim. Continental Commentaries. Minneapolis: Augsburg, 1986.

Lipinski, E. "Macarismes et Psaumes de congratulation." *RB* 75 (1968) 321–67.

Lohfink, N., and E. Zenger. *Der Gott Israels und die Völker: Untersuchungen zum Jesajabuch und zu den Psalmen*. SBS 154. Stuttgart: Verlag Katholisches Bibelwerk, 1994.

———. *The God of Israel and the Nations: Studies in Isaiah and the Psalms*. Collegeville, MN: Liturgical, 2000.

Martin-Achard, R. *A Light to the Nations: A Study of the Old Testament Conception of Israel's Mission to the World*. London: Oliver and Boyd, 1962.

Mays, J. L. *The Lord Reigns: A Theological Handbook to the Psalms*. Louisville: Westminster John Knox, 1994.

———. "The Place of the Torah-Psalms in the Psalter." *JBL* 106 (1987) 3–12.

McCann, J. C. "Books I–III and the Editorial Purpose of the Hebrew Psalter." In *Shape and Shaping of the Psalter*, edited by J. C. McCann, 93–107. JSOTSup 159. Sheffield: JSOT Press, 1993.

———. *The Shape and Shaping of the Psalter*. JSOTSup 159. Sheffield: JSOT Press, 1993.

McCann, J. C., and N. R. McCann. *A Theological Introduction to the Book of Psalms: The Psalms as Torah*. Nashville: Abingdon, 1993.

McGinn, A. "The Divine Council and Israelite Monotheism." ThM thesis, McMaster Divinity College, McMaster University, 2005.

Miller, P. D. "The Beginning of the Psalter." In *Shape and Shaping of the Psalter*, edited by J. C. McCann, 83–92. JSOTSup 159. Sheffield: JSOT Press, 1993.

Morgenstern, J. "The Mythological Background of Psalm 82." *HUCA* 14 (1939) 29–126.
Mowinckel, S. *The Psalms in Israel's Worship*. 2 vols. New York: Abingdon, 1962.
Moyise, S., and M. J. J. Menken, eds. *The Psalms in the New Testament*. TNTS 1. London: T. & T. Clark, 2004.
Mullen, E. T. *The Divine Council in Canaanite and Early Hebrew Literature*. HSM 24. Chico, CA: Scholars, 1980.
Nasuti, H. P. *Defining the Sacred Songs: Genre, Tradition and the Post-Critical Interpretation of the Psalms*. JSOTSup 218. Sheffield: Sheffield Academic, 1999.
Riedel, L. T. W. "Zur Redaktion des Psalters." *ZAW* 19 (1899) 169–72.
Rogerson, J. W., and J. W. McKay. *Psalms*. 3 vols. CBC. Cambridge: Cambridge University Press, 1977.
Ryken, L., J. C. Wilhoit, and T. Longman, eds. "Horn." In *Dictionary of Biblical Imagery*, 400. Downers Grove, IL: InterVarsity, 1997.
Sheppard, G. T. *Wisdom as a Hermeneutical Construct: A Study in the Sapientializing of the Old Testament*. BZAW 151. New York: de Gruyter, 1980.
Smith, M. S. "The Theology of the Redaction of the Psalter: Some Observations." *ZAW* 104 (1992) 408–12.
Tate, M. E. *Psalms 51–100*. WBC 20. Dallas: Word, 1990.
VanGemeren, W. A. "Psalms." In *The Expositor's Bible Commentary*, edited by F. E. Gaebelein, 5:1–880. Grand Rapids: Zondervan, 1991.
Weiser, A. *The Psalms: A Commentary*. OTL. Philadelphia: Westminster, 1962.
Westermann, C. *Praise and Lament in the Psalms*. Atlanta: John Knox, 1981.
Whybray, R. N. *Reading the Psalms as a Book*. JSOTSup 222. Sheffield: Sheffield Academic, 1996.
Willis, J. T. "Psalm 1: An Entity." *ZAW* 91 (1979) 381–401.
Wilson, G. H. *The Editing of the Hebrew Psalter*. Chico, CA: Scholars, 1985.
———. "Shaping the Psalter: A Consideration of Editorial Linkage in the Book of Psalms." In *Shape and Shaping of the Psalter*, edited by J. C. McCann, 72–82. JSOTSup 159. Sheffield: JSOT Press, 1993.
———. "Understanding the Purposeful Arrangement of Psalms in the Psalter: Pitfalls and Promises." In *Shape and Shaping of the Psalter*, edited by J. C. McCann, 42–51. JSOTSup 159. Sheffield: JSOT Press, 1993.
———. "The Use of Royal Psalms at the 'Seams' of the Hebrew Psalter." *JSOT* 35 (1986) 85–94.
Zenger, Erich. "The God of Israel's Reign over the World (Psalms 90–106)." In *The God of Israel and the Nations: Studies in Isaiah and the Psalms*, edited by N. Lohfink and E. Zenger, 161–90. Collegeville, MN: Liturgical, 2000.
———. "Zion as Mother of the Nations in Psalm 87." In *The God of Israel and the Nations: Studies in Isaiah and the Psalms*, edited by N. Lohfink and E. Zenger, 123–60. Collegeville, MN: Liturgical, 2000.

2

The Book of Daniel and the Roots of New Testament Mission

BRIAN P. IRWIN

INTRODUCTION

IN HIS BOOK, *The End of Christendom and the Future of Christianity*, McGill theologian Douglas John Hall addresses the question of how the mission of the church might be realized in the twenty-first century. Hall foresees a future North American church that will continue on a trajectory of numerical decline and loss of influence. In attempting to imagine what relevance the faithful will continue to have in society, Hall argues that the best hope for the church is to abandon the model of Christendom—in which the church identifies with the dominant secular power—and return to its biblical roots. For the church in Canada, argues Hall, this will mean accepting the status of a marginalized group. Far from being a disadvantage, however, this marginalization of the church will allow it to identify with other marginalized groups in society and occupy a place from which it can effectively critique society's power structures. Hall's view of the future church is of a body of authentic believers, serious about its role as an agent of change in the world. For many, however, the picture of numerical decline that Hall accepts without protest will seem unnecessarily pessimistic.

Since Hall's vision of the near future calls for a return to biblical roots, it seems fitting to ask what model the Bible might offer for being church. When we approach Scripture with this question in mind, the overwhelming image that presents itself is that of kingdom. In both testaments, the faithful are identified as members of an unseen kingdom—as people whose existence is on earth, but whose citizenship is elsewhere. In the New Testament, the news that the kingdom of God had arrived was the defining message of Jesus' ministry.[1] Even before the start of Jesus' public ministry, this message was seeded by his cousin John, who enjoined the people of Judaea to "Repent, for the kingdom of heaven is near" (Matt 3:2). At the very start of his own ministry, prior even to the calling of the disciples, Jesus preaches this same message (Matt 4:17). As he approaches Jerusalem and impending death, Jesus offers the cheering throngs the Parable of the Ten Minas as a corrective to their misconceptions about the kingdom (Luke 19:11–27).[2] In his last recorded words before ascending to heaven, Jesus uses kingdom language when he reminds the disciples that he has been granted "all authority in heaven and on earth" and that their duty now is to "make disciples," "teaching them to obey everything I have commanded you" (Matt 28:18–20).

The basic meaning of what constitutes the "kingdom of God" is clear from the Hebraic poetic parallelism of the Lord's Prayer in Matt 6:9–13.[3] There, the coming of the kingdom is explained in terms of God's

---

1. See Bruce, *New Testament History*, 163–77; and Bartholomew and Goheen, *Drama of Scripture,* 134–49.

2. At Passover, the great feast of national independence, Jesus is aware that the people are expecting him to usher in the kingdom at once (Luke 19:11). The Parable of the Minas shows the danger of this misguided expectation by focusing on a style of kingship that is characterized by grasping and violence. The details of the parable show it to be a retelling of how Herod Archelaus went to Rome to be made Ethnarch and returned to rule Judaea with unprecedented brutality (Josephus, *J.W.* 2.1–100). Against this backdrop, Luke consciously portrays the march of Christ to the cross as the act that will truly usher in the kingdom (Luke 19:1). See also Green, *Luke*, 676; and Marshall, *Luke*, 703–4. For a defense of the idea that the ruler represents Jesus, see Johnson, *Luke*, 294.

3. While the prayer is present also in Luke 11:2–4, it has been rendered there without most of its parallelism, presumably to make it more readily understood by the Gentile believers Luke addresses. See, however, Fitzmyer, *Luke*, 897–901, who argues that the Lukan form is original and that the Matthean version is expansionist, and Bock, *Luke*, 2:1046, who suggests that the Matthean and Lukan prayers are distinct in their origin. The idea that Matthew's version is simply expansionist, however, fails to reckon fully with the parallel character of the so-called additions and with the Jewishness of Jesus. Concerning the idea that the Matthean and Lukan prayers arose separately, it may be offered that the Gospel writers were sufficiently creative in their arrangement of material that the distinct settings of the prayer in Matthew and in Luke need not suggest separate origins for the two prayers.

will being carried out on earth in the same way that it is in heaven.[4] Elsewhere, Matthew repeats this same idea when we find Jesus declaring, "Not everyone who says to me, 'Lord, Lord,' will enter the kingdom of heaven; but he who does the will of my Father who is in heaven" (Matt 7:21). From this basic idea comes Jesus' emphasis that the kingdom of God is not a place or an era, but something that resides within the faithful themselves as they carry out God's will on earth (Luke 17:20–21).[5] At its most basic, therefore, the kingdom of God is wherever God rules.[6] From the dominance of the idea of the kingdom in the Gospels, it is clear that living out an identity as members of the kingdom of God is a foundational mission for those who make up the church.

While the idea of the kingdom of God dominates the Gospels, it does not spring fully formed in the New Testament. When Israel enters covenant relationship with Yahweh they become "a kingdom of priests and a holy nation" (Exod 19:6).[7] The concept of the faithful as members of God's kingdom is deeply imbedded in the Old Testament, from the presentation of the covenant in treaty form to the shaping of the Psalter.[8] An often-overlooked illustration of what it means to live in the world as members of the kingdom is found in the book of Daniel.

---

4. The rest of the parallelism unfolds as follows: the Father's name is holy because of his place in heaven (Matt 6:9), the provision of bread and the forgiveness of debts both employ imperatives and deal with ways in which God graciously meets needs (Matt 6:10–11), and contrasting parallelism connects the ideas of avoidance of temptation and deliverance from evil (Matt 6:12).

5. "The kingdom of God does not come with your careful observation, nor will people say, 'Here it is,' or 'There it is,' because the kingdom of God is within you" (Luke 17:20–21).

6. In light of this basic definition, it is clear that John is seen as preparing the way for Jesus because his message—that all must repent—is an essential first step in creating a place in which God's will is done (Matt 3:1–3; Mark 1:4–8; Luke 3:3–6; John 1:31).

7. On the relationship between covenant and kingdom in the Old Testament, see Bartholomew and Goheen, *Drama of Scripture,* 24.

8. Since Mendenhall, "Covenant Forms," studies of Deuteronomy have commonly emphasized its similarity in form to an ancient vassal treaty. See more recently, Weinfeld, "Deuteronomy." An appreciation of the final form of the Psalter—particularly of Book IV—has drawn attention to the message that Yahweh is Israel's true king. See Wilson, "Book of Psalms."

THE KINGDOM OF GOD IN DANIEL

For most people in the church, the book of Daniel does not elicit much interest. For those who are acquainted with the book, it is often understood to be an insider's guide to how the world wraps up—sort of an eschatological odds-maker's dream. As Stanley Walters has observed, however, Daniel is a much more practical book than the church at large has recognized. It is a work that chronicles what it means to live as the people of God through times of openness and times of persecution.[9]

Linguistically and form critically, Daniel is a composite text, with six chapters of Aramaic narratives surrounded by an introduction and a series of visions in Hebrew.[10] The first six chapters of Daniel emphasize that there is an unseen kingdom with an omnipotent ruler who exercises authority over all—over even the greatest kings of the earth. In this relatively open setting, the faithful are able to engage culture with only periodic threat from the temporal powers. When the faithful are threatened, the power of God intrudes to rescue them and humble their oppressors. For its part, the second half of Daniel (7/8–12) reckons with the fact that despite this divine authority, wickedness sometimes seems to advance unrestrained. In this visionary material, the attacks of the wicked go largely unanswered. Here, however, the fact that this persecution is disclosed in advance shows that its days have been numbered by God.

---

9. Walters, "The End (of What?)." The presentation of the basic structure and theme of Daniel offered here owes much to Walters's analysis.

10. See fig. 1.

Figure 1: The Structure and Shape of Daniel

Chapter	1	2	3	4	5	6
Language	Hebrew	Aramaic				
Outline	Intro	Narratives of Engagement				
Incident	Food	Vision of Four Kingdoms	Furnace (placed in and emerge unscathed)	Tree and Madness of Nebuchadnezzar	Writing Hand	Lion's Den (placed in and emerges unscathed)
Pattern		*Crisis* Vindication *Acknowledgment of God*: Daniel worshipped; God reveals *Promotion*: Daniel and friends	*Crisis* Vindication *Acknowledgment of God*: praises God; he delivers; no disrespect *Promotion*: Daniel's friends	*Acknowledgment of God*: eternal kingdom *Crisis*: king *Vindication* *Acknowledgment of God*: eternal kingdom; praises God; he is right, just *Promotion*: Nebuchadnezzar	*Crisis*: king *Vindication*: none *Acknowledgment of God*: none; did not honor God *Promotion*: Daniel *Demotion*: Belshazzar	*Crisis* *Vindication* *Acknowledgment of God*: all should fear God; imperishable kingdom; he rescues *Promotion*: Daniel
God	God quietly controls human affairs	Kingdom of God displaces earthly kingdoms (God alone "sets up kings and deposes them," vv. 20–21)	Narratives of chs. 3–6 illustrate the point of ch. 2 by emphasizing God's sovereignty and showing the quiet advance of the Kingdom of God			

46

Chapter	7	8	9	10	11	12
Language	Aramaic	Hebrew				
Outline	Transition	Visions of Persecution				
Contents	Four Beasts	Ram and Goat	70 sevens	Kings of the North and south		
Pattern	Arrogant enemy dominates. Faithful killed. God intervenes and judges	Arrogant enemy dominates. Faithful killed. God intervenes and judges	Faithful suffer as a result of past sin. Arrogant enemy dominates. Faithful killed. God intervenes and judges	Arrogant enemy dominates. Faithful killed. God intervenes and judges		
God	Kingdom of God overcomes earthly kingdoms and would-be gods. (God alone has authority and eternal dominion, vv. 14, 27)	Visions illustrate the point of ch. 7 by showing how kingdoms persecute the faithful, challenge God and are eventually judged.				

Narratives of Engagement

Daniel 1 serves as an introduction to the collections of stories and visions that comprise the book.[11] As an introduction, it supplies a historical and social setting, explains the rise of the Judahites to prominence, and establishes theme. In captivity in Babylon, four Judaean nobles are faced with a complete loss of control, unable to determine things so basic as their names or diet (Dan 1:5–7). It is at this point that a key theme of the book is first introduced. It is quickly demonstrated that while there has been a loss of control on the part of the Judaeans, there has been no corresponding loss of control on the part of God. Working invisibly, God controls the mind of the Babylonian official[12] so that he risks royal sanction and allows Daniel and his companions to set their own diet (Dan 1:9–10). From the outset, therefore, it is clear that the book of Daniel is going to be a story of the faithful striving to live in a foreign world, and God working both visibly and invisibly on their behalf.

If Daniel 1 serves as an introduction to the book as a whole, chapter 2 serves this same function for the first half of the book. In chapter 2, Nebuchadnezzar's dream introduces a pattern that will provide the framework for the narrative episodes that run from chapters 2 to 6. These narratives are marked by a pattern of *crisis > vindication > royal acknowledgment of God > promotion*.[13]

In Daniel 2, the *crisis* is initiated by Nebuchadnezzar's demand that advisors relate to him the substance of his dream along with its interpretation. The impossibility of this task leaves the astrologers protesting, "No one can reveal it to the king except the gods, and they do not live among humans" (2:11). When the king's dream is later revealed to Daniel, the Judaean prince utters a short hymn that acknowledges that it is God who "sets up kings and deposes them" (2:21). *Vindication* for the faithful comes when Daniel successfully relates the dream and its interpretation

---

11. That this is the case is clear not only from the content, but also from the summary of Daniel's career conveyed by the notation that Daniel entered foreign service in the reign of Nebuchadnezzar (Dan 1:5–6) and that he continued to serve until the reign of Cyrus the Persian (Dan 1:21).

12. 1:9, *wayyittēn hāʾĕlōhîm ʾet-dāniyēʾl lĕḥesed ûlĕraḥămîm lipnê śar hassāērîsîm* ("God granted Daniel favor and compassion before the chief of the officials"). Unless otherwise specified, all Hebrew quotations are from Elliger and Rudolph, eds., *BHS*. Septuagint quotations are based on Rahlfs, ed., *Septuaginta*. Greek New Testament quotations are taken from Aland et al., eds., *Greek New Testament*.

13. See fig. 1.

to the king's satisfaction (2:27–45). Nebuchadnezzar's *acknowledgment of God* comes in 2:46–47 when he falls prostrate before Daniel, orders offerings to be made to the Judaean, and affirms Daniel's god as "the God of gods and the Lord of kings" (2:47). In this first narrative, the Babylonian king's affirmation represents a far from perfect expression of Yahwistic orthodoxy. Sacrifices are made, for example, to Daniel and not to Yahweh. This action seems to be a natural, but naïve, response to Daniel's success in light of the earlier universal declaration that only a god could reveal the dream to the king (2:11).[14] Nebuchadnezzar's declaration that Daniel's god is "the God of gods and the Lord of kings" (2:47) is a better expression of Yahwistic belief, mirroring as it does Daniel's earlier affirmation that God "sets up kings and deposes them" (2:21). The substance of the chapter is summarized in the king's acknowledgment that the god of Daniel is the "revealer of mysteries" (2:47). The cycle concludes with 2:48–49 and the *promotion* of Daniel and his friends to positions of authority and power within the kingdom. By the end of this first cycle, it is clear that God *does* live among humans and that he exercises authority over earthly kings. The faithful living in a hostile setting can know that, even in such circumstances, God does speak and exercise authority.

Two elements of this passage stand out as important for everything that follows in the book. The first is Daniel's brief hymn of praise that lists key attributes of God that will be important later in the chapter and throughout the rest of the book: "wisdom and power are his. He changes times and seasons; he sets up kings and deposes them" (2:20–21). God is sovereign and those who reign do so at his pleasure. God also establishes the patterns by which the world operates; those who attempt to change these patterns are attempting to take the place of God himself and will be dealt with accordingly.

A second key element of this chapter, and one that is important for the chapters that follow, is the vision of the statue and the rock that destroys it. Without warning, a divinely-hewn rock[15] strikes the feet of the statue, destroying the entire figure. Having destroyed these kingdoms,

---

14. It is also possible that this action is intended by the king to humiliate the astrologers who were so quick to shrink from the royal challenge.

15. The designation of the rock as "not carved by human hands" (*hitgĕzeret ʾeben dî-lāʾ bîdayin*) establishes that these kingdoms are not destroyed by accident or human power, but by divine intent.

the rock grows to become a huge mountain that fills the earth.[16] The interpretation that Daniel provides (2:36–45) makes clear that the destroying and ever-expanding rock is a kingdom that God will establish among humans. While the rock strikes the last of the earthly kingdoms, in reality it destroys and displaces them all (2:35, 44–45). What the narratives of chs. 2 to 6 clarify and develop is the reality of this kingdom and the manner in which it grows. Throughout the episodes of the first half of the book, rulers will be judged on the extent to which they recognize the reality of this kingdom and the authority of its ruler. In this way, the narratives of the first half of Daniel demonstrate how the faithful engage a foreign and sometimes hostile realm that gradually gives ground to the expanding kingdom of God.

In Daniel 3, the cycle of *crisis* through *promotion* is once again present, and here too it serves to signal the presence and growth of the invisible kingdom of God. The *crisis* of this narrative comes in the form of a royal command to worship a colossal, golden statue of the king and the refusal of Shadrach, Meshach, and Abednego to comply with the royal decree (3:1–23). *Vindication* for the faithful comes when the three are rescued by the divine hand so that they are able to withstand the fire and even walk out of the furnace under their own power (3:24–27). In response to this act of God, Nebuchadnezzar once again *acknowledges* the hand of God but goes further to offer a now appropriately-directed expression of praise ("Blessed be the God of Shadrach, Meshach, and Abednego, who has sent his angel and delivered his servants who trusted in him") (3:28). The king's affirmation is further expressed negatively by the threat he issues to those who would denigrate the God of the Judaeans (3:29). The cycle is completed with the *promotion* of the three Judaeans within the province of Babylon (3:30). In this second narrative, the words of the Babylonian king show that even in a hostile setting, God is present and powerful, and can rescue the faithful.

Chapter 4 sees the reappearance of Daniel as the interpreter of yet another royal dream. This narrative represents a culmination of sorts in that the entire chapter is framed as a *royal acknowledgment* of God's au-

---

16. The fact that the stone grows into a mountain likely reflects a dependence on the same Sinai imagery found in the New Testament in contexts such as the Transfiguration (Matt 17:1–13; Mark 9:2–13; Luke 9:28–36). For a summary of the connections between Matt 17:1–13 and Sinai see Davies and Allison, *Matthew*, 2:684–709; and Donaldson, *Jesus on the Mountain*, 142–43.

thority with the expected cycle embedded within it. The progression of the kingdom of God and the positive influence of the faithful are made clear by the fact that, while the cycle begins with a challenge, there is *no crisis* or threat to the safety of the faithful. In fact, this episode illustrates the advancing power of the kingdom by placing the earthly king Nebuchadnezzar in the position of the one facing *crisis*. In his dream, Nebuchadnezzar sees a massive tree that provides shelter and sustenance for a vast array of animal life. Suddenly, and without explanation, this tree is destroyed by divine decree.[17] The dream itself makes it clear that the events that befall Nebuchadnezzar are intended to demonstrate the sovereignty of God who appoints human monarchs at will (4:14; ET 4:17). The sovereignty of Daniel's God is further emphasized by the fact that Nebuchadnezzar's *vindication* is achieved not by any action on his own part, but by the simple fact that the divine prediction of madness runs its course.[18] The status of this narrative as a culmination is related by the fact that here royal acknowledgment of God not only concludes the episode, it frames the entire narrative.[19] In his opening address to the peoples of the world, Nebuchadnezzar candidly acknowledges the existence of God's eternal kingdom and the fact of God's authority (3:33; ET 4:3). The close of the narrative includes the most thorough acknowledgment of God to this point in the book, going so far as to include a hymn declaring the eternal nature of God's kingdom and his sovereignty over heaven and earth (4:31–32; ET 4:34–35). The king also acknowledges God's righteousness and his own subservient status (4:34; ET 4:37). The appearance of *promotion* in this narrative parallels the earlier element of crisis as it is Nebuchadnezzar who is promoted when his officials seek

---

17. As noted above, the extent to which the kingdom of God has begun to intrude into the earthly realm is indicated by the fact that the king himself receives a partial interpretation of the dream. In 4:12b–14 (ET 4:15b–17), the angel announcing the destruction of the tree abandons the image of the tree and declares that an unnamed person will be temporarily deposed and given over to madness. This will be accomplished, the angel continues, to establish "that the Most High is sovereign over human kingdoms" (4:14; ET 4:17).

18. This is indicated in 4:31 (ET 4:34) by the phrase *wĕliqṣāt yômayyâ* ("At the end of that time").

19. This framing is emphasized by the use of *inclusio* in which the expression *malkûtēh malkût ʿolam wĕšolṭānēh ʿim-dār wĕdār* ("his kingdom is eternal and his dominion exists generation to generation") (3:33; ET 4:3) is inversely repeated in 4:31 (ET 4:34) as *šolṭānēh šolṭān ʿolam ûmalkûtēh ʿim-dār wĕdār* ("his dominion is eternal and his kingdom exists generation to generation").

him out and restore him to the throne (4:33b; ET 4:36b). With the conclusion of this narrative, it is clear that God's kingdom is present in the world and that human kings do well to acknowledge the authority of the one who establishes and deposes them at will.

The counterpoint to Daniel 4 and the acknowledgment that God establishes earthly kings comes in ch. 5 and the story of how Belshazzar is deposed. Here, too, the pattern of *crisis* through *promotion* is altered. As was the case in the previous episode, the one in crisis is not the follower of God, but the Babylonian monarch. Hosting a banquet, Belshazzar issues a drunken command that the vessels pillaged from the Jerusalem temple be brought and distributed among the guests. Whereas Belshazzar's predecessor had readily acknowledged the sovereignty of God, now drunken revelers praise idols even as they drink from cups once dedicated to Yahweh. At this point, the fingers of a hand appear and begin to write upon the wall. Soon Daniel is summoned to interpret the message for the terrified king. Before complying, Daniel informs the king that his father Nebuchadnezzar had occupied his position of authority only at the pleasure of the Most High God and had humbled himself and recognized the sovereignty of that God (5:18–21). The writing has been sent because Belshazzar has not humbled himself, but rather has desecrated God's property by using his vessels in the praise of idols (5:22–24). Such actions preclude any *vindication* in his case and so his reign is to be ended. In place of the expected *acknowledgment of God*, there is only Daniel's chastisement that the king had *failed* to acknowledge God (5:22–24). The narrative ends with *promotion* for Daniel (5:29) and the ultimate *demotion*—in the form of death—for Belshazzar (5:30). In this passage, the dramatic, physical intrusion of the disembodied hand marks the increasing way in which the authority of the kingdom of God is making itself felt in the human realm. The God of Daniel who reinstated a penitent Nebuchadnezzar in ch. 4 can, with equal ease, depose an arrogant Belshazzar in ch. 5.

The final narrative of the first half of the book provides the clearest evidence of the manner in which the kingdom of God has been growing, displacing, and influencing the powers of the temporal sphere. Here, God has swept aside Belshazzar and the Babylonian empire and replaced them with Darius. Here, the cycle of *crisis > vindication > royal acknowledgment of God > promotion* reverts to its expected form. Daniel is once again serving in the royal administration, but despite his integrity and competence, is victimized by scheming rivals. The result of this is that a sympathetic Darius is forced to sentence Daniel to be devoured by lions. When Daniel is rescued and hence *vindicated*, the king produces the expected *acknowledgment of God*. This acknowledgment, however, goes beyond any of the three issued earlier by Nebuchadnezzar in that it not only declares the sovereignty and saving power of God, but also commands the people of *all* nations to fear him (6:26–28; ET 6:25–27). The final occurrence of this cycle ends with the expected *promotion* of Daniel (6:29; ET 6:28). In this clearest example of the advancing presence of the divine kingdom, the rulers of the earth not only recognise the authority of God, but also enjoin their subjects to do the same.

Visions of Persecution

As a vision presented in Aramaic, ch. 7 mirrors much of the material in ch. 2 and so functions to close off the first half of the book. In ch. 7, Daniel receives a vision of four kingdoms (7:2–14) that stands in parallel to the dream concerning four kingdoms experienced earlier by Nebuchadnezzar (2:31–35). In both chapters, the final kingdom is destroyed and all are displaced by the kingdom of God. In addition, specific phraseology connects the two sections.[20]

In the present form of the book, the shape and language of ch. 7 of Daniel suggest that it also has a transitional function. While written in Aramaic like the preceding narratives of engagement, this section is a terrifying vision of bestial empires that persecute the faithful. This vision employs some of the features that are common to the second half of the book and to apocalyptic literature generally.[21] In this vision, four human kingdoms devour and destroy before any divine action takes place. Only when the fourth beast successfully wages war against the saints and challenges divine authority by attempting to change the "times and the seasons"[22] does the heavenly court sit and decree the beast's destruction

20. See the repetition in 2:21 and 7:25 of the terms *šn'* ("to change"), *zĕmān* ("fixed time/season"), and *ʿiddān* ("time"). Present also in both passages are near identical phrases emphasizing the eternal nature of God's kingdom. Compare *malkû dî lĕ ʾolmîn lāʾ titḥabbal* ("his kingdom is an eternal one, not to be destroyed," 2:44) and *dî-lāʾ titḥabbal* ("his kingdom is one which will not be destroyed," 7:14).

21. On the characteristics of apocalyptic, see Collins, *Apocalyptic Imagination*, 1–8; and Hanson, *Old Testament Apocalyptic*, 25–34.

22. The attempt on the part of the fourth beast to "alter the seasons" (*wĕyisbar lĕhašĕnāyâ zimnîn*) represents a direct challenge to the sovereignty of God whose right

(7:25). While the faithful are ultimately vindicated, this final section of the Aramaic portion of the book makes it clear that rescue will not always come to the faithful immediately. What this chapter establishes is that, while God is present and his kingdom real, there will be circumstances in which earthly kingdoms will claim divine authority and actively war against God's followers. Thus, this chapter prepares the reader for the visions to come and an era of ongoing persecution and justice delayed.

The era of persecution without immediate vindication is conveyed through the three visions that comprise the second half of the book (chs. 8–12). Chapter 8 marks an abrupt shift in language and content that clearly indicates that something new is happening. Here, Aramaic gives way to Hebrew. Simple narratives are replaced by visions filled with complex imagery. While Daniel continues to figure prominently in chs. 8 to 12, he is no longer the confident wise man who had ably served the kings of Babylon and Persia. Here he is reduced to the status of bewildered and quivering recipient of terrifying visions.

In the first of these visions (ch. 8), Daniel sees a two-horned ram representing the Medes and the Persians. This animal charges to and fro, conquering everything in its path. Next, Daniel observes a shaggy goat with a single, prominent horn that charges from the west and destroys the ram. The image of the triumphant goat clearly represents Alexander the Great and the Diadochi who defeat and supplant the Persian Empire. The last of these powers defies the sovereignty of God by attacking the saints, appropriating the sacrifices, destroying the sanctuary, and throwing "truth to the ground" (wĕtašlēk ʾĕmet ʾarṣâ) (8:11–12). When this enemy is destroyed, it is by the hand of God.[23]

The knowledge that the suffering of the faithful comes as a consequence of their rebellion (8:12) spurs Daniel to penitence and so the next section of the book opens with Daniel fasting and in prayer, pleading to God on behalf of his people (9:3–19). Here, the words of Daniel's prayer reflect the specific vocabulary of the previous vision in which

---

to exercise this kind of authority has already been recognized in Nebuchadnezzar's declaration that only God "changes the times and the seasons" (wĕhûʾ mĕhašnēʾ ʿiddānayyāʾ wĕzimnayyāʾ)(2:21). The connection between these two sections is further confirmed by the presence in 7:25 of various forms of ʿiddān ("time") (which appears also in 2:21).

23. This is the obvious implication of the statement that this kingdom will be destroyed, "but not by human power" (8:25). See also Dan 2:34, 45.

the heavenly messengers discuss the desolation of the sanctuary (8:13).²⁴ The interpretation given to Daniel by Gabriel also parallels in part the interpretation that accompanied the previous vision. In both cases, deliverance will come only after the faithful have endured great persecution. Here, Daniel is informed that while the end of the desolation has been decreed, the end is far off and will be preceded by much violence and suffering (9:24–27). As in the previous vision, the enemy will defy God by defiling his temple. Although many of the faithful will suffer and die unvindicated, God will eventually intervene.

The final vision of the book carries on the theme of how earthly powers challenge God and his kingdom, kill the faithful, and are ultimately judged by God. The vision begins with the notation that it concerns a "great conflict" (*wĕṣābāʾ gādôl*) (10:1)—a fact that sends Daniel into a three-week period of mourning.²⁵ The messenger's words reveal that the heavenly powers have been engaged in a difficult and unseen battle against earthly kingdoms (10:13, 20). Gabriel relates a long and detailed story of kingdoms, alliances, and warfare that will result in the arrival of a king from the North who will occupy Judaea (a.k.a. "the Beautiful Land") and will be given the power to destroy it (11:16).²⁶ The successor to this figure will oppose the "holy covenant," desecrate the temple, and put an end to the regular sacrifices (11:28, 31). The truly faithful will oppose this figure, but at enormous cost. Those who resist will "fall by the sword or be burned or captured or plundered" (11:33).

24. In 8:13, one angel asks of another, *ʿad-mātay heḥāzôn hattāmîd wĕhappešaʿ šōmēm tēt wĕqōdeš wĕṣābāʾ mirmās* ("How long will the vision of the regular sacrifice and the rebellion that causes desolation, and the trampling of the holy place and the host endure?). In response to this, Daniel uses the same key vocabulary to ask God to rectify this situation (*wĕhāʾēr pānêkā ʿal-miqdōškā haššāmēm*; "Shine your face upon your desolate holy place") (9:17).

25. If the first month mentioned in 10:4 is Tishri, then the three weeks of mourning undertaken by Daniel coincide with both the Day of Atonement and the Feast of Tabernacles, the former being an appropriate backdrop for Daniel's time of penitence.

26. The vision that begins in ch. 11 comes from the "Book of Truth" (11:21) and is a chronicle of the history of the ancient Near East from the end of the Persian Empire to the Hasmonaean era. Figures and events which seem to be indicated here are Alexander the Great (336–323 BC) (11:3); the Diadochi (322–301 BC) (11:4); the Ptolemies and the Syrian Wars (ca. 274–198 BC) (11:5–13); Antiochus III (223–187 BC); the battle of Ipsus (301 BC); the Peace of Apamaea (188 BC) (11:14–19); Seleucus IV Philapator (187–175 BC) (11:20); and Antiochus IV Epiphanes (175–163 BC) (11:21–45). See in general Goldingay, *Daniel*, 292–305. For the history of this period in general, see Bruce, *Israel and the Nations*, 116–43.

When the king of the North comes again to invade the "Beautiful Land," Michael, the protector of Israel, will step in to rescue the people of God. Within this complex vision, the picture is one of an enemy that will challenge God's authority and kill the faithful. God is sovereign, however, and has placed a limit to the suffering of his people and will eventually intervene on their behalf.

What the narratives and visions of the two halves of Daniel illustrate is that there is no single way to live as members of the kingdom of God. While the kingdom and power of God are always present and active, they are not always seen to be so. In some times and places, the faithful will find that they are able to engage an essentially alien and sometimes hostile culture and witness the advancing influence of God over it. This is the pattern that unfolds in the first half of the book. At other times, however, the kingdoms of the earth will be so hostile and unreceptive that engagement is impossible. It may even be the case that these kingdoms will actively war against God. In such circumstances, it falls to the followers of God to remain faithful and know that while unseen, the kingdom of God does exist and will someday be acknowledged by all. This is the message of the transitional ch. 7 and the second half of the book.

THE KINGDOM OF GOD IN THE NEW TESTAMENT

The Kingdom in Times of Persecution

As noted at the outset, the idea of the kingdom of God is one that permeates both Testaments. In the New Testament, images of the kingdom can be observed that comport with, and in some cases are even inspired by, the uses seen in the book of Daniel. The New Testament use of Daniel is most obvious in the case of the book of Revelation. This territory has been so well traversed by others that I will remain general in my treatment of it.[27] What is of particular interest to us, however, is where and how the material from Daniel related to the kingdom of God is used in Revelation and elsewhere in the New Testament. The possibility of an affinity between the portrayal of life in the kingdom in Daniel 7/8–12 and the book of Revelation is evident from Rev 1:9 and John's admission that suffering and membership in the kingdom can, and do, go hand

---

27. For a detailed treatment of the use of Daniel in Revelation, see Beale, *Use of Daniel*. On Old Testament references in general, see Beale, *Revelation*, 76–99.

in hand. Indeed, the entire message of Revelation—that Jesus is returning and that until then the faithful must endure to the end—is one that finds a parallel in the emphasis on endurance found in the latter half of Daniel.

In Rev 13, John describes a beast that arises from the sea (*ek tēs thalassēs thērion anabainon*) (Rev 13:1). This beast combines the features of leopard (*pardalei*), bear (*arkou*), and lion (*leontos*) (Rev 13:2), speaks boastful words (*megala*) (Rev. 13:5), and successfully wars against the saints (*kai edothē autō poiēsai polemon meta tōn hagiōn kai nikēsai autous*) (Rev 13:7). This figure that so opposes the faithful draws heavily on the imagery of the beasts from the transitional ch. 7 of Daniel.[28] There, Daniel sees a series of beasts rising consecutively from the sea (LXX: *kai tessara thēria anebainon ek tēs thalassēs*) (Dan 7:3). The first three resemble a lioness (*leaina*) (Dan 7:4), bear (*arkou*) (Dan 7:5), and leopard (*pardalin*) (Dan 7:6) respectively. The fourth beast in this series sprouts a horn that speaks boastful words (*megala*) (Dan 7:8) and wars against and conquers the faithful (*polemon synistamenon pros tous hagious kai tropoumenon*) (Dan 7:21). In Daniel, this period of martyrdom ends only when the Ancient of Days intervenes on behalf of the saints who then possess the kingdom (Dan 7:22). By his reuse of the material from Daniel, John emphasises that the faithful may be part of the kingdom even if they do not fully possess it. This distinction means that kingdom living can mean living in a hostile context where the faithful are persecuted and *not* rescued.

In Matthew 24, Jesus alludes to material from Daniel in order to talk about his someday return and the end of the age. In so doing, he describes a future characterized by messianic impostors and warfare among kingdoms (Matt 24:5–7). When this occurs, the faithful will suffer persecution and death. A sign that this time of persecution is near will be the installation in the temple of "the abomination that causes desolation" (*to bdelygma tēs erēmōseōs*) (Matt 24:15). This era is brought to a close by the arrival on the clouds of heaven of the "Son of Man" (*ton huion tou anthrōpou erchomenon epi tōn nephelōn tou ouranou*) (Matt 24:30), at which time the elect will be rescued and the good news of the kingdom universally proclaimed (Matt 24:9–14, 31). In his description of the future suffering of the faithful, the Gospel writer draws generally on the theme of martyred faithful found in Daniel 7/8–12. More specifically,

---

28. See further Beale, *Revelation*, 683–703.

Matthew draws upon Dan 9:26–27, 11:31, and 12:11, which describe the "abomination that causes desolation" (*bdelygma tōn erēmōseōn*) that the King of the North will establish in God's holy sanctuary. Along with this image, Matthew adds one from the transitional ch. 7 of Daniel in which it is one "like a son of man" whose arrival on the clouds of heaven (*epi tōn nephelōn tou oupanou hōs huios anthrōpou*) marks the end of the war against the faithful and the arrival of a kingdom that will never be destroyed (Dan 7:13–14). By his reuse of material from Daniel, Matthew affirms the reality of God's kingdom even in a setting where the faithful die at the hands of their oppressors.

Kingdom in Times of Engagement

Throughout the Gospels, the kingdom parables reflect a general view of the kingdom that is remarkably consistent with that presented in Daniel 1–7. In both cases, for example, the kingdom is an often-hidden reality. In Daniel, the rock that falls to earth and grows to become a great mountain crushes *all* of the kingdoms of the statue even if it only becomes visible in the time of the final one (Dan 2:44). In the narratives that follow, God's sovereignty is present and his power real even when Babylon and Persia seem dominant. Similarly, in the Gospels, the presence of the kingdom of God is not always obvious. In Matthew, it is likened to a treasure that is hidden in a field or a merchant seeking pearls (Matt 13:44–46). In both cases, the presence of the kingdom is not immediately evident. In the parable of the Net, the kingdom is likened to a net that does its work hidden beneath the surface. Only when it is raised is the final result obvious and the wicked and the righteous are separated (Matt 13:47–50). In this parable, the consigning of the wicked to the flames includes an obvious allusion to Daniel 3.[29] In the supplement to this parable, Jesus remarks that the one instructed in the things of the kingdom is like one who brings out treasures hidden in a storeroom (Matt 13:52).

---

29. In this parable and in the explanation of the parable of the weeds (Matt 13:36–43), the reference to the wicked being thrown into a fiery furnace (*kai balousin autous eis tēn kaminon tou pyros*; "and they shall be thrown into the furnace of fire," Matt 13:50) draws upon the vocabulary of Dan 3 where the righteous Shadrach, Meshach, and Abednego are preserved from the flames (*emblēthēsesthe eis tēn kaminon tou pyros*; "you shall be thrown into the furnace of fire," Dan 3:15). In the New Testament, however, this image is adapted to emphasize that, unlike the righteous Judaeans of old, the wicked will not be preserved.

In both Daniel 1–7 and the New Testament, the kingdom is something that is planted by God and subsequently grows, eventually resulting in a wider awareness of God. Again in Daniel, the kingdom begins as a stone that grows into a mountain (Dan 2:35). In the subsequent narratives, this growth is reflected in the increasingly orthodox testimony of the Babylonian and Persian monarchs.[30] In the parable of the Mustard Seed in Matt 13:31–32, Jesus likens the growth of the kingdom of God[31] to the way in which a tiny seed can eventually become a tree that is substantive enough to provide shelter for the birds. In this concise parable, Matthew combines several terms and phrases that show that he is drawing directly on Daniel for inspiration. These terms, *dendron* (tree), *tois kladois autou* (its branches),[32] and *peteina tou ouranou* (birds of heaven), appear together in the LXX only in Daniel 4 where they are part of the vision of the tree that represents Nebuchadnezzar.[33] The term *kataskēnoun* (live, settle, nest) found in the parable finds a parallel in Theodotion in Dan 4:12. What the parable in Matthew reflects is not only a reuse, but also a reapplication of the material from Daniel 4. What originally spoke of the growth of Nebuchadnezzar's kingdom and the sustenance provided by it is reused by Matthew to speak of the same things in relation to the kingdom of God. In the parable of the Yeast (Matt 13:33), the kingdom of God is likened to yeast that works its way through the dough, bringing about growth as it does so.

In both Daniel 1–7 and the New Testament, the faithful are called to engage society. In Daniel 1–7, the faithful are participants in structures that are not part of the kingdom of God. Their presence there creates a testimony that sometimes puts them at odds with the power structures, but that also transforms those structures. In each case, the faithful

---

30. This development is made most obvious by comparing Nebuchadnezzar's initial well-intentioned, but misguided, worship of Daniel (Dan 2:46) with Darius's decree that all citizens of his kingdom should fear the God of Daniel (Dan 6:26).

31. Where the other Synoptic Gospels use the phrase "kingdom of God," Matthew prefers the more conservative Jewish expression, "kingdom of Heaven." For the purposes of this discussion, the former term will be used even in those instances where Matthew uses the latter.

32. The form in Daniel LXX varies only slightly, appearing as *hoi kladoi autou* (its branches) (4:12).

33. Within this chapter, the term *dendron* (tree) appears five times (Dan 4:10, 20, 22, 23, 26), *klados* (branch) twice (Dan 4:12, 17), and *petaina tou ouranou* (birds of heaven) twice (Dan 4:12, 21).

are rescued from crisis and witness a royal acknowledgment of God. A basic example of how members of the kingdom are to be engaged in society comes in Jesus' response to the question, "Should we pay taxes to Caesar?" (Matt 22:15–22).

An example of how the spread of the kingdom results in an acknowledgment of God is found in Matt 8:5–13, where Jesus heals the servant of the Roman centurion. As Jesus enters Capernaum, he is met by a Roman centurion whose servant is gravely ill. When Jesus offers to go to heal the sick man, the officer demurs, declaring that he understands that Jesus possesses authority over the illness and thus is able to heal the sick regardless of his proximity to them. This acknowledgment by a member of the Roman authority then forms the basis for Jesus' declaration that many from outside Israel will be present in the kingdom of God (Matt 8:11). What makes this acknowledgment by a Gentile all the more significant is the fact that in the preceding narrative, Jesus attempts to prevent the spread of news regarding his healing powers (Matt 8:4). It is the work of Jesus in healing the sick, itself a sign of the arrival of God's kingdom,[34] that leads to the acknowledgment of God on the part of the representative of the ruling authority. This basic pattern is reflected again in the sending of the Twelve to preach the arrival of the kingdom (Matt 10:5–20). As the disciples undertake this work, Jesus warns, they will become the objects of persecution. This, however, will allow them to present divinely given words to governors and kings (Matt 10:17–20). Throughout this opposition, the faithful will be provided with a way of escape (Matt 10:23). Another example of this basic pattern may be found in Acts 16:19–34, the incident in which Paul and Silas are jailed, delivered, and testify to the jailer with the result that he becomes a Christian.

---

34. The arrival of the kingdom as an event marked by acts of healing is indicated in Matt 11:2–6. When John dispatches his disciples to ask Jesus if he is the Messiah, Jesus responds by indicating that his acts of healing answer in the affirmative ("The blind receive sight, the lame walk, those who have leprosy are cured, the deaf hear, the dead are raised, and the good news is preached to the poor," Matt 11:5). As other have noted, Jesus is here alluding to Isa 35, where God's future arrival in power will be marked by healing (Isa 35:5–6) (e.g., Hagner, *Matthew 1–13*, 300–301). In Matt 4:23, Jesus' preaching of the kingdom and healing go hand in hand (also Matt 9:35; Luke 9:2, 11; 10:9). In Matt 9:27, the appeal for healing on the part of the two blind men and their plea to Jesus using the messianic title "Son of David" again links the concept of healing with the presence of the kingdom.

CONCLUSION

For North American Christians, the preceding survey should be a reminder that we are living in the context of engagement, not of martyrdom without vindication. The rhetoric of End Times experts that identifies groups from the United Nations to the Shriners as fronts for the Antichrist, however, suggests that many North American Christians identify most closely with the faithful of Daniel 7/8–12. The explosion in popularity of the *Left Behind* series during the Clinton era is consistent with this basic self-understanding. The reality, however, is markedly different. It is difficult to see how a nation that is home to some of the wealthiest churches on the planet and where public officials from the chief executive down end speeches with "God Bless America" can be regarded as a system at war with the faithful. The consequence of this defensive posture has been a disengagement from the popular culture for a wide swath of Evangelicalism. The extent of this withdrawal is evident in the existence of Christian alternatives to almost everything, including something as innocuous as the diet book. *What Would Jesus Eat?* is simply the latest in a long line of sanctified health and weight-loss tomes that has included such memorable titles as *Slim for Him* and *More of Jesus, Less of Me*.[35] By embracing the Daniel 7/8–12 model of kingdom living, many North Americans, unfortunately, have chosen "hunkering down" like theological survivalists over being "salt and light." For much of the church, the effect has been stultifying. By identifying themselves with the faithful of Daniel 7/8–12, many North American Christians have declined the kind of engagement with society that promotes the kingdom by seeing that God's "will is done on earth as it is in heaven." If there is a segment of the church today that may reasonably identify with the model of Daniel 7/8–12, it is those Christians who live in societies where they are a minority and where anti-blasphemy laws and family honor can mean persecution and death for those who make the radical decision to abandon the dominant religion in favor of following Christ.

---

35. Colbert, *What Would Jesus Eat?*; Kreml, *Slim for Him*; Cavanaugh and Forseth, *More of Jesus, Less of Me*. A further example of such substitution is evident in the way in which End Times teachers such as Jack Van Impe and Hal Lindsey have fashioned their television programs after secular news magazine shows. In addition, North American Christians have access to specifically "Christian" or "biblically-based" home school curricula, internet and long distance phone service, network radio and television, children's community sports, cancer treatment, financial planning, retirement facilities, vacation services, etc.

While he sits at the opposite end of the theological spectrum from North American conservative Christians, Douglas John Hall takes a view of the future of the faithful that shares curious similarities with the defensive posture outlined above. In Hall's analysis, however, it is demographics that conspire against the church. As noted in the introduction, the silver lining that Hall sees in this numerical decline is embodied in his hope that as a marginalized entity, the church will identify with other marginalized groups in society to more effectively critique its power structures. While Hall's view preserves the principle of engaging and testifying to the powers that be, it seems to abandon the biblical idea of the growth of the kingdom.

What the preceding survey should tell us is that there has never been only one way to live out our status as members of the kingdom of God. Indeed, there is nothing to say that the available models should be limited to the two that have been outlined here. What is critical is that the faithful are appropriately reflective regarding themselves and society and careful in thinking about how best they should act out their identity as members of God's kingdom. To apply the wrong model may lead to ineffectiveness in engaging culture or an unwarranted pessimism when imagining the church's future.

BIBLIOGRAPHY

Aland, Kurt, et al., eds. *The Greek New Testament*. Nestle-Aland 27th ed., 4th rev. ed. Stuttgart: Deutsche Bibelgesellschaft, 1994.

Bartholomew, Craig D., and Michael W. Goheen. *The Drama of Scripture: Finding Our Place in the Biblical Story*. Grand Rapids: Baker, 2004.

Beale, G. K. *The Book of Revelation: A Commentary on the Greek Text*. NIGTC. Grand Rapids: Eerdmans, 1999.

———. *The Use of Daniel in Jewish Apocalyptic Literature and in the Revelation of St. John*. Lanham, MD: University Press of America, 1984.

Bock, Darrell L. *Luke*. 2 vols. BECNT 3. Grand Rapids: Baker, 1996.

Bruce, F. F. *Israel and the Nations: The History of Israel from the Exodus to the Fall of the Second Temple*. Rev. ed. Carlisle: Paternoster, 1997.

———. *New Testament History*. Garden City, NY: Doubleday, 1980.

Cavanaugh, Joan, and Pat Forseth. *More of Jesus, Less of Me*. Plainfield, NJ: Logos, 1976.

Colbert, Don. *What Would Jesus Eat? The Ultimate Program for Eating Well, Feeling Great, and Living Longer*. Nashville: Nelson, 2005.

Collins, John J. *The Apocalyptic Imagination: An Introduction to the Jewish Matrix of Christianity*. New York: Crossroad, 1984.

Davies, W. D., and Dale C. Allison Jr. *The Gospel according to Saint Matthew*. 3 vols. ICC. Edinburgh: T. & T. Clark, 1991.

Donaldson, Terence L. *Jesus on the Mountain: A Study in Matthean Theology.* JSNTSup 8. Sheffield: JSOT Press, 1985.

Elliger, Karl, and W. Rudolph, eds. *Biblia Hebraica Stuttgartensia.* Minor ed. Stuttgart: Deutsche Bibelgesellschaft, 1984.

Fitzmyer, Joseph A. *The Gospel according to Luke [X–XXIV]: Introduction, Translation, and Notes.* AB 28A. Garden City, NY: Doubleday, 1985.

Goldingay, John. *Daniel.* WBC 30. Dallas: Word, 1989.

Green, Joel B. *The Gospel of Luke.* NICNT. Grand Rapids: Eerdmans, 1997.

Hagner, Donald A. *Matthew 1–13.* WBC 33A. Dallas: Word, 1993.

Hall, Douglas John. *The End of Christendom and the Future of Christianity.* Valley Forge, PA: Trinity Press International, 1997.

Hanson, Paul D. *Old Testament Apocalyptic.* Nashville: Abingdon, 1987.

Johnson, Luke Timothy. *The Gospel of Luke.* SP 3. Collegeville, MN: Liturgical, 1991.

Kreml, Patricia Banta. *Slim for Him.* Plainfield, NJ: Logos, 1976.

Marshall, I. Howard. *The Gospel of Luke.* NIGTC 3. Grand Rapids: Eerdmans, 1978.

Mendenhall, George E. "Covenant Forms in Israelite Tradition." *BA* 17.3 (1954) 50–76.

Rahlfs, Alfred, ed. *Septuaginta.* Stuttgart: Deutsche Bibelgesellschaft, 1935. Repr. 1979.

Walters, Stanley D. "The End (of What?) Has Come." *TJT* 2 (1986) 23–46.

Weinfeld, Moshe. "Deuteronomy, Book of." In *ABD* 2:168–83.

Wilson, Gerald H. "The Shape of the Book of Psalms." *Int* 46 (1992) 129–42.

3

Mark, Matthew, and Mission

Faith, Failure, and the Fidelity of Jesus

MICHAEL P. KNOWLES

INTRODUCTION

IF THE BIBLE IS the church's book, then Christians read the Gospels as ancient accounts of their own history. Reading Scripture is an exercise in communal self-reflection, however great the distance in time, geography, or culture from one's present situation. Examining missiology in particular amounts to an inquiry into the origins of one's own existence: it is a study in religious identity as much as an exercise in theological, historical, or literary methodology. Thus the question Jesus puts to his immediate disciples—"Who do people say that I am?" (Mark 8:27)—finds its counterpart in the question later followers ask themselves: "Who do the Gospels say that *we* are?" As it turns out, the two questions (and their answers) are intimately connected, but not always in the manner we expect. Our examination of mission in Mark will pursue a series of literary and thematic links connecting the Evangelist's programmatic opening statement (1:1) to the beginning of Jesus' Galilean ministry (1:14–15) and the call of the first four disciples (1:16–20), to the choosing of the Twelve (3:13–19), and finally to Jesus' sending of them into the villages of Galilee (6:7–13). Our study of Matthew will concentrate on points of departure from Mark, and on the delineation of a distinct missiology following the failure of the mission to Israel, in the aftermath of the First Jewish War.

MARK'S "GOSPEL OF JESUS CHRIST" AND THE ANNOUNCEMENT OF GOD'S KINGDOM

Mark opens with a bold declaration: "The beginning of the gospel of Jesus Christ, son of God." On the face of it, this is a statement about the identity of Jesus and the εὐαγγέλιον (*euangelion*) that he proclaims. But to what does the phrase ἀρχὴ τοῦ εὐαγγελίου (*archē tou euangeliou*) refer: is this the beginning of *Mark's* Gospel document, or a reference to the historical origins of Jesus' message, the beginning of the gospel that Jesus proclaims? The answer, surely, is both. For Mark's text is part and product of that which he chronicles, both consequence and cause of gospel proclamation, an example of the engaged testimony that Jesus both embodies in his own person and enjoins on those whom he draws to himself.

The link to Mark's literary opening is obvious in the words with which Jesus commences his public ministry: "Now after John was arrested, Jesus came to Galilee, proclaiming the good news of God, and saying, 'The time is fulfilled, and the kingdom of God has come near; repent, and believe in the good news'" (Mark 1:14–15). Where Mark proclaims the εὐαγγελίου Ἰησοῦ Χριστοῦ (*euangeliou Iēsou Christou*, the gospel of Jesus Christ), Jesus, he says, preaches the εὐαγγέλιον τοῦ θεοῦ (*euangelion tou theou*, the gospel of God), calling those who hear him to turn and trust in this "good news" (μετανοεῖτε καὶ πιστεύετε ἐν τῷ εὐαγγελίῳ, *metanoeite kai pisteuete en tō euangeliō*). Mark's literary mission reflects that of Jesus, even as Jesus' own mission is rooted in the antecedent purposes of God, the *missio dei*.[1] That is, Mark reports Jesus' mission as a direct expression and re-assertion of the divine reign: "The time is fulfilled, and the kingdom of God has come near." This announcement seems unexpected in several senses: the declaration of God's dominion occurs away from Jerusalem, the theo-political heart of the nation. It is proclaimed by a teacher who relies on charismatic authority instead of formal training or authorization; rather than vindicating God's people against their oppressors, it calls them to repentance. In short, this announcement is prophetically counter-intuitive in several respects. But it is also definitively and authoritatively *revelatory*, intended by Mark as an unambiguous declaration of God's saving purpose.[2]

---

1. On this concept, see Bosch, *Transforming Mission*, 390–92. Unless otherwise indicated, scriptural quotations follow the text of the NRSV.

2. On the definitively revelatory character of Mark 1:14–15, see Webster, "Disciple-

The sense of Jesus' proclamation is that "The time is fulfilled, the kingdom of God draws near; *therefore* repent and trust the good news." He announces God's reign in terms that are neither abstract nor impersonal, but call into being a new community with a new identity. God's engagement in the history of his people calls, paradoxically, for reciprocal engagement on their part. The call to submit to God's reign places the onus on those who have, Jesus implies, rebelled against it and are now called to return: out of this return from spiritual exile the new community of God's people will emerge.[3] Our long familiarity with these words is liable to obscure their subversive, even revolutionary character, for Caesar, not Jesus, was "Savior," "Son of God," and especially *Kyrios*, "Lord."[4] The only contemporary *basileia* (kingdom or dominion) to be reckoned with was, of course, Imperial Rome, as the Zealots of the first Jewish revolt would discover in irrefutable fashion. Yet even God's chosen nation, suffering under foreign domination—victims of ungodliness rather than ungodly themselves—Jesus calls to repentance! Such an appeal is audacious, to say the least. Yet the kingdom Christ declares is so powerful, so contrary to human standards and human understanding, that it calls *all* humanity, Jew and Gentile, pious and pagan alike, to turn from their customary ways and trust anew in God.

Even so, Mark understands Jesus' call not in generic or nationalist terms, but as immediate, specific, and individual. Bosch notes the intentional juxtaposition of Jesus' declaration of the kingdom's advent and the calling of the first four disciples, quoting Pesch to this effect: "Calling, discipleship and mission belong together."[5] Mark's repeated καί (*kai*, "and") is all-important in this regard:

> *And* passing along by the Sea of Galilee, he saw Simon and Andrew . . . casting a net into the sea . . . *And* Jesus said to them, "Follow me *and* I will make you become fishers of men." (Mark 1:16–17; RSV)

---

ship and Calling," 137, "The good news of God is from God, about God, enacted and made known by God."

3. That Second Temple Judaism conceived of itself as continuing in exile, given foreign domination of the land of Israel, is generally acknowledged: see summary discussion in Wright, *New Testament and the People of God*, 268–72.

4. See, e.g., Kim, "The Anarthrous *huios theou*"; Mowery, "Son of God"; Evans, "Beginning of the Good News."

5. Bosch, *Transforming Mission*, 36; and, further, Harris, *Mission in the Gospels*, 78–82.

This is less stylistic sloppiness than theological continuity, directly linking Jesus' proclamation (vv. 14–15) to the call of the fishermen (vv. 16–17a) and a missional commissioning of their own (v. 17b). But while the call to discipleship entails a call to mission, the two cannot simply be collapsed into each other. Rather, the sequence and theological priority of the different elements must be preserved, for the mission of the disciples (and, by implication, of the church) is the product of Jesus' mission, not identical with it. Only by virtue of having first been the object of God's missionary intent, expressed in Jesus, does the community of disciples become the instrument and further extension of that mission. This, at the very least, is the significance of the striking contrast between more typical contemporary patterns of discipleship, according to which it was the prerogative of the disciple to attach himself to a teacher of his own choosing, and Jesus' insistence on selecting disciples for himself.[6] This has interesting, if perhaps uncomfortable, implications for models of conversion that prevail within Western pietist spirituality. Likewise it runs counter to the general outlook of much Christian activism, for Jesus' irreplaceable initiative clearly implies that because the in-breaking of God's reign is the cause of the disciples' mission, Christian mission (however faithful) can never be the cause of the kingdom.

The mission of Jesus, and therefore also the mission of his disciples, is expressly eschatological. We see this, first, in Jesus' declaration that "the time is fulfilled." Accordingly, "the hearers are called to turn away from the old age that is now on its deathbed . . . [and] to turn in faith toward the new age that is dawning, in which God will reign as king."[7] The eschatological character of the disciples' mission emerges especially in the call for them to become ἁλιεῖς ἀνθρώπων (*halieis anthrōpon*, fishers of people). As at Qumran, the metaphor of fishing for people (likely alluding to Jer 16:16) portrays the disciples as agents of God's ingathering for final judgment.[8] The force and authority of Jesus' call is reflected also in the response of Simon and Andrew, and subsequently James and John:

---

6. Bosch, *Transforming Mission*, 36–37.
7. Marcus, *Mark 1–8*, 175.
8. See further Wuellner, *Meaning of "Fishers of Men."* Notwithstanding the fact that "In the Greco-Roman environment a fisher of people is often a teacher" (Marcus, *Mark 1–8*, 184), the overtones of eschatological conquest might seem apt for Roman subjects familiar with the popular gladiatorial pairing of the *retiarius* (net-thrower) and the *murmillo*, whose name and role in combat derived from the stylized fish (μόρμυλος, *mormylos*) represented on his helmet.

"*immediately* they left their nets and followed him" (Mark 1:18; cf. 1:20). Their abrupt departure, abandoning kinship ties and economic responsibilities, implies the adoption of a new circle of primary relationships (cf. 3:31–35) as well as a new means of sustenance.

The location, moreover, is all-important: Jesus' call to fishermen in "Galilee of the Gentiles," on the shores of the lake itself, suggests (once more quoting Bosch's use of Pesch) that "Their mission would take the fishers of humans across the lake to the Gentiles, to the people for whom Jesus was to die."[9] Yet that is not the immediate focus of Jesus' own ministry: instead Mark relates Jesus' call of Levi, son of Alphaeus (2:14), and of the remainder of the inner Twelve (3:13–19), even though the circumstances of the latter are not described in detail. What does emerge clearly, however, are the conditions of discipleship, which are equally the conditions of mission: "[Jesus] appointed twelve, whom he also named apostles, to be with him, and to be sent out to preach and have authority to cast out demons" (Mark 3:14–15, RSV mg.; cf. NRSV).

The number of disciples is hardly accidental: they are to constitute a renewed Israel.[10] Viewed in historical context, this is a deeply shocking and offensive gesture, for (much like the call to repent in general) it implies the inadequacy (even infidelity) of the previous "twelve" tribes of God's choosing. The theological significance of this gesture should be obvious to Christians who are themselves offended by the supersessionist claims of, for example, Islam or Mormonism. For now, in Jesus, God makes a surprising new choice, focusing not on the traditionally pious, but on a handful of obscure individuals whose lives have been to this point unremarkable either for good or for ill. Thus, much as their calling and identity depend on factors outside their own initiative or control, so the disciples' initial mandate is simply to rest in the presence of Jesus, to be "with him" and to share in all his experiences (cf. 5:18; 8:2; 9:2; 14:18–20, 67, etc.). The principle is so simple as to risk, once more, being overlooked: just as the call of the disciples relies on the initiative

---

9. Bosch, *Transforming Mission*, 36.

10. According to Schnabel, *Early Christian Mission*, 1:271, "The symbolism of the number 'twelve' shows that Jesus intended right from the beginning a necessary missionary activity: the twelve disciples are called to contribute . . . to the restoration of God's people promised by the prophets, and it implies at the same time the success of their mission." Both Mark and Matthew, however, acknowledge the effective *failure* of the disciples' mission to Israel, in which case the numerical designation can have only a prophetic or proleptic value.

of Jesus, and the mission of Jesus in turn expresses the purposes of God, so the mission of Jesus' followers is in the first instance theologically passive, open, and receptive: before they are to "accomplish" anything, they merely live out a new identity as companions of the Messiah, witnesses of God's in-breaking reign, those who learn by following, watching, and receiving for themselves all that they will later offer to others. This much is implied already in Jesus' designation of them (if textually authentic) as "apostles." In any event, the disciples share in Jesus' authority as the basis for their own words and actions.

The first element of their missional task is that they are sent out "to proclaim," κηρύσσειν (*kēryssein*). In this, of course, they imitate the activity of the one who sends them, who, we recall, came into Galilee "preaching the evangel of God" (1:14), and has apparently continued to do so ever since: "he went throughout Galilee, preaching in their synagogues and casting out demons" (Mark 1:39). The Twelve are to imitate Jesus in the latter respect also, for he grants them "authority to cast out demons" (3:15; cf. 6:7). This is something the disciples are said to accomplish only once, in the summary statement of 6:13 ("they cast out many demons, and anointed with oil many who were sick and healed them"), to which we will return in due course. More prominent by far is their failure to heal the boy with the unclean spirit while Jesus and the inner three are on the Mount of Transfiguration, a failing that elicits from Jesus both exasperation and rebuke (9:14–29).

Parenthetically, it is instructive to note a further, inverse connection between preaching and healing that emerges on at least three occasions in Mark's Gospel. Where the emissaries of the Messiah are instructed to preach and cast out demons, as corresponding verbal and practical expressions of God's reign, so healing itself leads to preaching in the case of the Galilean leper (1:45), the Gerasene demoniac (5:20), and the deaf-mute's companions (7:36). In each instance the person who is healed or those who have witnessed the healing go out to preach or proclaim (κηρύσσειν, *kēryssein*) all that Jesus has done. Even the example of the woman of Bethany who anoints Jesus' head with costly nard—a "good work" (καλὸν ἔργον, *kalon ergon*) performed in the service of the Messiah—becomes part of the preaching of the gospel (14:6–9). What seems curious, in any event, is that Mark uses κηρύσσειν (*kēryssein*) to describe the activity of John the Baptist twice (1:4, 7), Jesus three times (1:14, 38, 39), and the newly-healed or their companions on a further three occasions (1:45, 5:20, 7:36); but only once (6:12, cf. v. 30) do the newly-minted disciples actually engage in preaching, despite Jesus' commissioning in 3:12 and more general references at 13:10 and 14:9.

THE COMMISSIONING OF THE TWELVE

If Mark's opening statement (1:1) anticipates Jesus' Galilean declaration of his mission (1:14–15), with the latter echoed in turn by his commissioning of the Twelve (3:14–15), the sending of the twelve disciples (6:7–13, 30) forms yet another link in this chain by repeating earlier themes of authority and exorcism. The language of these four passages is by no means identical: rather, each picks up at least one theme or strand from the one immediately prior, creating a series of meaningful theological linkages. The links extend beyond the limits of the text itself, as Mark likely understands these instructions to apply to his own church as well. For, he writes, Jesus "called the twelve and *began* (ἤρξατο, *ērxato*) to send them out two by two" (6:7), implying (as with Luke's ἤρξατο, *ērxato*, in Acts 1:1) that the process of commissioning and sending is ongoing.

Here, then, Jesus fulfills his earlier promise to make them "fishers of people," actually sending out his closest disciples in six pairs and imposing on them a telling set of conditions:

> He ordered them to take nothing for their journey except a staff; no bread, no bag, no money in their belts; but to wear sandals and not to put on two tunics. He said to them, "Wherever you enter a house, stay there until you leave the place. If any place will not welcome you and they refuse to hear you, as you leave, shake off the dust that is on your feet as a testimony against them." (Mark 6:8–11)

Although it does not appear at the head of the list, the injunction to wear sandals (6:9) stands out by virtue of its superfluity: surely the disciples would not otherwise have wandered the Galilean hill country barefoot?[11] Yet the explanation for this instruction may be theological rather than literal if, as Joel Marcus proposes, these directions are in-

---

11. Citing *b. Ta'an.* 13a, Mealand, *Poverty and Expectation*, 67 and 121 n. 29, observes that "It was rabbinic practice to go barefoot on fast days, although that rule was relaxed for longer journeys between towns." Both the late date of the source and the inapplicability of the injunction to extended travel obviate this reference for the situation envisaged in Mark.

tended as allusions to the conditions of the Exodus.[12] For it is striking, as Marcus notes, that the instructions are less concerned with what they should bring than with what they should not, for, as with Israel in the wilderness, God may be relied on to furnish their needs.

Two Torah passages in particular supply the details necessary for comparison. The first, Exod 12:11, concerns the manner in which the departing Israelites are to eat the Passover lamb: "This is how you shall eat it: your loins girded, your sandals on your feet, and your staff in your hand; and you shall eat it hurriedly. It is the Passover of the LORD."[13] Perhaps, then, the reference to sandals and staff implies that the disciples are engaged in God's new work of redemption, although such comparison might seem more obvious were it related to the Last Supper. A more general parallel appears in the covenant renewal ceremony from Deut 29, as Moses (speaking for God) recites the conditions of Israel's wilderness journeying:

> I have led you forty years in the wilderness. The clothes on your back have not worn out, and the sandals on your feet have not worn out; you have not eaten bread, and you have not drunk wine or strong drink—so that you may know that I am the LORD your God.[14]

To state the implications of these parallels in maximal terms, God will sustain the Twelve in their mission as a renewed Israel celebrating a reconstituted Passover in a new Exodus, furnishing bread for the journey, together with the clothing and footwear they will need.[15]

---

12. Marcus, *Mark 1–8*, 388–89.

13. The likelihood that a Passover motif is operative in Mark 6:8–9 is heightened by the apparent influence of an early Passover liturgy on the structure of 12:13–37: see Daube, "Earliest Structure."

14. Deut 29:5–6; cf. Deut 8:2–4: "Remember the long way that the LORD your God has led you these forty years in the wilderness, in order to humble you, testing you to know what was in your heart, whether or not you would keep his commandments. He humbled you by letting you hunger, then by feeding you with manna . . . in order to make you understand that one does not live by bread alone, but by every word that comes from the mouth of the LORD. The clothes on your back did not wear out and your feet did not swell these forty years."

15. It is important to note, however, that for both Mark and Matthew, "New Exodus" motifs are mediated and governed by the vision of promised deliverance articulated in Isa 40–55, interpreted christologically: see esp. Watts, *New Exodus*; Harris, *Mission in the Gospels*, 37–69 (on Matthew, emphasizing the eschatological ingathering of the nations).

We may glimpse here a possible reference to early Christian hospitality. But that this is not the primary intent emerges in particular from Jesus' miraculous provision of food for five thousand (6:35–44) then another four thousand (8:1–10) in the "wilderness" (ἔρημος, *erēmos*, 6:31; ἐρημία, *erēmia*, 8:4). Not only does Jesus expect the disciples to trust God likewise for their own needs, he challenges them to provide for the crowds as well (6:37), in both instances demonstrating his ability to satisfy the hungry.[16] Mark then records in painful detail the disciples' concern that they will run short of supplies, their lack of insight, and Jesus' repeated challenge for them to understand (8:14–21). What they fail to see is that Jesus does not expect them to sustain themselves and God's mission. Rather, as his own provision implies, it is God's mission that sustains them: their ministry is possible only because they have been swept up by a new act of divine judgment and liberation, the advent of which is theirs to proclaim and enact as emissaries of the Messiah and the vanguard of a new or renewed Israel.

This explains the severity of the judgment that Jesus pronounces on those who fail to welcome them: "Wherever you enter a house, stay there until you leave the place. If any place will not welcome you and they refuse to hear you, as you leave, shake off the dust that is on your feet as a testimony against them" (6:10–11). Those who fail to hear or welcome the messengers are rejecting nothing less than God's new Exodus and new Israel. With regard to his own church, Mark is not necessarily envisaging a network of Christian safe-houses to welcome the itinerant Evangelists.[17] Rather, his point is theological: the forewarning of rejection (and the lack of an extra tunic for warmth at night) makes even more pressing the spiritual discipline of reliance on God.

---

16. Marcus observes further Exodus allusions in the fact that the five thousand are seated "by hundreds and by fifties" (6:40), recalling the military arrangements of Israel in the wilderness (Exod 18:21, 25; Deut 1:15), and especially in the themes of leaven, testing, and hardness of heart that are integral to the feeding of the four thousand. See Marcus, *Mark 1–8*, 408–9, 482–86.

17. *Pace* Robinson, "Safe House," who proposes a complex historical etiology whereby the earliest itinerant evangelists "at first approached blindly some completely unknown house with the familiar greeting, 'Shalom!', 'Peace!'" (188), but by the time of the canonical Gospels, the missionaries would have developed a regular circuit of "safe-houses," with these eventually developing into house churches of the sort assumed in the Book of Acts.

Mission and Failure

According to Mark 6:12–13, and again 6:30, the disciples are initially successful even beyond the strict letter of Jesus' instructions: they not only preach repentance and cast out "many demons," but also succeed in healing the sick by anointing them with oil, an activity not previously mentioned even in Jesus' own work. But this proves to be their only achievement: from this point onward the disciples are noted more for their failures than for any success in following or imitating their master. According to Mark, this is a failure not only of the disciples' representative mission and ministry—their failure to win more disciples—it represents the failure of their own discipleship as well. We might even say that it represents the failure of Jesus' word and preaching in them. Specifically, Mark depicts the disciples in terms that recall one of the first and most famous parables that Jesus tells in this Gospel, that of seed falling on different kinds of soil. Three times the seed fails to bear fruit: when it is eaten by hungry birds, scorched by the hot sun, and choked by thorns. The relevance of the parable for Jesus' mission lies in the fact that, as we read in 4:14, "The sower sows the word" (τὸν λόγον, *ton logon*). The sower, in other words, is like Jesus himself, who "speaks the word" (2:2; 4:33) to the listening crowds.

Like the three failed sowings, the disciples' own inability to understand Jesus' "word" is set forth in a three-fold cycle demarcated by predictions of Jesus' death (8:27—9:29; 9:30—10:31; 10:32–45) and bracketed, appropriately enough, by accounts of blind men being healed (8:22–26; 10:46–52). In each section, the prediction itself (8:31; 9:31; 10:33–34) is followed by notable error or incomprehension on the part of the disciples, which elicits correction and explanation from their master; the first two incorporate conscious verbal echoes of the parable's interpretation.[18] Thus, in the first cycle, just as "the sower sows the word" only to have Satan snatch it away (4:14–15), so Jesus openly declares the "word" of his impending crucifixion (καὶ παρρησίᾳ τὸν λόγον ἐλάλει, *kai parrēsia ton logon elalei*), only to have a disciple identified with "Satan" attempt to dissuade him (8:32–33). Reiterating their lack of power over evil, this cycle concludes with the disciples unable to cast out an unclean spirit

---

18. For a similar application of categories from the Parable of the Sower to the narrative of Mark's Gospel (although postulating a more complex series of rhetorical correspondences than is proposed here), see Tolbert, *Sowing the Gospel*, esp. 121–230, and, more briefly, Drury, *Parables in the Gospels*, 51–52.

(9:14–29). In the course of the second cycle, Jesus tells an enquirer with "much property" to sell all that he owns in order to find treasure in heaven. But the man is shocked at the word (ἐπὶ τῷ λόγῳ, *epi tō logō*), and goes away disappointed (10:21–22). Jesus then warns that the wealthy will be unable to enter the kingdom, but his disciples fail to understand and are likewise astounded "at his words" (ἐπὶ τοῖς λόγοις αὐτοῦ, *epi tois logois autou*). So Jesus must repeat himself, making the link to the interpretation of the Sower more explicit: "It is easier for a camel to pass through the eye of a needle than for a rich man (πλούσιον, *plousion*) to enter the kingdom of God" (10:23–25; cf. the seduction of weath, ἡ ἀπάτη τοῦ πλούτου, *hē apatē tou ploutou*, 4:19).[19] The cycle comes to an end with Jesus promising, in terms that reflect the vocabulary of 4:17 (when tribulation or persecution comes, γενομένης θλίψεως ἢ διωγμοῦ, *genomenēs thlipseōs ē diōgmou*) and 4:20 (one hundred, ἐν ἑκατόν, *hen hekaton*), that those who have left everything for his sake will "receive a hundredfold" (λάβῃ ἑκατονταπλασίονα, *labē hekatontaplasiona*) of the same in return, albeit "with persecutions" (μετὰ διωγμῶν, *meta diōgmōn*) (so 10:30; cf. 13:19, 24: θλῖψις, *thlipsis*). Against the objection that this particular saying does not anticipate failure on the part of the disciples, we need only look ahead to 14:50 where, faced with the prospect of their own arrest, "All of them deserted him and fled" (compare Jesus' earlier warning not to be "ashamed of me *and my words*" [καὶ τοὺς ἐμοὺς λόγους, *kai tous emous logous*, 8:38]).[20] In fact it is Peter who initiates this debate (10:28), and Peter who will later most explicitly deny his Lord (14:66–72), in anticipation of which Jesus exhorts him in 14:38 to "Stay awake and pray ἵνα μὴ ἔλθητε εἰς πειρασμόν (*hina mē elthēte eis peirasmon*); meaning, lest he should come to trial, have his faithfulness put to the test. For Jesus must know—Mark certainly knows, as the parable has foretold—that he, like all the rest, will fail utterly. The third prediction cycle consists largely of the request by James and John to sit at Jesus' right and left hand in glory. The Lord's reply indicates that to be accorded such an honor, were it possible, would require them to share his "baptism" and "cup" of suffering, something he himself is barely able to undergo (cf. 14:36). If previous responses have underscored their

---

19. Elsewhere in Mark, compare 12:41–44 (the widow's pittance is more than all that the wealthy [πλούσιοι] contribute to the temple treasury) or 14:10–11 (Judas succumbs to the "seduction of wealth").

20. λόγους (*logous*) is omitted by 𝔓45 W copsa *et al.*: see *TCGNT*4, 84.

failure to heed Jesus' words, this exchange highlights their imminent and even more momentous failure to follow Jesus' example at the moment of his betrayal and crucifixion.

The language of the parable of the Sower and its interpretation thus correspond to features of thematic content and specific wording within the three-fold cycle of prediction, failure, and correction that constitute Mark 8:27—10:45. This section repeatedly demonstrates the disciples' failure even to understand Jesus' words, much less remain true to them. But despite these initial challenges, the parable of the Sower's seed does not end with failure, any more than does Mark's vision of the gospel. On the contrary, some seed is said to multiply "thirty, sixty, and a hundredfold." The significance of the historically unrealistic yield ratios of the fruitful seed has been the subject of much debate. Most interpreters take the point of the multiplication to be its miraculous greatness, eschatological in dimension.[21] For those familiar with the grinding hardships of agrarian life, the emphasis on divine intervention would have been unmistakable, since the envisaged yields were well beyond the ability of even the most diligent and successful farmer. Notwithstanding occasional exaggerations on the part of some classical authors, more realistic estimates suggest that "a four-fold or five-fold yield is probably typical of much of the Mediterranean world in antiquity, especially in Palestine." Hence "even the grain that gave a yield of thirty-fold . . . was not only exceptional, it was miraculous in first-century Palestine."[22] Douglas Oakman confirms this reading on socio-economic grounds, pointing out that contrary to the emphasis on diligent care and strenuous physical labor required of a peasant farmer, divine providence alone can triumph over the impediments of nature and cause the seed to bear fruit.[23] Certainly this is the sense conveyed by the parable immediately following, which concerns seed that bears fruit "of itself (αὐτομάτη, *automatē*)," even while the weary farmer sleeps. Growth is a mystery: the sower himself "does not know how" the seed bears fruit (Mark 4:26–29).[24]

---

21. E.g., Jeremias, *Gleichnisse Jesu*, 149–50. Marcus (*Mark 1–8*, 297) astutely observes that the progression "30–60–100" is non-sequential (unlike "30–60–90" or "30–60–120"), which lends particular prominence to the concluding tally.

22. McIver, "One Hundred-Fold Yield"; cf. Marcus, *Mark 1–8*, 292–93. These estimates are confirmed by Hamel, *Poverty and Charity*, 125–37.

23. Oakman, *Economic Questions*, 100–108.

24. Cf. ibid., 109–14; Tolbert, *Sowing the Gospel*, 161–62.

The same mystery underlies the parable of the mustard seed, "which, when sown upon the ground, is the smallest of all the seeds on earth; yet when it is sown it grows up and becomes the greatest of all shrubs, and puts forth large branches, so that the birds of the air can make nests in its shade" (Mark 4:31–32). Neither the Twelve nor Mark's readers can entertain any illusion that they themselves are responsible for such wildly disproportionate growth. The life-giving divine fecundity that produces unexpectedly magnificent results from such meager beginnings, remaining constant "night and day" (4:27), recalls Jesus' description in Matthew of the gracious Father who "makes his sun rise on the evil and on the good, and sends rain on the just and on the unjust" (Matt 5:45), as well as the Johannine theme of the Father who continues to labor for the benefit of humanity even while the latter take their Sabbath rest (John 5:17). But there is more at stake here than divine providence in general or the bounty of creation in particular. These are, after all, parables of God's kingdom, the kingdom Jesus himself proclaims, to which the disciples bear witness, whose seeds are sown in the "word" that they preach. Taken together, the parables of the sower, the seed growing secretly, and the mustard seed suggest a possible solution to the much-vexed question of why Mark's Gospel portrays the disciples in such a negative light. In historical terms, Mark must account, on the one hand, for the disciples' partnership with Jesus in declaring the imminent reign and new exodus of God and, on the other, for their shameful betrayal and abandonment of him. The extent to which this portrayal also reflects the circumstances of Mark's church must remain a matter of speculation. But what emerges in any event is a clear relativizing of human—ecclesiastical—agency. Mark's readers are led to conclude that their own community exists partly *despite* and not simply because of the role of Jesus' first followers. Not unlike the weary farmer, slumbering while the seed comes to life, the disciples also sleep in Gethsemane. Yet the "word" that is the seed and "gospel" of God's kingdom flourishes and bears fruit in spite of them. What the disciples do initially accomplish reflects the authority of the one who has sent them, but when they subsequently fail to understand, obey, or take up their respective crosses and follow Jesus to his (Mark 8:34–35), he goes forward without them. Whatever gifts the disciples are accorded, in the end only Jesus can give sight to the blind, and only Jesus can inspire faith in those who have so little (so 4:40; 11:22–24; contrast 2:5; 5:34, 36; 9:23–24; 10:52). In both parable and practice, then, whether in the teaching of Jesus or the missionary endeavor of his followers, Mark unambiguously emphasizes the mysterious, all-powerful agency of God—not the disciples—as providing essential evidence of the kingdom at work.

By establishing this contrast between Jesus and his first followers, between divine agency and human endeavor, Mark portrays the ongoing task of the church as a kind of "mission *malgré soi*." He neither excuses failure nor sanctifies disobedience, but rather seeks to pinpoint the proper theological foundations of discipleship and mission alike. Only the authority of Jesus makes mission possible in the face of human inadequacy and half-hearted or uncomprehending discipleship. There is comfort for Mark's congregation—and hope for our own—in the assurance that, however obscure or ineffectual their efforts may seem, Christ's identity is unchanged, his call unvarying, his authorization undiminished. For a contemporary church with triumphalist tendencies, even as it struggles with a diminished sense of identity, direction, and power, Mark's message could hardly be more timely.

MATTHEW: THE PRESENCE OF JESUS AND THE ABSENCE OF MISSION

Where the missiology of Mark emerges clearly in the opening line of his Gospel, Matthew's missiology is most evident at his conclusion, as Jesus sends his followers out to "make disciples of all nations" while assuring them, "I am with you always, to the end of the age" (Matt 28:18, 20). For whereas Mark's Jesus typically calls the disciples to accompany and remain "with him" (Mark 3:14; cf. 5:18; 9:2; 14:33), Matthew emphasizes Jesus' presence—indeed, God's presence—with *them*. This theme emerges especially at three key moments in the Gospel: at the naming of the infant Messiah, in Jesus' instructions to the church, and in his departing words of commissioning for ministry. Thus Matthew explains that Joseph's dream (in which an angel tells him to name the boy "Jesus") "took place to fulfill what had been spoken by the Lord through the prophet: 'Look, the virgin shall conceive and bear a son, and they shall name him Emmanuel,' which means, '*God is with us*'" (1:22–23, emphasis added). In the fourth of Matthew's five blocks of teaching material, the one containing Jesus' instructions to the gathered church, he declares, "Where two or three are gathered in my name, I am there among them" (18:20). The third and final example has already been cited. Taken together, these passages indicate that, in Matthew's view, the theme of the divine presence is central, first, to Jesus' own identity as Messiah; second, to the life of the community that gathers around that indwelling presence; and third, to the continuing mission of making "disciples of all nations." Matthew thus depicts the infant church in terms that resemble Israel in the desert, guided and sustained by the presence of God in their midst.[25]

What implications does this have for Matthean missiology, especially given the Evangelist's tendency to add material on top rather than in place of his Markan source? Matthew too sees Jesus inaugurating his Galilean ministry with a call to repentance (Matt 4:17; cf. Mark 1:15), even preceding it with a report of identically-worded preaching by John the Baptist (Matt 3:2). Likewise he retains the call for Simon and Andrew (as well as, implicitly, James and John) to become fishermen for God's kingdom (Matt 4:18-22//Mark 1:16-20), as he does Jesus' choice and bestowal of authority on the Twelve (Matt 10:1-4//Mark 3:13-19). Whereas for Mark the calling and sending of the Twelve occur separately (4:13-19; 6:8-11), Matthew combines the two accounts into a single passage (Matt 10:1-14: see Figure 1). This implies, even more clearly than in Mark, that the disciples are called specifically for the purpose of imitating and extending Jesus' own ministry.

Accordingly, Matthew recasts the granting of authority to preach as an aspect of Jesus' mission charge, condensing Mark 3:14 ("he appointed twelve . . . to be sent out to preach") and 6:12 ("they went out and preached that all should repent") into a single command: "Preach as you go, saying, 'The kingdom of heaven is at hand'" (10:7). Repeating the phrasing of Matt 3:2 and 4:17 draws the message of the disciples into direct line with that of John the Baptist and Jesus, in addition to which Matthew deletes Mark's several uses of the verb κηρύσσειν (*kēryssein*, to preach) to describe testimony from recipients of or witnesses to healing (Mark 1:45; 5:20; 7:36; cf. Matt 8:4, 34; 15:31). Proclamation, in other words, is for Matthew the characteristic activity only of John, the Messiah, or those whom the Messiah has directly authorized. Similarly, Matthew makes more precise use of the verb διδάσκειν (*didaskein*, to teach) frequently deleting (Mark 2:13; 4:1-2; 8:31; 9:31; 11:17; 12:35) or replacing it (Mark 6:34; 10:1; cf. Matt 14:14; 19:2), even when referring to Jesus, and retaining such vocabulary only for

---

25. The most comprehensive recent study of this motif is Kupp, *Matthew's Emmanuel*.

FIGURE 1: The Mission Charge in Mark and Matthew

Mark 6	Matthew 10
7 He called the twelve and began to send them out two by two, and gave them authority over the unclean spirits.	1 Then Jesus summoned his twelve disciples and gave them authority over unclean spirits, to cast them out, and to cure every disease and every sickness … 5 These twelve Jesus sent out with the following instructions: "Go nowhere among the Gentiles, and enter no town of the Samaritans, 6 but go rather to the lost sheep of the house of Israel. 7 As you go, proclaim the good news, 'The kingdom of heaven has come near.' 8 Cure the sick, raise the dead, cleanse the lepers, cast out demons. You received without payment; give without payment.
8 He ordered them to take nothing for their journey except a staff; no bread, no bag, no copper [money] in their belts; 9 but to wear sandals and not to put on two tunics.	9 Take no gold, or silver, or copper in your belts, 10 no bag for your journey, or two tunics, or sandals, or a staff; for laborers deserve their food. 11 Whatever town or village you enter, find out who in it is worthy, and stay there until you leave.
10 He said to them, "Wherever you enter a house, stay there until you leave the place.	12 As you enter the house, greet it. 13 If the house is worthy, let your peace come upon it; but if it is not worthy, let your peace return to you.
11 If any place will not welcome you and they refuse to hear you, as you leave, shake off the dust that is on your feet as a testimony against them."	14 If anyone will not welcome you or listen to your words, shake off the dust from your feet as you leave that house or town. 15 Truly I tell you, it will be more tolerable for the land of Sodom and Gomorrah on the day of judgment than for that town."

Jesus' activity in synagogue (Mark 6:2//Matt 13:54; Mark 6:6 cf. Matt 9:35) or Temple (Mark 14:49//Matt 26:65; Matt 21:23 cf. Mark 11:27; Matt 22:33) or—in the case of the Sermon on the Mount—employing it to frame a significant block of halachic instruction (Matt 7:28–29 with 5:2; cf. Mark 1:21–22).[26] Indeed, for Matthew the combination of "teaching," "preaching," and "healing" provides a characteristic summary of Jesus' ministry (Matt 4:23; 9:35; 11:1).

By contrast, the disciples are not once said to "teach" in the course of their time with Jesus (with Matt 14:12 deleting "they taught," ἐδίδαξαν, *edidaxan*, from Mark 6:30), for he alone is rightfully called "rabbi" and "teacher" (διδάσκαλος, καθηγητής, *didaskalos, kathēgētēs*: Matt 23:7–10). *Their* teaching is a distinctly post-Easter activity ("teaching them to obey all that I have commanded you," 28:20). The same appears true of the disciples' testimony (μαρτύριον, *martyrion*, 10:18; 24:14; cf. 18:16),[27] preaching (κηρύσσειν, *kēryssein*, 24:14; 26:13), and proclamation of the evangel (εὐαγγέλιον, *euangelion*, Matt 24:14; 26:13): notwithstanding the language of Jesus' charge, not once does Matthew portray the disciples actually carrying out these activities; so also with the disciples' ministry of healing. According to Matthew, Jesus imparts "authority over unclean spirits, to cast them out, and to cure every disease and every sickness (ἐξουσίαν πνευμάτων ἀκαθάρτων ὥστε ἐκβάλλειν αὐτὰ καὶ θεραπεύειν πᾶσαν νόσον καὶ πᾶσαν μαλακίαν, *exsousian pneumatōn akathartōn hōste ekballein auta kai therapeuein pasan noson kai pasan malakian*, 10:1), directly echoing the Messiah's own task of "curing every disease and every sickness among the people" (καὶ θεραπεύων πᾶσαν νόσον καὶ πᾶσαν μαλακίαν, *kai therapeuōn pasan noson kai pasan malakian*, Matt 4:23; so 9:35). Jesus' actual charge to them is both detailed and explicit: "As you go, proclaim the good news, 'The kingdom of heaven has come near.' Cure the sick, raise the dead, cleanse the lepers, cast out demons" (Matt 10:7–8). As noted earlier, Mark reports that the Twelve indeed "cast out many demons, and anointed with oil many who were sick and healed them," returning to tell Jesus "all that they had done and taught" (Mark 6:13, 30). But neither passage appears in Matthew.

26. Conversely, Matt 22:41 deletes the specification from Mark 12:35 that Jesus is teaching in the temple, while Matt 22:33 does the opposite (cf. Mark 12:27), perhaps because his location has already been indicated, i.e., he enters the temple in 21:33 and departs at 24:1.

27. Note in this regard the deletion of εἰς μαρτύριον αὐτοῖς (*eis martyrion autois*, Mark 6:11) from Matt 10:14.

Jesus' response, shortly thereafter, to the question of an imprisoned John, "the blind receive their sight, the lame walk, the lepers are cleansed, the deaf hear, the dead are raised, and the poor have good news brought to them," closely echoes the language of Jesus' commissioning (Matt 11:5). But this answer refers only to "the deeds of the Christ" (11:2). In this Gospel, the only healing we see the disciples attempt ends in abject failure (Matt 17:14–16//Mark 9:14–17), an outcome Jesus blames on their lack of faith (Matt 17:20, as distinct from Jesus' response in Mark, "This kind can come out only through prayer," 9:29). In sum, while the disciples are charged with accomplishing nothing less than a conscious imitation and continuation of Jesus' ministry, the actual fulfillment of this weighty responsibility seems to lie on the other side of 28:20, presumably in the life of the community to and for which the Evangelist writes.

If the failure of the Markan disciples is related in some measure to the circumstances of Jesus' betrayal and abandonment, Matthew also has in view the subsequent fate of Jerusalem and Judea. Composing his Gospel in the dark shadow of abortive revolt and the catastrophic destruction to which it has led, Matthew is conscious that Jesus and his followers alike have failed to win over the people of the land of Israel.[28] Perhaps this is the best explanation for the much-controverted difference between Jesus' initial command, "Go nowhere among the Gentiles (εἰς ὁδὸν ἐθνῶν, *eis hodon ethnōn*) but go rather to the lost sheep of the house of Israel" (10:5–6), and that with which the Gospel concludes: "Make disciples of all nations" (πάντα τὰ ἔθνη, *panta ta ethnē*, 28:19). Accordingly, Jesus laments over Chorazin, Bethsaida, and Capernaum in the north (Matt 11:20–24); his own city of Nazareth takes offense at him (Matt 13:53–58//Mark 6:1–6); and he grieves deeply over Jerusalem's rejection of past prophets and present Messiah alike (Matt 23:37–39). However we interpret the term "lost sheep," it is evident that both Jesus' own mission to Israel and that of his followers have been of limited effect. Both have now been overtaken by political realities on the ground, for "the kingdoms of the world" (4:8) have triumphed decisively over "the city of the great King" (5:35), and even "the kingdom of heaven

---

28. Nor is such concern obviated if Matthew and his community are located in Syrian Antioch, which served as a staging ground and supply center for Rome's response to the Jewish rebellion (so Carter, "Matthaean Christology," 153), and where popular reaction to the war expressed itself in the form of furious repression and pogroms against the Antiochene Jews (Josephus, *J.W.* 7.47–62).

suffers violence" (11:12). Following the First Jewish War it has become painfully obvious, to borrow a line from John, that whatever kingdom Jesus proclaims is surely "not of this world" (John 18:36): this inescapable reality requires a redefinition of the Christian mission, now directed not to "the house of Israel" alone (at least in any geopolitical sense), but to "all nations."

The paradox, of course, is that—however redefined—the mission of the church is now expanded rather than diminished. Yet even if the religious, social, political, and ethnic scope of their proclamation incorporates "all nations," the terms and conditions of its conduct remain unchanged. That is, the simple fact of Matthew having (like Mark) retained such powerful words of commissioning amidst the failure of Jesus, of the Twelve, and of the pre-70 church to fully convince and convert their first audience—ethnic Israel—argues forcefully for their ongoing validity in a changed situation. With this in mind, we return to the terms of that commissioning to discover how mission is to be conducted in the community for which Matthew writes.

SANDALS AND STAFF: WITH OR WITHOUT?

As we saw earlier, Mark's Jesus instructs the disciples, "to take nothing for their journey except a staff; no bread, no bag, no copper in their belts; but to wear sandals and not to put on two tunics" (Mark 6:7–8). In other words, they may take only staff, sandals, and a single tunic. Matthew 10:9–10 deletes the reference to bread, expands the monetary references, and flatly contradicts the instructions regarding sandals and staff: "Take no gold, or silver, or copper in your belts, no bag for your journey, or two tunics, *or sandals, or a staff*; for laborers deserve their food." Taken literally, Matthew envisages a journey with neither walking-stick nor footwear. Neither stipulation makes much sense: while the former is found also in Luke 9:3, the latter is, at the very least, impracticable for anything more than a short trip.[29] It is possible, nonetheless, that Matthew found in Q a reversal of the Markan injunction, and added to it because it re-

---

29. The structure of the phrase in Matt 10:10 μὴ πήραν εἰς ὁδὸν μηδὲ δύο χιτῶνας μηδὲ ὑποδήματα μηδὲ ῥάβδον (*mē pēran eis hodon mēde duo chitōnas mēde hypodēmata mēde hrabdon*) does not indicate that ὑποδήματα is governed by the δύο of δύο χιτῶνας (i.e., that Jesus is forbidding them from carrying two tunics *and* a second pair of sandals).

called for him traditional instructions describing conduct appropriate to the Temple precincts:

> A man may not behave himself unseemly while opposite the Eastern Gate [of the Temple] since it faces toward the Holy of Holies. He may not enter into the Temple Mount *with his staff or his sandal or his wallet*, or with the dust upon his feet, nor may he make of it a short by-path; still less may he spit there.[30]

Even if it represents a certain idealization, the antiquity of the Mishnaic reference is probable for the simple reason that it refers to the architecture and orientation of a Temple that is no longer standing. The relevance for Matthew is heightened because Jesus sends the disciples out in pairs (Mark 6:7), a detail Matthew knows from his source even if he does not include it in his text, since according to Matt 18:20 the agreement of "two or three" is sufficient to testify to the Divine presence, namely Jesus (cf. Deut 19:15). Hence to preach and heal on Jesus' behalf is the functional equivalent of being in the Temple: "Whoever receives you receives me," says Jesus, "and whoever receives me receives the One who sent me" (Matt 10:40). Even more obvious in this regard is the promise of 28:18–20: "Go and make disciples of all nations . . . and I am with you always, to the end of the age." In addition to the passage from *Mishnah Berakhot*, Hamel cites *m. Shabb.* 6.4 and 24.1 to the effect that the prohibition against carrying money, sandals, and extra clothing applied in particular to the Sabbath: "In that sense, disciples were actually required to consider every day a Sabbath."[31] He also quotes Mealand with approval: "The approach of the Kingdom makes the time a holy season, and the whole land a holy place."[32] But the sanctity of Sabbath, Temple,

---

30. *m. Ber.* 9.5 (Danby, *Mishnah*, 10); cf. *t. Ber.* 7.19 (17); *y. Ber.* 9.8; *b. Ber.* 62b. The parallel between Matt 10:10 and *m. Ber.* 9.5 is noted by, e.g., Manson, *Sayings of Jesus*, 181; Taylor, *Mark*, 304; Mealand, *Poverty and Expectation*, 67 n. 31 (p. 121); cf. Schweizer, *Evangelium nach Matthäus*, 154. While acknowledging "Jesus' fondness for parabolic actions," Davies and Allison, *Matthew*, 2:173, are non-committal, averring that "it is hard to assess the probability of this conjecture." My colleague James C. Peterson suggests that the prohibition of sandals may also reflect a literal reading of Josh 1:3 ("Every place that the sole of your foot will tread upon I have given to you, as I promised to Moses"), a proposal that might seem superfluous were it not for the fact that in the LXX, "Joshua" is also Ἰησοῦς (*Iēsous*, Jesus).

31. Hamel, *Poverty and Charity*, 69.

32. Hamel, *Poverty and Charity*, 69 n. 85, citing Mealand, *Poverty and Expectation*, 69.

and land alike is anchored in and superseded by that of the Messiah, who is "Lord of the Sabbath" and "greater than the Temple" (Matt 12:6, 8). This, then, is the christological foundation of the Matthean mission, which is carried out not only with messianic authority, in imitation of the Messiah, but in the very presence of the Risen Lord: hence the— theologically symbolic—prohibition of staff or sandals.[33]

Although such proposals are necessarily speculative, reference to the divine presence may shed light on two further details in this account. Matthew's expansion of Mark's "no copper in the belt" (μὴ εἰς τὴν ζώνην χαλκόν, *mē eis tēn zōnēn chalkon,* Mark 6:8) to read "do not take gold or silver or copper in your belts" (μὴ κτήσησθε χρυσὸν μηδὲ ἄργυρον μηδὲ χαλκὸν εἰς τὰς ζώνας ὑμῶν (*mē ktēsesthe chryson mēde argyron mēde chalkon eis tas zōnas hymōn,* Matt 10:9) is sometimes understood as a clue to the greater wealth of the Matthean church.[34] While this is certainly plausible, the references may also be of symbolic value: "gold, silver, and bronze" are among the freewill offerings from which the Tabernacle and its furnishings were cast. Granted, the disciples are bidden *not* to receive or bear such valuables with them (the verb has a range of possible meanings),[35] yet it seems striking that in the Septuagint the specific combination of χρυσόν ... ἄργυρον ... χαλκόν appears most frequently in connection with the sanctuary furnishings (Exod 25:3; 31:4; 35:5, 32; 1 Chr 29:2; cf. 22:14–16; 2 Chr 2:6, 14; 1 Esd 8:54–60//2 Esd 8:24–30), or as a designation of that which is "sacred to the LORD" (Josh 6:19, 24).[36] Second, whereas for Mark the action of shaking dust from one's feet is intended "as a testimony against them" (εἰς μαρτύριον αὐτοῖς, *eis martyrion autois,* Mark 6:11), this qualification is absent from Matt 10:14. Perhaps the omission can also be explained in terms of Matthew's emphasis on conduct that befits the divine presence, as suggested by *m. Ber.* 9.5: the disciples cast off the dust of any towns that refuse to acknowledge the presence of the Holy One who

---

33. But such an explanation need not obviate considerations of poverty, defenselessness, and radical dependence on God, since these too are expressions of the *basileia* that the disciples proclaim (so Schnabel, *Early Christian Mission*, 1:297–98).

34. E.g., Beare, *Matthew,* 243.

35. So Luz, *Matthew 8–20,* 76–77.

36. Elsewhere only at Num 31:22; Isa 60:17; Dan 2:32–45; the adjectival forms appear in conjunction at 2 Kgs 8:10 and Dan 5:4, 23.

both authorizes and accompanies them.³⁷ Or in terms implied by Matt 10:40, whoever rejects them rejects the Messiah, and whoever rejects the Messiah rejects the One who sent him. Interpreting the Matthean mission charge in light of Matt 18:20 and 28:20—with the risen Jesus as God's presence³⁸—thus represents a further parallel between the disciples and their Lord, whose own concern for honoring God's sanctity is indicated by his teaching (e.g., "hallowed be your name," ἁγιασθήτω τὸ ὄνομά σου, *hagiasthētō to onoma sou*, 6:9) and his prophetic actions (Matt 21:12–13//Mark 11:15–17) alike.³⁹

PEACE AND PROVISION: THE CONDITIONS OF MISSION

In Matthew's formulation, the prohibition of money, begging bag, tunics, sandals, and staff is explained by the phrase "for the worker is worthy of his food" (ἄξιος γὰρ ὁ ἐργάτης τῆς τροφῆς αὐτοῦ, *axios gar ho ergatēs tēs trophēs autou*, Matt 10:10). No doubt this implies that the missionaries will need to rely on the hospitality of strangers or fellow Christians, and carries with it the prospect of hunger and cold should their message be rejected. According to Josephus, traveling Essenes relied on those of like conviction to provide for their needs, thereby avoiding contact with non-members (*J.W.* 2.124–125).⁴⁰ Gundry, followed by Davies and Allison, suggests that Matthew has in view the re-evangelization of settlements in which the good news of Jesus has already been successfully proclaimed: "Whatever town or village you enter, *find out who in it is worthy*, and stay there until you leave."⁴¹ Certainly the fact that Matthew typically uses ἄξιος (*axios*) to describe pious conduct argues in favor of this proposal (cf. Matt 3:8//Luke 3:8; Matt 10:37–38,

---

37. Building on studies by Neusner and Chilton, Wright, *Jesus and the Victory of God*, 557–58 and n. 77, tentatively suggests interpreting Jesus' washing of the disciples' feet (John 13:1–20) in similar terms: Jesus is preparing his followers for the Last Supper and the sacrificial death that it foreshadows, which will parallel and supersede the Temple cultus. Compare also Matt 18:20 and 28:20 with John 1:14, ἐσκήνωσεν ἐν ἡμῖν (*eskēnōsen en hēmin*).

38. Although it is tempting to refer to Jesus as *Shekinah*, given Matthew's allusions to Temple worship, Kupp is extremely cautious in this regard (see *Matthew's Emmanuel*, 192–96).

39. On the significance of the Temple action in Matthew, see Keener, *Matthew*, 495–501.

40. Cited in Keener, *Matthew*, 317.

41. Gundry, *Matthew*, 188; cf. Davies and Allison, *Matthew*, 2:175.

diff. Luke 14:26–27; Matt 22:8, diff. Luke 14:21). Yet it is equally clear that when it comes to choosing specific lodgings, Jesus envisages the possibility that the household in question will *not* prove worthy (10:13), and will *not* welcome them or listen to their words. Far from acknowledging the disciples or their Messiah, "that house or town" deserves only to have its dust shaken from the feet of the departing missionaries (10:14). It seems more likely, then, that in this instance we must interpret "worthiness" in a more general fashion: the missionaries are to seek out those with a reputation for piety, perhaps those who "seek first the kingdom of God and his righteousness" (Matt 6:33), even if such hosts prove ultimately unwilling to receive their message and the Messiah who accompanies them. The ensuing warnings about suffering and rejection (10:16–31, 34–36) only serve to underscore this danger.

In any event, the overriding concern here is on divine provision: if the disciples are agents and emissaries of the Christ, then it is the responsibility of the one of who has engaged and sent them to provide for their needs, as stipulated by Scripture (e.g., LXX Ps 110[111]:5: "He provides food [τροφήν, *trophēn*] for those who fear him; he is ever mindful of his covenant") and tradition (*m. B. Mezia* 7.1) alike.[42] Indeed, if Jesus promises as much to any and all who hear him ("Do not worry about your life, what you will eat or what you will drink, or about your body, what you will wear. Is not life more than food [τροφῆς, *trophēs*], and the body more than clothing?" Matt 6:25), how much more so does this apply to those who bear his name.

Yet despite the murder of the Messiah, the persecution of his followers, and the devastating failure of the mission to Israel in the destruction of Jerusalem, it must not escape our notice that those whom Jesus commissions are bearers—arbiters, even—of peace: "If the house is worthy, let your peace come upon it; but if it is not worthy, let your peace return to you" (Matt 10:13). As commentators note, this is neither psychological, social, nor political "peace," but the all-encompassing eschatological *shalom* characteristic of God's reign. The fact that the disciples convey its blessing directly contradicts both the words of Jesus later in the same discourse ("Do not think that I have come to bring peace to the earth; I have not come to bring peace, but a sword," Matt 10:34) and the immediate historical experience of the disciples and Israel alike.

---

42. Similarly LXX Ps 64:9 [65:10]; 103[104]:27; 135[136]:25; 144[145]:15; 145[146]:7; 146[147]:9; Job 36:1; Wis 16:20, etc.

But the contradiction provides the key to its meaning, summarizing the conditions under which later believers (especially those of Matthew's circle) continue Christ's work. They follow a crucified insurrectionist, in imitation of his largely ineffective apostles, on a mission that has failed to win the majority in Israel. They themselves anticipate rejection, even persecution, in a political situation for which God's promised "peace" is—at least for Palestinian Judaism—a shattered hope. Yet this victim of judicial injustice is also Lord and Messiah; the faltering disciples and their failed mission are the foundation of Matthew's own community, providing immediate evidence of the kingdom they proclaim; and far from being dead or absent, the risen Christ actually accompanies them with peace and power, enabling them to speak and minister with the authority of God's eschatological reign. We may press the paradox even further, for the nature of the missionaries' authority bespeaks the graciousness that is characteristic of the gospel itself. The missionaries have authority to declare God's peace or to accept it back when others will not receive it (cf. Matt 16:19; 18:18). That is, they have power to administer the eschatological blessing of God's reign. But they do not have authority to pronounce condemnation, for that right is reserved for God and the day of judgment alone (10:15).[43] Despite the opposition they encounter and the tribulation they must undergo (Matt 5:10–12; 7:14; 10:16–23; 24:9), the disciples are granted only the gracious and benevolent aspects of Jesus' authority, not its full measure. Herein lies the difference between the brutality of an ill-named *Pax Romana* and the subversive potency of Christ's kingdom and *shalom*.

The relevance of this portrayal for today's church lies largely in its central emphasis on the enabling presence of Christ. In the West, Christian mission is typically undertaken with the support of a full panoply of personal, fiscal, ecclesiastical, and professional resources. We are more likely, that is, to be conscious of our assets and abilities than of any weakness or inability. For Matthew, by contrast, Christian mission relies on the Christ whose power and presence reverse the failures of history, and make effective proclamation possible in a situation of individual

---

43. This contrast is more marked in Luke's narrative sequence, which juxtaposes Jesus' rebuke of the disciples' attempt to call down fire on an unwelcoming Samaritan village (Luke 9:52–55) with the mission of the seventy, whose task is to bestow peace, grant healing, and announce God's reign (10:1–9), followed by the warning of final judgment on those who reject them (10:10–12) and on the unrepentant cities of Galilee in particular (10:13–15).

persecution and national defeat. The key principle that emerges from our study of his mission charge is that of contingency, of the absence of self-reliance or, in specifically theological terms, of dependence on divine grace. This represents a profound challenge to the implicit cultural imperialism of much Western missiology, both past and present, and should cause us to question the degree to which the "peace," "authority," or "blessing" we seek to convey operates according to social, cultural, or political—rather than radically Christological and theocentric—principles. More specifically, although in the immediate context Matthew's emphasis appears more doxological and eschatological than explicitly ethical, the theological premise of ministering in the presence of Christ as *God's* presence poses the question of how sanctity, holiness, and the divine character inform contemporary missiology, whether in terms of personal ethics, ecclesiology, or methodology itself. At the very least, adopting a Matthean perspective will draw mission and missiology into the ambit of worship, encouraging such endeavors to be undertaken less as expressions of cultural or doctrinal triumphalism, and more as obedient submission to the gracious initiative of Christ.

MISSION BETWEEN JESUS AND THE GOSPELS

As in all studies concerning the historical Jesus, we are faced with the difficulty of sorting out which aspects of Markan or Matthean missiology are historically original, and which derive from the Evangelists themselves. In what measure does each writer chronicle the causes or consequences, respectively, of Christian mission, and how far behind the texts themselves may we trace the origins of our own religious identity? Notwithstanding clear redactional tendencies, the sobering estimate of human agency offered by both accounts, and the surprising lack of communal self-congratulation, seems to imply a firmer historical basis than is sometimes assumed. Conversely, both Gospels emphasize the ability of Jesus to accomplish what his followers cannot, although they do so in quite distinctive ways. The question posed of such texts by Jesus' followers—"Who do the Gospels say that we are?"—is thus answered by the question Jesus poses of them: "Who do people say that I am?" In short, the missiology of the first two Gospels clearly indicates that the person and purpose of the Messiah are what determine the mission of the disciples, not the other way around.

Other contemporary texts provide at least a few clues to help bridge the historical gap between the ministry of Jesus and the writing of the Gospels. For instance, 1 Tim 5:18 quotes the Lukan version ("The worker is worthy of his *wage*" [μισθός, *misthos*], Luke 10:7) of Matt 10:10b, in tandem with Deut 25:4, "You shall not muzzle an ox when it is treading out the grain." This proof from Torah is also central to Paul's claim that he and Barnabas, like the other apostles, deserve to be supported by the congregations they serve (1 Cor 9:3–12, esp. v. 9). Nonetheless, he insists, the only recompense (μισθός, 9:18) he claims is the right to make the gospel available free of charge. This implies, first, that Jesus' instructions were widely known and acknowledged within twenty years of his death, even outside Palestine (cf. also *Did.* 11:6; 13:1–2).[44] Second, and perhaps more significantly, Paul appears to know the Lukan (presumably Q) version of this saying (concerning μισθός rather than τροφή), yet submits in practice to a contrary injunction which appears only in Matt 10:8: "You received without payment; give without payment." Whatever implications this may have for the transmission of Synoptic traditions,[45] Paul's own custom provides an example of how dominical instructions came to be implemented in the missionary endeavor of the post-Easter church (cf. Acts 8:20; 20:33). In this regard it may also be instructive to recall that, according to Acts 13:51, Paul and Barnabas signify their turn from a Jewish to a Gentile mission by shaking the dust from their feet (similarly, Acts 18:6). Likewise, the constant suffering and trials endured by Paul and his companions prove the accuracy of Jesus' grave warning:

> They will hand you over to councils and flog you in their synagogues; and you will be dragged before governors and kings because of me, as a testimony to them and the Gentiles . . . you will be hated by all because of my name. (Matt 10:17–18, 22; cf. Mark 13:9)

Finally, reflecting the ambiguity of his own biography—and notwithstanding the sometimes contradictory nature of his testimony—we may discern in Paul the same contrast between apostolic failure and the faithfulness of Christ that later emerges in the work of the Evangelists:

---

44. Paul is, in fact, explicit on this point: "The Lord commanded that those who proclaim the gospel should get their living by the gospel" (1 Cor 9:14).
45. Cf. the discussion in Robinson, "Safe House," 191–92.

> For I am the least of the apostles, unfit to be called an apostle . . . But by the grace of God I am what I am, and his grace toward me has not been in vain. On the contrary, I worked harder than any of them—though it was not I, but the grace of God that is with me. (1 Cor 15:9-10)

Paul thus provides a kind of "middle term," a living example linking the mission of Jesus and that of earlier and later apostles with the mission for which Mark and Matthew write.

CONCLUSION

Although at some risk of oversimplification, we may summarize our findings in the following terms. Both Mark and Matthew stress the theological priority of Jesus' mission as he proclaims God's immediate sovereignty and gives concrete form to that dynamic by calling a community of followers into existence, authorizing them to function in word and deed as his—and God's—representatives. Paul, whether in his own correspondence or as subsequently depicted by Luke, provides an example of how Jesus' instructions continue to be implemented by Christian missionaries a generation after the death of their leader. Writing later in the first century, Mark reckons with the initial failure both of Jesus' ministry and the ministry of his disciples (one follower actively betrays the Messiah and the remainder simply abandon him to his fate) *narratologically* by means of allusions to the Sower and Seed, and *theologically* by appeal to the priority of divine action—grace—that the parable implies. Matthew, who must also come to terms with the destruction of the Temple and the collapse of the Jewish state, stresses yet more strongly the significance of Jesus' resurrection: the church's ongoing mission is enabled by the enduring presence of the risen Lord. While we may not minimize the differences between these different stages of development, they together provide a critical foundation for assessing the missionary practices of our own church, the theological presuppositions that undergird its enterprise, and the degree to which such ministry may claim to follow Christ.[46]

---

46. I wish to thank Matt Lowe for his meticulous assistance in researching background materials for this study, and Anders Runesson for proposing several important qualifications, particularly with regard to theological vocabulary.

BIBLIOGRAPHY

Beare, F. W. *The Gospel according to Matthew*. Peabody, MA: Hendrickson, 1987.

Bosch, David J. *Transforming Mission: Paradigm Shifts in Theology of Mission*. American Society of Missiology Series 16. Maryknoll, NY: Orbis, 1991.

Carter, Warren. "Matthaean Christology in Roman Imperial Key: Matthew 1.1." In *The Gospel of Matthew in Its Roman Imperial Context*, edited by John Riches and David C. Sim, 143–65; JSNTSup 276. London/New York: T. & T. Clark, 2005.

Danby, Herbert. *The Mishnah: Translated from the Hebrew with Introduction and Brief Explanatory Notes*. Oxford: Oxford University Press, 1977.

Daube, David. "The Earliest Structure of the Gospels." *NTS* 5 (1959) 174–89.

Davies, W. D., and Dale C. Allison Jr. *The Gospel according to Saint Matthew*. 3 vols. ICC. Edinburgh: T. & T. Clark, 1988–1997.

Drury, John. *The Parables in the Gospels: History and Allegory*. New York: Crossroad, 1985.

Evans, Craig A. "The Beginning of the Good News and the Fulfillment of Scripture in the Gospel of Mark." In *Hearing the Old Testament through the New Testament*, edited by Stanley E. Porter, 83–103. Grand Rapids: Eerdmans, 2006.

Gundry, Robert H. *Matthew: A Commentary on His Handbook for a Mixed Church under Persecution*. Grand Rapids: Eerdmans, 1994.

Hamel, Gildas H. *Poverty and Charity in Roman Palestine: First Three Centuries C.E.* Berkeley: University of California Press, 1990.

Harris, Geoffrey R. *Mission in the Gospels*. London: Epworth, 2004.

Jeremias, Joachim. *Die Gleichnisse Jesu*. Göttingen: Vandenhoeck & Ruprecht, 1965.

Keener, Craig S. *A Commentary on the Gospel of Matthew*. Grand Rapids: Eerdmans, 1999.

Kim, T. H. "The Anarthrous *huios theou* in Mark 15,39 and the Roman Imperial Cult." *Bib* 79 (1998) 226–38.

Kupp, David D. *Matthew's Emmanuel: Divine Presence and God's People in the First Gospel*. SNTSMS 90. Cambridge: Cambridge University Press, 1996.

Luz, Ulrich. *Matthew 8–20: A Commentary*. Translated by James E. Crouch. Edited by Helmut Koester. Hermeneia. Minneapolis: Fortress, 2001.

Manson, T. W. *The Sayings of Jesus: As Recorded in the Gospels according to St. Matthew and St. Luke*. London: SCM, 1949.

Marcus, Joel. *Mark 1–8: A New Translation with Introduction and Commentary*. AB 27. New York: Doubleday, 2000.

McIver, Robert K. "One Hundred-Fold Yield—Miraculous or Mundane? Matthew 13.8, 23; Mark 4:8, 20; Luke 8:8." *NTS* 40 (1994) 607–8.

Mealand, David L. *Poverty and Expectation in the Gospels*. London: SPCK, 1980.

Mowery, Robert L. "Son of God in Roman Imperial Titles and Matthew." *Bib* 83 (2002) 100–110.

Oakman, Douglas E. *Jesus and the Economic Questions of His Day*. SBEC 8. Lewiston, NY: Mellen, 1986.

Robinson, James M. "From Safe House to House Church: From Q to Matthew." In *Das Ende der Tage und die Gegenwart des Heils: Begegnungen mit dem Neuen Testament und seiner Umwelt. Festschrift für Heinz-Wolfgang Kuhn zum 65. Geburtstag*, edited by M. Becker and W. Fenske, 183–99. Leiden: Brill, 1999.

Schnabel, Eckhard J. *Early Christian Mission*. I. *Jesus and the Twelve*. Downers Grove: InterVarsity, 2004.

Schweizer, Eduard. *Das Evangelium nach Matthäus*. Göttingen: Vandenhoeck & Ruprecht, 1973.

Taylor, Vincent. *The Gospel according to St. Mark: The Greek Text with Introduction, Notes, and Indexes*. London: Macmillan, 1955.

Tolbert, Mary Ann. *Sowing the Gospel: Mark's World in Literary-Historical Perspective*. Minneapolis: Fortress, 1989.

Watts, Ricki E. *Isaiah's New Exodus and Mark*. WUNT 2.88. Tübingen: Mohr Siebeck, 1997.

Webster, John. "Discipleship and Calling." *Scottish Bulletin of Evangelical Theology* 23 (2005) 133–47.

Wright, N. T. *Jesus and the Victory of God*. Minneapolis: Fortress, 1996.

———. *The New Testament and the People of God*. Minneapolis: Fortress, 1992.

Wuellner, W. *The Meaning of 'Fishers of Men.'* Philadelphia: Westminster, 1967.

4

A Light to the Nations

Isaiah and Mission in Luke

CRAIG A. EVANS

INTRODUCTION

THE CHRISTIAN MISSIONARY EFFORT in Luke–Acts is rooted in the prophetic Scriptures of Israel. Foremost of these Scriptures is the prophecy of Isaiah, especially in the second half of the book, beginning with ch. 40, which announces the good news of God's reign and the redemption of Israel. None of this is lost on the Evangelist Luke, who begins his first volume (i.e., the Gospel of Luke) with important allusions to Isaiah and ends his second volume (i.e., the book of Acts) with more allusions to Isaiah. This is no proof from any prophecy scheme (as in one form or another we see at work in Matthew and John). For the Evangelist Luke, prophecy has explanatory power and provides the framework structurally and hermeneutically by which the story of Jesus and his church may be told.[1] It is from this perspective that Luke's understanding of Christian mission must be understood.

The present study discerns this important function of Isaiah in five sections or developments in Luke–Acts: (1) in the infancy narratives, (2) in the Baptist narrative, (3) in the proclamation of Jesus, (4) in the

---

1. Two books that perceptively explore the influence of Isaiah in Luke's development of the theme of evangelism and salvation are Tiede, *Prophecy and History in Luke–Acts*; and Pao, *Acts and the Isaianic New Exodus*. See also the briefer, but very helpful studies by Seccombe, "Luke and Isaiah," and Sanders, "Isaiah in Luke."

missionary commissions in Luke and Acts, and (5) in the proclamation of the apostles in Acts.

ISAIAH IN LUKE'S INFANCY NARRATIVE

Important words and phrases from Isaiah appear in three of Luke's infancy songs: (1) in the song of Mary, or the Magnificat (1:46–55), (2) the song of Zechariah, or the Benedictus (1:67–79), and (3) the song of Simeon, or the Nunc Dimittis (2:29–32, 34–35). Allusions to Isaiah appear in the final two verses of the Magnificat (Luke 1:54–55):[2]

> He has helped his *servant Israel*, in remembrance of his mercy,
> as he spoke to our fathers, to *Abraham* and to his *posterity* for ever.

Mary's words allude to Isaiah 41:8–9 (with italics indicating the parallels):

> But you, *Israel*, my *servant*,
>   Jacob, whom I have chosen,
>   the *offspring* of *Abraham*, my friend;
> you whom I took from the ends of the earth,
>   and called from its farthest corners,
> saying to you, "You are my *servant*,
>   I have chosen you and not cast you off."

The similar language of Ps 98:3 ("He has remembered his mercy to Jacob, and his truth to the house of Israel") and Mic 7:20 ("He shall give blessings truly to Jacob, and mercy to Abraham, as you swore to our fathers") has probably contributed to the wording of this part of the Magnificat.

The song of Zechariah also alludes to important passages from Isaiah.[3] Luke 1:76 ("you, child, will be called the prophet of the Most High; for you will go before the Lord to prepare his ways") surely reflects Isa 40:3 ("In the wilderness prepare the way of the Lord"). Isaiah 58:8 and 60:1–2 are also echoed in Luke 1:78–79. According to Isa 58:8: "Then shall your light break forth like the dawn, and your healing shall spring up speedily; your righteousness shall go before you." To this Luke 1:78

---

2. The song of Mary has been traditionally called the Magnificat because in the Latin version, or Vulgate, the song begins with *magnificat* (magnifies).

3. The song of Zechariah is also called the Benedictus, once again because in the Latin version, the song begins with *benedictus* (blessed).

alludes: "through the tender mercy of our God, when the day shall dawn upon us from on high"; while Luke 1:79 ("to give light to those who sit in darkness and in the shadow of death, to guide our feet into the way of peace") recalls language and imagery from Isa 9:1–2 (MT and LXX: 8:23–9:1) and especially 60:1–2. The latter passage reads:

> Arise, shine; for your light has come,
>   and the glory of the Lord has risen upon you.
> For behold, darkness shall cover the earth,
>   and thick darkness the peoples;
> but the Lord will arise upon you,
>   and his glory will be seen upon you.

Finally, the concluding words of Zechariah's song, "to guide our feet into the way of peace" (Luke 1:79) surely alludes to Isa 59:8 ("the way of peace they know not").

In the song of Simeon, we have important echoes of passages from Isaiah.[4] Indeed, Luke's introduction of Simeon brings to mind the first verse of the second half of Isaiah. The Evangelist Luke tells us that Simeon "was righteous and devout, looking for the consolation (παράκλησιν, *paraklēsin*) of Israel" (Luke 2:25). Given the allusions to Isaiah in the song itself, it is probable that readers are to think of Isa 40:1, which enjoins the nations: "Comfort, comfort (*or* Console, console; Greek: παρακαλεῖτε παρακαλεῖτε, *parakaleite, parakaleite*) my people, says God." We may have an echo of Isa 49:13 as well: "For the Lord has had mercy on his people, and has comforted (*or* consoled; Greek: παρεκάλεσεν, *parekalesen*) the lowly ones of his people." Righteous Simeon is ready to depart from this life. "For," he says in Luke 2:30–31,

> my eyes have seen your salvation (ὅτι εἶδον οἱ ὀφθαλμοί μου τὸ σωτήριόν σου, *hoti eidon hoi ophthalmoi mou to sōtērion sou*)
>
> which you have prepared in the presence of all (πρόσωπον πάντων, *prosōpon pantōn*) peoples.

These words echo Isa 40:5 and 52:10:

> 40:5 And the glory of the Lord shall appear, and all flesh shall see the salvation of God (LXX, ὄψεται πᾶσα σὰρξ τὸ σωτήριον τοῦ θεοῦ, *opsetai pasa sarx to sōtērion tou theou*): for the Lord has spoken.

---

4. The song of Simeon is called the Nunc Dimittis, because in the Latin version, the song begins with the words *nunc dimittis* (now let depart).

> 52:10 The Lord has bared his holy arm before the eyes of all the nations (LXX, ἐνώπιον πάντων τῶν ἐθνῶν, *enōpion pantōn tōn ethnōn*); and all the ends of the earth shall see the salvation that (is) from God (τὴν σωτηρίαν τὴν παρὰ τοῦ θεοῦ, *tēn sōtērian tēn para tou theou*)

The salvation, of which Isaiah the prophet spoke long ago, the righteous Simeon has finally seen, in fulfillment of an assurance given to him by the Holy Spirit. Simeon goes on to say in his song that God's salvation is (Luke 2:32):

> a light for revelation to the Gentiles (φῶς εἰς ἀποκάλυψιν ἐθνῶν, *phōs eis apokalypsin ethnōn*), and for glory to your people Israel (δόξαν λαοῦ σου Ἰσραήλ, *doxan laou sou Israēl*).

These words allude to at least three passages from Isaiah LXX (i.e., 42:6; 46:13 and 49:6):

> 42:6 I have given you as a covenant to the people, a light of nations (φῶς ἐθνῶν, *phōs ethnōn*).
>
> 49:6 I will give you as a light to the nations (φῶς ἐθνῶν, *phōs ethnōn*), that you should be for salvation (σωτηρίαν, *sōtērian*) to the end of the earth.
>
> 46:13 I have given salvation in Zion to Israel for glory (ἐν Σιων σωτηρίαν τῷ Ισραηλ εἰς δόξασμα, *en Siōn sōtērian tō Israēl eis doxasma*).

The salvation of the Lord will be as a light for the nations, or Gentiles, and it will redound to the glory of God's people Israel.

The brief notice of Anna the prophetess also contains an important allusion to Isaiah, even though no actual words of this elderly woman, of the tribe of Asher, are reported. The Evangelist says that she "spoke of [Jesus] to all who were looking for the redemption of Jerusalem" (Luke 2:38). Luke's words surely allude to Isa 52:9 "the Lord has had mercy upon (Jerusalem), and has delivered (LXX: ἐρρύσατο, *errysato*)/redeemed (MT: גָּאַל, *gā'al*) Jerusalem."

The language of the three infancy songs stands out in comparison with the three angelic annunciations (Luke 1:14–17; 1:32–33, 35; 2:14). Whereas the three songs contain important allusions to the second half of Isaiah—the part of the prophecy that speaks of the time of salvation, the three annunciations allude to other Scriptures.[5] The language of the songs is intended to recall the saving promises of Isaiah and to suggest that these promises are now being fulfilled in the birth of Jesus. Joel Green has rightly remarked that Luke 1–2 "initiates a narrative centered above all on God whose aim it is to bring salvation in all its fullness to all."[6]

ISAIAH IN THE BAPTIST NARRATIVE

Luke the Evangelist edits and enriches the story of John the Baptist in several interesting ways. For our purposes there are four items that call for comment. The first three are relatively minor, but they are important for understanding how the Evangelist has contextualized the story. Both of these details are seen in way that Luke establishes the setting of John: "In the fifteenth year of the reign of Tiberius Caesar . . . in the high-priesthood of Annas and Caiaphas, the word of God came to John, the son of Zechariah, in the wilderness" (Luke 3:1–2). First, the temporal notices "in the fifteenth year" and "in the high-priesthood of" are reminiscent of temporal notices in the prophets: "In the year that King Uzziah died I saw the Lord" (Isa 6:1); "The year in which Ahaz the king died" (Isa 14:28); "in the days of Josiah the son of Amon, king of Judah, in the thirteenth year of his reign" (Jer 1:2). Second, the language "the word of God came to (ἐγένετο ῥῆμα θεοῦ ἐπί, *egeneto rhēma theou epi*) John" is reminiscent of the classic prophets (LXX): "The year in which Ahaz the king died this word came" (ἐγενήθη τὸ ῥῆμα τοῦτο, *egenēthē to rhēma touto*) (Isa 14:28); "The word of God, which came to (τὸ ῥῆμα τοῦ θεοῦ ὃ ἐγένετο ἐπί, *to rhēma tou theou ho egeneto epi*) Jeremiah" (Jer 1:1); "Behold, the word of the Lord came to them (ἰδοὺ τὸ ῥῆμα κυρίου

---

5. The annunciation of John's birth (Luke 1:14–17) alludes to the birth announcements of Isaac (Gen 17:19) and Samson (Judg 13:2–21), to the Nazirite law (Num 6:1–3), and to Malachi's prophecy of the return of Elijah (Mal 4:5–6). The annunciation of the birth of Jesus (Luke 1:32–33, 35) alludes to the birth announcements in the first half of Isaiah (7:14; 9:6–7) and to the Davidic Covenant (2 Sam 7:12–16; cf. 4Q246). The annunciation to the shepherds (Luke 2:14) may allude to liturgical elements in circulation in Palestine at the turn of the era; cf. *Pss. Sol.* 18:10 ("Great is our God and glorious, dwelling in the highest"), *T. Levi* 5:1 ("and upon the throne of glory the Most High"), and *1 En.* 1:8 ("And with the righteous he will make peace, and upon the elect will be preservation and peace, and mercy will be given to them, and all will be of God, and he will give approval to them and he will bless all, and he will take hold of all, and he will help me, and light will appear to them and upon them he will make peace").

6. Green, "The Problem of a Beginning," 63.

ἐγένετο αὐτοῖς, *idou to rhēma kyriou egeneto autois*)" (Jer 6:10). Third, the Evangelist Luke says that the word of the Lord came to John "in the wilderness" (ἐν τῇ ἐρήμῳ, *en tē erēmō*). The Evangelist has reminded his readers that it was in the wilderness that John remained "until the day of his manifestation to Israel" (Luke 1:80). We are reminded of John's location in the wilderness because of the citation of Isa 40:3 that follows.

We come now to the fourth and most important detail in Luke's editing and enrichment of the Baptist's story. As does Matthew (Matt 3:3), Luke omits the quotation of Mal 3:1 that prefaces the quotation of Isa 40:3 (cf. Mark 1:2–3). But unlike Matthew (and Mark), Luke extends the quotation of Isaiah 40 to include v. 5. The quotation therefore ends with the words: "and all flesh shall see the salvation of God (ὄψεται πᾶσα σάρξ τὸ σωτήριον τοῦ θεοῦ, *opsetai pasa sarx to sōtērion tou theou*)" (Luke 3:6). The passage reads in Luke 3:4–6:

> As it is written in the book of the words of Isaiah the prophet,
> "The voice of one crying in the wilderness:
> Prepare the way of the Lord,
>   make his paths straight.
> Every valley shall be filled,
>   and every mountain and hill shall be brought low,
> and the crooked shall be made straight,
>   and the rough ways shall be made smooth;
> and all flesh shall see the salvation of God."

The formal quotation of Isa 40:5 reminds the reader of the oracle spoken by Simeon years before, when he looked upon the infant Jesus: "my eyes have seen your salvation (εἶδον οἱ ὀφθαλμοί μου τὸ σωτήριόν σου, *eidon hoi ophthalmoi mou to sōtērion sou*), which you have prepared in the presence of all (πρόσωπον πάντων, *prosōpon pantōn*) peoples" (Luke 2:30–31). With the appearance of John the Baptist, the prophecy of Isaiah 40 begins its fulfillment. The salvation promised long ago is at last at hand.

Of course, for Luke, Isaiah's prophetic "all flesh shall see the salvation of God" (ὄψεται πᾶσα σάρξ τὸ σωτήριον τοῦ θεοῦ) portends good things for Gentiles; it complements Simeon's "a light of revelation to the Gentiles" (Luke 2:32). But not all understood Isa 40:5 in this sense. After all, the text might mean that all flesh will see God *saving Israel*; all Gentile flesh, in contrast, may well face judgment. This seems to be the understanding in *1 En.* 1:6–9, parts of which read:

> And the mountain shall be shaken and will fall and will be scattered, and the high and lofty mountains will be brought low ... And the earth will be torn asunder (into) a split crevice, and all that is on the earth will be destroyed, and judgment will be upon all. And with the righteous he will make peace, and upon the elect will be preservation and peace, and mercy will be given to them ... and light will appear to them and upon them he will make peace. He comes with his myriads and with his holy ones, to make judgment against all, and he will destroy all the ungodly, and convict all flesh (πᾶσαν σάρκα) concerning all works of their ungodliness.

The allusion to Isa 40:4 is quite clear in *1 En.* 1:6 ("the high and lofty mountains will be brought low"). *First Enoch* 1:9 ("He comes with his myriads and with his holy ones, to make judgment against all") echoes Isa 40:10 ("Behold, the Lord God will come with might ... behold, his reward is with him, and his recompense before him"), while *Enoch's* "all flesh" may also allude to Isa 40:5 ("all flesh shall see the salvation of God").

The next passage from Isaiah presents similar interpretive ambiguities. Is the good news of the anointed messenger for Israel only, or is it also for the Gentiles?

ISAIAH IN THE PROCLAMATION OF JESUS

In Mark's version of Jesus' teaching in the Nazareth synagogue (Mark 6:1–6) we are not told what Jesus actually said. His only words ("A prophet is not without honor, except in his own country," etc.) are in response to the skepticism and criticism of the village ("Where did this man get all this?" etc.). But in Luke's greatly expanded version (Luke 4:16–30) we are given a text and a sermon.

The text is from Isaiah 61 (cited in Luke 4:18–19), a passage that is alluded to in the beatitudes (Matt 5:3–4; Luke 6:20) and in the reply to the imprisoned John the Baptist (Matt 11:5; Luke 7:22). Luke's version of Isa 61:1–2, enriched with a phrase from Isa 58:6, reads as follows:

> "The Spirit of the Lord is upon me,
>   because he has anointed me
>   to preach good news to the poor.
> He has sent me to proclaim release to the captives
>   and recovering of sight to the blind,
> to set at liberty those who are oppressed,
>   to proclaim the acceptable year of the Lord."

Given the omission of the last phrase of Isa 61:2 ("and the day of vengeance of our God") and the addition of the interpretive illustrations from the ministries of Elijah and Elisha,[7] it is clear that Luke understands Isaiah 61 as promising good news for Gentiles, as much as for ethnic Israel. Many Jews were not in agreement with this interpretation, however. The Nazareth congregation was not at all happy with it, as the conclusion of the story makes clear (Luke 4:28 "When they heard this, all in the synagogue were filled with wrath"). It is likely that the author of Qumran's Melchizedek Scroll (i.e., 11Q13) would not have agreed with it either. According to this scroll only the righteous will benefit from the good news; the wicked will be visited with God's vengeance (and this part of Isa 61:2 is not omitted in the scroll; it is emphasized).

In the midst of the quotation of Isa 61:1–2a, the Evangelist Luke has inserted a phrase from Isa 58:6 "set at liberty (or send away) those who are oppressed (ἀπόστελλε τεθραυσμένους ἐν ἀφέσει, *apostelle tethrausmenous en aphesai*)." The insertion enriches the quotation taken from Isaiah 61 and perhaps hints at healings and exorcisms to come, whereby those who are sick or oppressed by Satan are healed and set at liberty. But Isa 58:6, the phrase inserted into the quotation of Isaiah 61, also recalls the earlier allusion to Isaiah 58 in the song of Zechariah (esp. Luke 1:78–79), where language from Isa 58:8 ("Then shall your light break forth like the dawn, and your healing shall spring up speedily") was utilized.

All of this may strike us moderns as mysterious. We are not accustomed to memorizing numbers of texts and then quoting, conflating, or alluding to them in our discourse. But there is ample evidence from late antiquity of this very thing. Throughout his work, the Evangelist Luke weaves words and phrases from the Old Greek version of Scripture into his narrative, including the speeches, sermons, and songs of his characters. The Evangelist has done this with key passages from Isaiah at several points, with which the present paper is concerned.

In looking upon the infant Jesus, the Lord's Messiah (Luke 2:26), righteous Simeon declares that he has seen God's salvation (2:30). Later, in reference to the ministry of John the Baptist, the Evangelist Luke will extend the quotation of Isaiah 40, to conclude with v. 5 "all flesh will see

---

7. The story of Elijah's ministry to the widow (1 Kgs 17:1–16) is mentioned in Luke 4:25–26, the story of Elisha's ministry to Naaman the Syrian (2 Kgs 5:1–14) is mentioned in Luke 4:27.

the salvation of God" (Luke 3:6). In his song of thanksgiving for the birth of his son John, Zechariah alludes to Isa 40:3 (cf. Luke 1:76), which will later be associated with John. Zechariah's song also alludes to part of an oracle from Isaiah 58, a phrase of which will appear in Jesus' quotation of Isaiah 61, which Jesus will interpret as portending salvation for Gentiles, as well as for the people of Israel. This interpretive orientation is completely in step with the earlier quotation of Isa 40:5—all flesh, including Gentiles, will indeed see the salvation of God, just as surely as it had been foreshadowed in the ministries of Elijah and Elisha long ago.

Luke's infancy narratives of John and Jesus adumbrate important scriptural themes in the inaugural proclamations of John and Jesus. One of these themes is that the good news foretold by Isaiah is also good news for the Gentiles. The establishment of this theme at the outset of the Gospel of Luke, buttressed with the important witness of Isaiah, prepares for the commissioning of the disciples at the end of the Gospel and the beginning of the book of Acts, to which we now turn.

ISAIAH IN THE MISSIONARY COMMISSIONS

The Evangelist Luke presents his version of the Great Commission in two parts: at the end of the Gospel (Luke 24) and at the beginning of the Acts of the Apostles (Acts 1). The two passages should be studied together. We shall find that once again there are words and phrases that take us back to the earlier songs in the infancy narratives and also look forward to strategic turning points in the narrative of Acts.

Twice in Luke 24 the risen Jesus informs his disciples that the events of Passion Week and Easter were foretold in the Law and the Prophets (vv. 25–27, 44–49). The disciples are told:

> "Thus it is written, that the Christ should suffer and on the third day rise from the dead, and that repentance and forgiveness of sins should be preached in his name to all nations, beginning from Jerusalem. You are witnesses of these things." (Luke 24:46–48)

Most of the elements in this utterance can be traced to various scriptural passages, some of them obviously known to Luke the Evangelist. For example, the statement that "the Christ (or Messiah) should suffer" probably alludes to Isa 53:7–8, which is quoted in Acts 8:32–33 and applied to Jesus. (In the *Targum Isaiah*, the Suffering Servant is understood to be the Messiah.) The statement "on the third day rise from the dead" probably alludes to Hos 6:2 (which the Evangelist Luke may not have known) and to Ps 16:8–11, which is quoted in Acts 2:27 and applied to Jesus (in Acts 2:29–32), not only by Peter, but also by Paul (Acts 13:35). (In the *Targum of the Prophets*, Hos 6:2 is understood as referring to the resurrection of the dead in the last days.) Even the phrase "beginning from Jerusalem" may allude to Isa 2:2–3.

But of more relevance to the concerns of this paper is that the message of repentance and forgiveness of sins is to be preached "to all nations" or "all Gentiles." The phrase "to the nations" probably alludes to Isa 42:6 and 49:6 ("a light to the nations"), which was heard echoed in the infancy narrative, in Simeon's song: "a light for revelation to the Gentiles" or "nations" (Luke 2:32). Most striking is the declaration of the risen Jesus: "You are witnesses of these things." Given the contribution that the prophecy of Isaiah has made to Luke's understanding of mission, it is very probable that the Evangelist would have us think of the Lord's solemn declarations in Isaiah: "You are my witnesses" (Isa 43:10, 12; 44:8). The disciples of Jesus now fulfill the task of being the Lord's witnesses. They are witnesses of what God has accomplished in his Son, Jesus the Messiah, whose death and resurrection have made salvation possible. This is what is meant by the words "witnesses of these things." The disciples have witnessed in Jesus the fulfillment of the Isaianic prophecies. They are now to proclaim this fulfillment to the world.

The book of Acts begins where the Gospel of Luke ends—with the last words of Jesus just before his ascension. In Acts 1:8, the risen Jesus promises his disciples "power when the Holy Spirit has come" upon them. In the Pentecost sermon (Acts 2:16–21), Peter will, of course, appeal to Joel 2:28–32, but the promise of the Spirit may also recall the prophecy in Isaiah, where God promises Israel: "I will pour my Spirit upon your descendants, and my blessing on your offspring" (Isa 44:3); and "this is my covenant with them, says the Lord: my spirit which is upon you, and my words which I have put in your mouth, shall not depart out of your mouth, or out of the mouth of your children, or out of the mouth of your children's children" (59:21).

The risen Jesus goes on to remind his disciples, "you shall be my witnesses," which recalls his words in Luke 24:48, words that may allude to important declarations in Isaiah, as mentioned above. The disciples will be Jesus' witnesses "in Jerusalem and in all Judea and Samaria and to the end of the earth." Beginning "in Jerusalem" recalls "beginning from

Jerusalem" in Luke 24:47. Most interesting is the last phrase, "to the end of the earth (ἕως ἐσχάτου τῆς γῆς, *heōs eschatou tēs gēs*)." Some interpreters think we have an allusion to *Pss. Sol.* 8:15 "He brought him that is from the end of the earth (ἀπ' ἐσχάτου τῆς γῆς, *ap' eschatou tēs gēs*), that strikes mightily. He decreed war against Jerusalem, and against her land." The reference is to Pompey, whom God brought from Rome, to make war against Jerusalem. The expression, "end of the earth," may allude to Rome, and that is precisely the place where the narrative of the book of Acts comes to a conclusion (Acts 28:14 "and so we came to Rome"). But the language of Luke the Evangelist agrees exactly with the Greek version of Isa 49:6 "I will give you as a light to the nations, that my salvation may reach to the end of the earth (ἕως ἐσχάτου τῆς γῆς, *heōs eschatou tēs gēs*)." The Paul of Acts will quote Isa 49:6 (in Acts 13:47) as providing scriptural justification for "turning to the Gentiles" (Acts 13:46). And, as argued earlier in this study, the song of Simeon (Luke 2:32 "a light of revelation to the Gentiles") alludes to Isa 49:6.

Thus the Acts of the Apostles begins with words of the risen Jesus that take the thoughts of attentive readers and hearers back to the infancy narratives, where we find the first hints of global mission, a mission grounded in the prophecies of the book of Isaiah. The allusion to Isa 49:6 in the words of the risen but not yet ascended Jesus adumbrates the Gentile mission to come.

ISAIAH IN THE PROCLAMATION OF THE APOSTLES

The "light" of Isa 49:6 runs throughout the book of Acts. The passage is quoted formally in Acts 13:47 and it is alluded to many times, from the words of the risen Jesus, who commands his disciples to bear witness in Jerusalem, even "to the end of the earth" (Acts 1:8), to the very end of the Acts narrative, where the imprisoned Paul warns the Jewish elders that "this salvation of God has been sent to the Gentiles" (Acts 28:28). Let us consider a few of the key passages.

Given Paul's mission to the Gentiles, it is not surprising that the light of Isa 49:6 is so closely tied to him in the narrative of Acts. One cannot help but wonder if the Evangelist Luke intends his readers to link the light of Paul's conversion to the light of Isaiah. On the road to Damascus, as part of the pogrom against Jews and proselytes who have expressed faith in Jesus as Israel's Messiah, Paul encounters the risen Jesus: "suddenly a light from heaven flashed about him" (9:3; cf. 22:6, 9,

11; 26:13). What makes me associate the light of Paul's conversion with the light of Isa 49:6 is what the risen Jesus says to Ananias a few verses later: "Go, for he is a chosen instrument of mine to carry my name before the Gentiles and kings and the sons of Israel" (9:15; cf. 22:21; 26:17–18). Thus, in the context of Paul's conversion we have *light* and taking the gospel *to the Gentiles*. Indeed, even the mention of "the sons of Israel" coheres with Isa 49:6, which speaks of raising up the tribes of Jacob and restoring Israel. One should recall also the words of Simeon's song: "a *light* . . . to the *Gentiles*, and for glory to your people *Israel*" (Luke 2:32, with emphasis added).

Paul's apostolic commission is confirmed by Peter, whose testimony results in the conversion of Cornelius and his household and the pouring out of the Holy Spirit "even on the Gentiles" (Acts 10:45). This remarkable experience is reported at the first Jerusalem Council (Acts 11:1, 18 "to the Gentiles God has granted repentance to life"). In the plot of Acts, Paul is now free to roam about the Gentile world.

After encountering stiff resistance to their preaching in the synagogue of Pisidian Antioch, Paul and Barnabas declare (in Acts 13:46–47):

> It was necessary that the word of God should be spoken first to you. Since you thrust it from you, and judge yourselves unworthy of eternal life, behold, we turn to the Gentiles. For so the Lord has commanded us, saying, "I have set you to be a light for the Gentiles, that you may bring salvation to the uttermost parts of the earth."

Not only does Isa 49:6 provide justification for taking the light of salvation to the Gentiles, the expression, "to the uttermost part of the earth (ἕως ἐσχάτου τῆς γῆς, *heōs eschatou tēs gēs*)," harkens back to the commission in Acts 1:8 and, if the interpretive orientation of *Pss. Sol.* 8:15 is a proper guide, looks forward to Paul's eventual arrival in Rome.

Paul's interpretation of Isa 49:6 is confirmed along the way. Gentiles respond in faith (Acts 13:48). Paul and Barnabas return home and report "all that God had done with them, and how he had opened a door of faith to the Gentiles" (14:27). Paul and Barnabas later share their experiences with the second Jerusalem Council (15:12). Their report is well received and it is decided that the Council "not trouble those of the Gentiles who turn to God" (15:19). Indeed, the conversion of the Gentiles is seen as part of the fulfillment of Amos 9:11–12 (Acts 15:15–18), which is primarily concerned with the restoration of the house of David.

Later, when Paul returns to Jerusalem, he and his companions are "received gladly" (Acts 21:17). In the presence of James and all the elders, Paul "related one by one the things that God had done among the Gentiles through his ministry" (21:19). Much later, standing before Agrippa II, Paul avers:

> I stand here testifying both to small and great, saying nothing but what the prophets and Moses said would come to pass: that the Christ must suffer, and that, by being the first to rise from the dead, he would proclaim light both to the people and to the Gentiles. (Acts 26:22–23)

We have here not only allusion to Isa 49:6, proclaiming light to the Gentiles, but we have a summary of the words of the risen Jesus in Luke 24:44–47: "everything written about me in the law of Moses and the prophets and psalms must be fulfilled . . . that the Christ should suffer and on the third day rise from the dead, and that repentance and forgiveness of sins should be preached in his name to all nations."

What was hinted at in the infancy narratives and then fulfilled with the events of the Passion and the Resurrection has been faithfully proclaimed by the disciples, especially in the case of Paul, in the book of Acts. The prophecy of Isaiah has played a foundational role from beginning to end, especially Isa 49:6, which foretold the light of God's truth going forth "to the Gentiles, to the uttermost parts of the earth," which in the context of the Acts narrative appears to be Rome, where the story ends.

A BRIEF EPILOGUE

I conclude with a brief epilogue. It concerns two important witnesses in Luke's infancy narratives, Zechariah and Simeon. The former sang in thanksgiving for John and the other sang in thanksgiving for Jesus. Both alluded to the light of Isa 49:6 (Luke 1:78–79; 2:30–32) and so commenced Luke's remarkable scriptural justification for and pattern of the Gentile mission.

In 2003, Joe Zias reported the discovery of what appear to be two fourth-century inscriptions on the upper side of the so-called Tomb of Absalom (or Absalom's Pillar), in the Kidron valley, which runs between the Temple Mount and the Mount of Olives. One inscription refers to Zechariah; the other refers to Simeon.[8] The inscriptions read as follows:

τόδε μνεμεῖον Ζακκαρίας μάρ[τυρος]
πρεσβητ[έρου] θεοσεβε[στάτου] παππέα[ς] Ἰοά[ννου]

Here is the tomb of Zacchariah, witness
old, very pious, father of John.

ὁ θάφος Συμεων ὁ ἦν
δικαιότατος ἄνθρωπ[ος]
καὶ γῆρας ἡ εὐσηβήστατος
καὶ παράκλησιν
λαοῦ
προσδεχ[όμενος]

The tomb of Simeon who was
a very just man
and a very devoted old (one),
and for the consolation
of the people
was waiting.

It is interesting that the fourth-century inscriber describes Zechariah and Simeon the way he does. He describes Zechariah, the father of John, as a μάρτυς (*martys*), which could be translated "martyr," in light of later tradition, in which it is said that he suffered martyrdom at the hands of Herod the Great (cf. *Prot. Jas.* 23:1–3). But is this what the inscriber means? The literal meaning of the word μάρτυς is "witness." Of course, it later came to be understood as referring to those who suffered for their witness. But even if we allow that the inscriber was referring to the tradition that Zechariah died at the hands of Herod, we should note what the text says. Facing the threatening Herod, Zechariah declares: μάρτυς εἰμὶ τοῦ θεοῦ (*martys eimi tou theou*) (*Prot. Jas.* 23:3). The context makes clear that μάρτυς here means witness, not martyr. The Greek should be translated, "I am a witness of God." Zechariah was indeed a "witness" of God's saving work, at its very point of inception. Surely this faithful man is numbered among the "witnesses of these things," foretold by the prophet Isaiah and recalled by the risen Jesus.

---

8. Zias made the announcement at the 2003 SBL meeting in Atlanta. The story was carried in several newspapers, including *The Atlanta Journal-Constitution* (21 Nov 2003) A3, which includes facsimile. See now Puech, "Le tombeau de Zacharie et Siméon."

The fourth-century inscriber also describes righteous Simeon in very fitting terms when he says that he was waiting for the "consolation" (παράκλησις, *paraklēsis*) of the people. It is with the promise of consolation that the second half of Isaiah begins (Isa 40:1 "Console, console my people, says God"), the promise that early Christians believed was fulfilled in the life, death, and resurrection of Jesus, and in the faithful preaching of his apostles, who brought the good news of this fulfillment to Jews and Gentiles alike.

BIBLIOGRAPHY

Green, J. B. "The Problem of a Beginning: Israel's Scriptures in Luke 1–2." *BBR* 4 (1994) 61–85.

Pao, D. W. *Acts and the Isaianic New Exodus*. WUNT 2.130. Tübingen: Mohr Siebeck, 2000. Repr. Biblical Studies Library. Grand Rapids: Baker Academic, 2002.

Puech, É. "Le tombeau de Zacharie et Siméon au monument funéraire dit d'Absalom dans la Vallée de Josaphat." *RB* 110 (2003) 321–35.

Sanders, J. A. "Isaiah in Luke." *Int* 36 (1982) 144–55. Repr. in *Luke and Scripture: The Function of Sacred Tradition in Luke–Acts*, edited by C. A. Evans and J. A. Sanders, 14–25. Minneapolis: Fortress, 1993.

Seccombe, D. P. "Luke and Isaiah." *NTS* 27 (1981) 252–59.

Tiede, D. L. *Prophecy and History in Luke–Acts*. Philadelphia: Fortress, 1980.

5

A Cord of Three Strands

Mission in Acts

STANLEY E. PORTER *and* CYNTHIA LONG WESTFALL

INTRODUCTION

IT IS GENERALLY AGREED that Luke[1] has selected his material and arranged his account in Luke–Acts with a theological purpose, so it stands to reason that the arrangement, design, and structure of Acts reveal that purpose as well. But what is the nature and implication of the design and what is the purpose in regards to the mission of the early church?[2] Some scholars have suggested that Acts would better be titled "The Acts of the Holy Spirit" or "The Continuing Acts of Jesus." However, if Acts were the authoritative and official account of mission as directed by the Holy Spirit or Jesus, the absence in the second half of the discourse of such important characters as Barnabas after his conflict with Paul (Acts 15:36–41) might be seen to indicate that his role in mission

---

1. While we acknowledge that some scholars find it impossible to believe that Luke is the author of Acts, Lukan authorship is assumed throughout this chapter. For discussion, see McDonald and Porter, *Early Christianity*, 291–95; and for detailed discussion, see Thornton, *Der Zeuge des Zeugen*, 8–81.

2. There are a number of proposals regarding Luke's ultimate purpose in composing Acts. For the spectrum of views on the purpose of Acts, see Powell, *What Are They Saying About Acts?*, 13–19. It is beyond the purpose of this paper to fully argue the issues of genre or the structural relationship between Luke and Acts. However, the text in Acts 1:1–2 indicates that Acts assumes the information and argument in the Gospel of Luke.

was revoked—even though he is given a very positive evaluation up to the point of his altercation with Paul. On the other hand, titles such as "The Acts of Peter and Paul" are also inappropriate, because of the absence of any accounts of Peter's work in the second half of the narrative other than his participation in the Jerusalem Council—this indicates a clear focus on Paul.[3] Luke styles his narrative so that the Twelve and every other significant character play a support role in ways that are relevant to Paul's mission to the Gentiles. Clearly, Acts is not "The Acts of the Apostles," since everyone whom Luke designates as an apostle, other than Paul, Barnabas, Peter, and John, are all but absent from the record after Acts 2. John disappears after Acts 8. After Acts 12, Peter has only a cameo appearance in Acts 15, after which both he and Barnabas disappear from the narrative with no effort to tell "the rest of the story." James, who is not explicitly designated as an apostle by Luke, comes to play a central role in Jerusalem rather than the Twelve (Acts 15:14–21; 21:18).[4] But by the end of the narrative in Acts 28, Paul alone occupies the stage.

One implication of the narrative plot is that Luke is focusing the reader's attention on Paul's mission. This focus must be given due weight as a primary factor in determining the purpose of the book of Acts. Luke could, for example, be writing a validation, vindication, or apologetic

---

3. However, the Marcionites did not accept Acts into the canon because they recognized that it vindicated Peter as well as Paul, and so Acts played an important part among the anti-Marcionites in the middle of the second century (see Bruce, *Acts*, 4–5). The unity that Acts depicts between the Jewish mission and Paul's mission is one of the bases of F. C. Baur's thesis that Luke's purpose was irenic, a thesis now recently revived and defended by Goulder (Baur, *Paul*; Goulder, *Tale of Two Missions*; Goulder, *Paul*).

4. In Luke–Acts, "apostle" is used almost exclusively to refer to the twelve disciples of Jesus Christ (for the two exceptions, see Acts 14:4 and 14 where Paul and Barnabas are called apostles), in contrast with the Pauline epistles, where Paul designates himself, his team, and others as apostles and identifies the function/office of apostle as a spiritual gift. W. Bienert sees a differentiation between Luke's tradition of the first witnesses as the "prototypes of church officials" and Paul's tradition of the "charismatic apostolate" that appeals to the Spirit (Bienert, "Apostelbild"). However, Bienert's view is mitigated by Luke's depiction of the sending of the Twelve as charismatic (Luke 9:1–2; 24:48–49; Acts 1:4–8), by Luke's designation of Paul and Barnabas as apostles (Acts 14:4, 14), and by Paul's equation of his apostleship with Peter's (Gal 2:7–8). See also E. J. Schnabel's discussion of the foundational significance of the term ἀπόστολος and further critique of Bienert (Schnabel, *Early Christian Mission*, 1:280–84).

for Paul personally,[5] or for Paul's ministry to the Gentiles.[6] He could be providing an apologetic for the Christian movement as a whole by following Paul's path as a prototype.[7] Acts is not, however, a treatise on the mission of the early church or the acts of all of the apostles. That is not to say that Acts is not a significant source in reconstructing the early church's mission, or that mission is not a central theme in Acts. It is to say that when all characters fade off the stage and only Paul remains, it is not Luke's purpose to indicate that the torch of the early church's mission had passed from the twelve apostles to Paul.[8] Rather, Luke effectively demonstrates continuity between Jesus' mission in Luke, the twelve apostles' mission in the first ten chapters of Acts, and Paul's mission to the Gentiles. At least in part, as Köstenberger and O'Brien indicate, "the account underscores the fundamental points that there are *not three distinct missions, but the one mission of God* who has sent his Son Jesus as the missionary *par excellence* and in whose mission the twelve apostles and Paul participate as 'witnesses.'"[9] However, as we already noted above, the focus of Acts is on the validity and continuity of Paul's participation, which assumes the validity of the mission of the twelve apostles and the mission in Jerusalem headed by James; rather than replacing or supplanting them, Acts develops them further by taking them beyond Judea and Samaria to the end of the earth (Acts 1:8).

In addition to the primary focus on the nature of Paul's participation in the mission, some questions remain to be answered about the narrative in Acts. How does Luke depict continuity between Jesus' mission and Paul's mission? What is the relationship of the Jewish mission (the twelve apostles) to Paul in the fulfillment of Jesus' programmatic charge in Acts 1:8, "you shall be my witnesses in Jerusalem and in all Judea and Samaria and to the end of the earth"? In what way does Luke

---

5. Suggestions for a defense of Paul vary from a defense brief for his trial (see, for example, Sahlin, *Der Messias*, 30–56) to a defense of Paul to the Jewish Christians (see Brawley, *Luke–Acts and the Jews*; Brawley, "Paul in Acts").

6. For a discussion of Luke's interest in the Gentile mission, see Dupont, *Salvation*, 11–34.

7. Some see Acts as an apologetic appeal or confirmation of Christianity directed toward the Roman Empire or Roman citizens (see, for example, Haenchen, *Acts*; Bruce, *Acts*; van Unnik, "Book of Acts").

8. Contra a view that is prominent in Lukan studies that the mission to the Gentiles replaces the mission to Israel. See, for example, Sanders, *Jews in Luke–Acts*.

9. Köstenberger and O'Brien, *Salvation to the Ends of the Earth*, 146–47.

display the continuity between Jesus and Paul in the first half of Acts before Paul appears, and then how do the paths of Peter, James, and Paul intersect in the subsequent narrative, before Paul's missionary journeys become dominant? In what ways does the Jewish mission play a role supportive of Paul's mission? We can locate the continuity between the first two missions and Paul's mission by identifying patterns of repetition in Luke's account of the missions in Acts. We treat these three missions as strands of one uniting cord of mission.

THE FIRST STRAND: JESUS' MISSION

Acts is the second volume of a two volume account written to Theophilus, and was originally circulated together with Luke's Gospel.[10] Luke–Acts constitutes an integral whole, and the purpose and design of Acts cannot be read apart from the Gospel of Luke and Jesus' mission. While more work can be done in finding patterns that constrain the Jewish mission and Paul's mission in Luke (such as the calling and sending of the Twelve and the Seventy-two in Luke 6:12–16; 9:1–2; 10:1), a focus on the conclusion of Luke and the beginning of Acts firmly establishes the continuity between Jesus' mission and the Jewish mission—the twelve disciples are designated as witnesses of the fulfillment of Scripture (Luke 24:48), which paraphrases the phrase "the things that have been fulfilled among us" in Luke 1:1 and hence invokes the entire Gospel. The Twelve are witnesses to the fulfillment of Scripture in Christ's suffering, resurrection, and the preaching of repentance and forgiveness of sins in his name to all nations beginning in Jerusalem (Luke 24:48) and then Judea, Samaria, and the end of the earth (Acts 1:8).

The content of Luke's witness (Luke 24:48) forms an interesting contrast to that of Matthew (Matt 28:19–20). Rather than emphasizing the teaching of all that Jesus commanded as in Matthew, the focus in Luke 24:46–48 is on being a witness of the suffering and resurrection of Christ as the basis of proclamation of forgiveness of sins—though the qualifications for Judas's replacement included witnessing to Jesus' entire ministry from the baptism of John to the ascension (Acts 1:21–22). This element of being a witness to the suffering and resurrection of Christ is picked up in Paul's own conversion. Paul's peculiar personal encoun-

---

10. See the prefaces from both Luke (1:1–4) and Acts (1:1–2). Theophilus is the explicit recipient of both the Gospel and Acts, and in Acts the author refers to the Gospel as the former book.

ter with the resurrected Christ, told and re-told three times, underlines its importance and its continuity with the focus of the Lukan mission (Acts 9:1–19; 22:3–16; 26:12–18). The first account, in narrative form, concludes with Ananias being told that Paul is God's chosen instrument to carry his name to the Gentiles and their rulers. The two later accounts are parts of Paul's testimony to the crowd in Jerusalem and to Festus, Agrippa, and Bernice. According to Paul's accounts, Ananias prophesied that he would be a witness to everyone of all that he had seen and heard (Acts 22:15), and he was told directly by Jesus that he was appointed as a witness and a servant of what he had seen of Christ and what he would show him (Acts 26:16). All three of these accounts underscore the continuity of Paul with the twelve apostles in his appointment to function as a witness to Jesus and his mission.

THE SECOND STRAND: THE JEWISH MISSION

The Jewish mission in Acts is composed of two identifiable groups: the Palestinian Jews and the Hellenistic Jewish Christians. The Palestinian Jews were identified with the twelve apostles and the temple. The Hellenistic Jewish Christians were identified with Hellenistic synagogues,[11] and the seven "deacons" appointed to oversee a non-prejudicial distribution of the food to the believers' widows in Acts 6 came from among the Hellenistic Jewish Christians. The continuity between Paul's mission and the mission of the Palestinian Jewish Christians concerning Jesus is created by a similar appointment. The Palestinian Jewish Christians were to be witnesses of what they had seen and heard, particularly in terms of the resurrected Christ. For both the twelve apostles and Paul, the experience of the risen Christ was followed by an empowerment by the baptism of the Holy Spirit, which led to a life that was explicitly changed by encountering the resurrected Jesus. There is also a connection between Paul and the spontaneous revivals that occurred as a result of the witness of the Hellenistic Jewish Christians, which further resulted in the geographic spread of the gospel beyond Jerusalem and Judea. Finally, there was an intertwining of Peter and Paul in the extension of the gos-

---

11. See Acts 6:9, where the primary opposition to Stephen came from "what was called the synagogue of the freedmen," which included Cyrenians and Alexandrians and people from Cilicia and Asia (ἀνέστησαν δέ τινες τῶν ἐκ τῆς συναγωγῆς τῆς λεγομένης Λιβερτίνων καὶ Κυρηναίων καὶ Ἀλεξανδρέων καὶ τῶν ἀπὸ Κιλικίας καὶ Ἀσίας).

pel to the Gentiles, capped by the endorsement of both by James at the Jerusalem Council (Acts 15). Several of these elements require further discussion.

Mission, the Baptism of the Holy Spirit, and Transformation

The baptism of the Holy Spirit is a repeated motif in Acts—initially it is described as power "from on high" and empowerment for witness (Acts 1:8). The disciples were instructed not to leave Jerusalem, but to wait for the promise of the Spirit (Luke 24:49; Acts 1:4). The day of Pentecost is the fulfillment of the promise to the Twelve by the filling with the Holy Spirit accompanied by the phenomena of wind, fire, and tongues that resulted in the preaching of repentance and forgiveness of sins in Jesus' name. Paul also experienced a filling with the Holy Spirit, which is specified in Luke's first account of his conversion (Acts 9:17).[12] A series of "mini Pentecosts" occurs throughout the book of Acts, associated with the significant advance of the gospel to Samaria (Acts 8), to the Gentiles (Acts 10), and to some of John the Baptist's followers (Acts 19). R. C. Tannehill demonstrates that, after encountering the risen Christ and particularly after Pentecost, the faults that the disciples displayed in Luke are overcome.[13] Of course, this motif of repenting after encountering the resurrected Christ and being filled by the Spirit is even more pronounced with Paul's encounter on the Damascus Road, where he turned from attempting to exterminate the church to being its advocate throughout the Roman Empire and in Rome itself.

Mission Expansion and the Twelve Apostles

One of the more potentially confusing issues in analyzing mission in Acts is that of determining why Paul alone appears to fulfill the instructions that were given to the twelve apostles in Acts 1:8 concerning being a witness to all nations, as the gospel geographically expands from Jerusalem to the end of the earth. The twelve apostles are depicted by Luke as continually located in Jerusalem, with the exception of John and Peter's trip to Samaria (Acts 8) and Peter's trips to Lydda, Joppa, and Caesarea

---

12. The terms "baptism of the Holy Spirit," "gift of the Holy Spirit," the Holy Spirit "coming on" one, the reception of the Holy Spirit, and the "filling of the Holy Spirit" are used interchangeably in Acts (Acts 1:4–5, 8; 2:4, 38–39; 10:44–45, 47; 11:15–17; 19:6).

13. Tannehill, *Narrative Unity*, 24–25.

(Acts 9:32—10:48). While Luke indicates that Peter left Jerusalem after his imprisonment (Acts 12:17), he does not trace his subsequent movements. When he refers to Peter again in Acts 15, he is again located in Jerusalem. However, rather than indicating that the disciples were disobedient or obtuse in regards to expansion, Luke portrays their orientation to Jerusalem as the eschatological fulfillment of the restoration of Israel and the centrality of Jerusalem in the expansion of the gospel. This is consistent both with Jewish expectation and Old Testament prophecies of restoration and the gathering of the nations on Mt. Zion, and with the early church's understanding of itself as the eschatological people of God.[14] On one level, the "witness to all nations" by the twelve apostles was fulfilled in Jerusalem in Acts 2, with the declaration of the wonders of God in the languages of "every nation under heaven" (Acts 2:5) to the Jews who were from those nations (Acts 2:5–12). Subsequently, when Luke records that the Jerusalem church sent out leaders on mission trips, sometimes in response to news about revivals and mission work (Acts 8:14, 25; 9:31–32; 10:1—11:18; 11:19–24), this may be taken as part of a larger pattern of expanding mission, even though the Jewish mission was more focused. The Jewish mission primarily targeted Jews, and, according to Luke, many thousands of Jews had come to believe through the Jewish mission, perhaps even to the point that these Jewish Christians misunderstood the nature of Paul's mission (Acts 21:20).[15]

The Twelve were no doubt involved in mission trips that were not recorded by Luke, even if he was probably aware of them.[16] Paul asserted that Peter, the other apostles, and Jesus' brothers took wives with them on such trips (1 Cor 9:5). By the time Luke wrote his Gospel, according to tradition, the twelve apostles had established missions in some

---

14. See Schnabel for further discussion of the initial activity of the Twelve in Jerusalem and their understanding of their responsibility to preach the good news to Gentiles, in Schnabel, *Early Christian Mission*, 1:521–27.

15. It is sometimes assumed that Christianity was a predominantly Gentile movement at the time that Luke wrote (see, for example, deSilva, *Introduction to the New Testament*, 354). However, it is highly unlikely that Jews were a minority in the Christian movement within the first half of the first century, given that the twelve apostles and the Hellenistic Jews primarily concentrated on evangelizing Jews in Palestine and the Diasopora during the same period as Paul's ministry, according to Luke.

16. Background details of Peter's mission trips apparently constituted shared information with the recipients of Galatians and the Corinthian letters, so that Paul could refer to Peter and his trips without elaboration concerning their purpose (Gal 2:11; 1 Cor 9:5). It is unlikely that Luke did not have the same understanding.

of the areas reached by Paul such as Rome and Ephesus, and in other areas such as regions in the east.[17] Later traditions indicate that, after the events in Acts 12, the twelve apostles each undertook more far-reaching missions in assigned regions, which may be validated to some extent by local traditions and legends in various places where churches had been planted.[18] It is possible that the twelve apostles' missionary work was respected and the details were already shared information in the Christian community and provided a recognizable prototype that included a call to witness, an encounter with the resurrected Christ, and Spirit baptism and transformation. The continuity between Jesus' mission and the apostles' work was probably transparently portrayed in any accounts of the ministry of Jesus that were circulating, whether written or oral. The story of Paul's mission work also needed to be told and grounded in the context of Jesus' mission and the Jewish mission.[19] If his work and status were being questioned and needed an explanation and defense, it would also reflect on the pedigree of the churches he planted. Read in this light, Theophilus's need to know the certainty of the things he had been taught (Luke 1:4) could have included insecurity about the validity of Paul's gospel in the face of criticism. Luke provides and demonstrates an important and intimate connection between the program of the apostolic mission and Paul's mission.

Geographic Expansion and the Hellenistic Jewish Christians

The expansion of Christianity to Samaria, the Diaspora, and the Gentiles initially occurred as a result of Stephen's martyrdom (Acts 7; 8:1) and the subsequent outreach of Hellenistic Jewish Christians. Persecution

---

17. Peter's arrival in Rome has multiple attestations—Eusebius places his arrival in the second year of Claudius in 42 CE (Eusebius, *Hist. eccl.* 2.14.6). These references may be an inference drawn from Acts 12:17, where Peter "went to another place." However, it is more likely that his arrival was later than the date of Paul's epistle to the Romans. There are also traditions of Philip and John going to Asia. See Duchesne, *Early History*, 1:98–99.

18. See Schnabel, *Early Christian Mission*, 1:527–33.

19. Paul felt forced to defend his call and commission in a number of his letters, such as in 2 Cor 12:11–12, because they were questioned (see Bruce, *Acts*, 14), and Paul's defensive attitude is almost embarrassing at points. If the pastoral epistles are taken as authentic, Paul ends his life in prison feeling justified in his mission (2 Tim 4:6–8) but abandoned by his supporters (2 Tim 4:16). The tendency to see Paul as the triumphant victor through the lens of the ultimate dominance of the Gentile church over the Jewish mission is anachronistic.

followed the martyrdom that was spearheaded by Saul/Paul and particularly targeted the Hellenistic Christian Jews.[20] As a result of the violent attacks on the Jerusalem church, Christianity spread to other Jews, half-Jews (Samaritans), those affiliated with Judaism (an Ethiopian eunuch), and ultimately the Gentiles, by means of the intended Hellenistic victims who fled throughout Judea, Samaria, Phoenicia, Cyprus, and Antioch (8:1-4; 11:19).

Philip, one of the seven Hellenistic church leaders in Acts 6, immediately initiated the wildly successful conversion of a city in Samaria (8:4-8) and, in response to direct divine guidance, converted and baptized an Ethiopian eunuch, perhaps indicating the origin of an African mission[21]—from the Greco-Roman point of view Ethiopia was "the end of the earth" (8:26-40).[22] Hellenistic Jewish Christians from Cyprus and Cyrene went to Antioch and began, with significant success, to intentionally target "Greeks" (Ἑλληνιστας, *Hellēnistas*) for conversion (11:20-21). In response to the new development, the Jerusalem church sent Barnabas to Antioch, who validated the Gentile conversions as evidence of the "grace of God" (11:22-24), and brought Paul from Tarsus to Antioch to assist him in this unusual development (11:25-26). According to Luke, the geographic spread of the gospel and crossing the racial barrier was not a Pauline innovation or initiative, but had precedent in divine guidance and what amounted to acts of God.

While Luke traces the expansion of the gospel in terms of the Pauline mission, he also provides an explanation for the exponential expansion by Hellenistic Jewish Christians into areas far beyond the delimitations of Paul's missionary journeys. In fact, the description of the audience at Pentecost in Acts 2:5-12 highlights many areas that Paul did not evangelize, including North Africa, the areas bordering the southern shore of the Black Sea, Mesopotamia, and eastern territories as far as India. According to Acts 8:4, the Hellenistic Jewish Christians scattered by the persecution "preached the word wherever they went." This dynamic suggests that Christianity spread throughout the Jewish population of the

---

20. Acts 8:1 states that "all except the apostles were scattered throughout Judea and Samaria." Many hold that the apostles represent Palestinian Christians who were not identified with Stephen's more radical view of the temple (see, for example, Bruce, *Acts*, 162).

21. In the spirit of the story, Irenaeus suggests that he became a missionary among his own people—but Irenaeus probably inferred this (Irenaeus, *Haer.* 3.12.10).

22. In Homer, *Od.* 1.23, Ethiopians are "the last of men" (ἔσχατοι ἀνδρῶν).

Diaspora to the countries of the audience's origin, which may well account for the existence of a church in Rome before Paul's arrival.[23]

Luke's account highlights and contextualizes relevant developments in the Pauline mission: the geographic spread of Christianity beyond Jerusalem was a direct act of God; the breaking of racial boundaries in the cases of the Samaritans and the Ethiopian eunuch were under divine guidance and confirmed by signs and wonders; there was apostolic confirmation of the Samaritan mission; and the spread of the gospel to the Gentiles was part of the pattern of expansion, demonstrated the hand of God, and was approved by an apostolic emissary. In other words, the basis of the Pauline mission had direct divine guidance, historic precedence, apostolic approval, and the confirmation of signs and wonders through the Hellenistic Jewish Christians before Paul and Barnabas were sent out by Antioch. The boundaries had already been crossed and the ground had been laid. Paul was not embarking on something entirely new or simply on his own, but he was part of a bigger story involving other characters as well. Paul, however, does have a unique place in Luke's narrative economy: Luke clearly depicts Paul as having a specific divine call to evangelize the Gentiles, uniquely articulating the mission to the Gentiles, and working out the theological implications of the addition of the Gentiles to the people of God.

The Mission to the Gentiles and the Jewish Mission

Luke strategically stages the extension of the gospel to the Gentiles in Antioch by inserting the account of Paul's conversion and the highly descriptive account of the conversion of Cornelius's household (Acts 8:32—11:18) in the middle of the account of the expansion of Christianity immediately following Stephen's death (Acts 8:1–31; 11:19–29), and thus make Acts 9–11 a central pivot point for the entire narrative. This confluence of indicators of the Gentile mission is reinforced by multiple accounts of Paul's Damascus road conversion, Peter's encounter with Cornelius (Acts 10:1–48; 11:4–17; 15:7–11) and the account of the apos-

---

23. Paul had never visited Rome when he wrote his epistle to the Romans, but it is the earliest document that attests to the presence of a Christian community in Rome. According to Paul, it had been there "for many years" (Rom 15:23). If the original Roman Christians were members of the Pentecost crowd, the founding of the church would date to as early as the 30s, and the church would have first been made up of Hellenistic Jewish Christians and God-fearing Gentiles that associated themselves with the Jewish community in Rome. See Fitzmyer, *Romans*, 29.

tolic decree (Acts 15:19–20, 29; 21:25)—each repeated three times in the Acts account. This pattern establishes the connection between the Jewish and Gentile missions, but also underlines the validity of the Gentile mission in general, and Paul's mission in particular.

Paul's conversion in Acts 9:1–31 takes place as part of the story of the spread of Christianity by the Hellenistic Jewish Christians. He is a Hellenistic Jew himself. He is ironically converted in the process of trying to stem the rising tide that he himself significantly contributed to by his zealous persecution. In this first account, he is designated as God's chosen instrument to carry God's name to the Gentiles, both the Gentile rulers and the Jews as well (vv. 15–16). This typifies Luke's accounts of Paul's missionary strategy of preaching first to the Jews in each city.[24] Luke's account of Paul's conversion and the subsequent trouble he stirred up in Antioch and Jerusalem is laced with further irony, but his eventual acceptance and protection by the Jerusalem church demonstrates solidarity between Paul and the apostolic mission (vv. 28–30).

Peter's encounter with Cornelius validates the mission to the Gentiles through direct divine guidance and the process of events (Acts 10:1–47). Luke depicts both participants as lacking any kind of agenda, so that God is portrayed as the sole initiator of the first conversion of Gentiles. Cornelius receives a vision to send for Peter and Peter receives a vision that overrides his reluctance to enter the home of a Gentile. He preaches to Cornelius's household with no apparent expectation for results. The conversion of the group of Gentiles with a "mini-Pentecost" is clearly counter to expectations—it humorously occurs before Peter is done speaking and certainly before he issues an invitation (it is not clear whether he intended to issue an invitation). Luke indicates that the contact with Gentiles, let alone Peter's decision to baptize them, is controversial. Peter's question, "Can anyone keep these people from being baptized?" is more than hypothetical. Peter is rebuked and confronted by the believers in Jerusalem (Acts 11:1–3). The experience of the replication of the baptism of the Holy Spirit is ultimately the decisive argument for the Jerusalem church. Their revolutionary conclusion is crucial for the argument of Acts: "So then, God has granted even the Gentiles

---

24. This may appear to contradict Paul's designation of himself as an apostle to the Gentiles (Gal 2:7). However, as we shall see below, it is entirely consistent with his statements elsewhere, in particular in Romans.

repentance unto life" (Acts 11:18). Peter will use this account and argument to support Paul's mission at the Jerusalem Council in Acts 15.

THE THIRD AND MOST FOCAL STRAND: PAUL'S MISSION

As we have demonstrated, the stage is set for Paul's mission long before Paul arrives on the scene to take up the mantle by joining the mission outlined and instigated by the Jewish Christians. There are a number of factors that indicate the continuity between the mission of Jesus, the mission of the disciples, and the mission of Paul. These include the fact that the gospel had already expanded beyond the confines of Jerusalem and the Jews to reach those in the outlying areas, including Samaritans, Ethiopians, and Gentile Roman soldiers. The spread of persecution had diffused the Christian mission to areas far outside of Jerusalem, and even beyond Judea. In the aftermath of Stephen's death (Acts 7), persecution spread to a number of areas (Acts 8:1). A further tangible sign of the continuity of mission is found in the fact that Paul was not the first to evangelize non-Jews. Besides Philip's testifying to the Ethiopian eunuch, Peter had gone to the household of the Gentile soldier Cornelius and eaten together with him. The ways in which these individual episodes are brought together in Acts 9–11, including Paul's conversion, indicate the lines of continuity between Jesus' exhortation to "be witnesses both in Jerusalem, and in all Judaea and Samaria, and even to the end of the earth" (Acts 1:8), the Jewish mission, and then the Gentile mission.

Even though all of this evidence is clear, there is also more to the story, especially as Luke wishes to convey it. Paul grasped the special significance of what it meant to be the apostle to the Gentiles in ways that, though continuous with the preceding actions and traditions, pressed their boundaries into new and challenging areas. Whereas Luke conveys the continuity of the traditions, he also does not hesitate to depict Paul as the most important figure in taking the gospel to the Gentiles in an intentional and focused way. There are three specific characteristics to note regarding Paul's mission: the strategy of Paul's missionary journeys, Paul's approach toward the Jews first and then the Gentiles, and the content of Paul's missionary preaching.

The Strategy of Paul's Missionary Journeys

Paul is depicted as bringing a sense of system and order to the spread of the gospel both to Jews and to Gentiles. As we have noted above, there is a gradual process of introduction of Paul into the missionary venture. At first the mission is carried forward by the Twelve. They do so in what can only be characterized as a haphazard or unsystematic way, influenced in great part by the fact of persecution. The missionary venture begins in Jerusalem at Pentecost, and focuses upon that city until persecution forces an expansion into new areas. This expansion is not systematic, but involves a venture into Samaria (Acts 8), the Ethiopian eunuch on the road to Gaza and possibly Egypt (Acts 8), Cornelius in Caesarea (Acts 10), and Barnabas going to Antioch (Act 11:22). Nevertheless, there is a pattern, no doubt intended to reveal the hand of God at work. The pattern is one of venturing ever further from Jerusalem, until Barnabas arrives at Antioch. While this decentralization is occurring, what at first appears to be only a minor theme is developed: the introduction of Saul/Paul. Saul/Paul first appears at the stoning of Stephen (Acts 7:58) in support of this action (Acts 8:1), and as engaging in his own persecution (Acts 8:3) following in the wake of the general persecution of Hellenistic Jewish Christians (Acts 8:1). Paul is re-introduced in Acts 9 when he gets the arrest warrants from the high priest and sets off toward Damascus to persecute the church, only to be stopped in his tracks by the Lord Jesus Christ (Acts 9:1–9). Paul, however, then again leaves the stage while he goes to Arabia and Tarsus, before he is found by Barnabas, who goes from Antioch looking for him (Acts 11:25). Barnabas and Paul are then sent to Jerusalem as envoys (Acts 11:30). Upon their return (Acts 12:25), in Antioch the Holy Spirit indicates that Barnabas and Paul should be set apart for a special endeavor (Acts 13:2): the first extended missionary journey recorded in detail in the New Testament. In a sense, it is as if the various partial and trial gestures have been made in preparation for this concerted and planned act of outreach. This is the beginning of the known missionary ventures of Paul as apostle to the Gentiles. Thus, there is a clear interweaving of the two strands—the major strand being that of missionary outreach, and the other of the developing life of Paul—until they come together in and around Antioch and become a single strand that joins with the two previous strands to form a single cord.

There is some critical discussion about the nature and number of Paul's missionary trips.[25] Some scholars believe that we cannot actually discern distinct missionary journeys in Acts, while others dispute whether there are three or some other number. Some of the dispute regarding the existence of the missionary journeys revolves around the failure to realize the extent of the journeys. Luke's focus upon Paul in the mission of Acts portrays the center of the missionary endeavor to the Gentiles as already moving from Jerusalem by a gradual process of growth until it is focused upon Antioch. Antioch then becomes the center of missionary outreach to the Gentiles. When Antioch is placed at the center of the analysis, definable patterns emerge more clearly.

The three missionary journeys each begin from Antioch. As in the earlier part of Acts, each journey takes Paul and his companions further from the center, while always returning to the centre.[26] Paul is the focus and the end of the earth is the goal (Acts 1:8). The first missionary journey begins as the journey of Barnabas and Paul (Acts 13:2), and extends as far as Cyprus and Asia Minor. This journey goes by way of Cyprus into southern Asia Minor and provincial (southern) Galatia, and then essentially retraces its steps (Acts 13:4—14:28), but along the way it becomes the journey of Paul and Barnabas (Acts 13:42, 43; cf. 14:14). The second missionary journey also begins from Antioch, proceeds through Asia Minor by way of Galatia and re-visits some of the churches created on the first journey (e.g., Derbe, Lystra, and Iconium), and then proceeds further west, moving beyond Asia Minor into Europe, more particularly Macedonia and then Achaia (Greece), before returning by way of the coast of Asia Minor and Jerusalem to Antioch (Acts 15:36—18:22). This second missionary journey extends the mission of Paul well beyond Judea, Samaria, Antioch, and even those areas conveniently reached. It extends the outreach as far as the heart of Gentile lands, especially Greece and such cities as Athens and Corinth. The third missionary journey also begins from Antioch, retraces Paul's steps through Asia Minor and the churches of Galatia, proceeds west to Ephesus, first visited on the second missionary journey (Acts 18:19–21), and then works its way up the coast of Asia Minor, across into Europe, and again down to Achaia and Athens and Corinth, before Paul retraces his steps all the way to Ephesus, and

---

25. For a Pauline Christology, see McDonald and Porter, *Early Christianity*, 365–72.

26. On the idea of the missionary journeys as an ever-expanding circle that retains its center, see Porter, *Paul of Acts*, 173.

then travels by sea back to Jerusalem, before what would appear to be an anticipated return to Antioch (Acts 18:23—21:17). The third missionary journey, though it does not extend the scope of Paul's mission significantly further than the second journey, does ensure deeper penetration, as Paul visits and then re-visits many of the places that he had evangelized on the second and even first missionary trips.

These three missionary trips of Paul reveal a pattern of increasing distance between the home base in Antioch and increasing penetration into the world further away from the eastern Mediterranean, including even Achaia. The result is that Paul spent a significant amount of time on a number of occasions in several of the cities visited. He spent the most time in Ephesus. He visited Ephesus and environs four times (the fourth time he intentionally skirted it but met the Ephesian elders at Miletus; Acts 20:13–38), and spent well over three years in that city (see esp. Acts 19:1–41). Paul visited Philippi on perhaps three occasions, even if the time was not lengthy (Acts 16:12-40; 20:1-2, 3-6), and visited Corinth on probably two occasions (Acts 18:1-18; 20:2-3) and spent over two years in that city. He also may have visited Athens on two occasions, even though we only know explicitly of one (Acts 17:15-34; cf. 20:2-3). There are probably a number of other cities that Paul visited on several occasions (e.g., Thessalonica, when it says that he went through Macedonia; Acts 20:1-2). We will turn to Paul's specific mission strategy in each city below, but often only the first account of his visit is given significant coverage in Acts. The implication is that on subsequent visits he reinforced the pattern that was outlined in the initial visit. If this is so, it indicates that Paul's subsequent visits to a city were devoted to further Gentile-based outreach, as he had moved on to the Gentiles after being rejected by the Jews in these cities—a pattern we will discuss in more detail below.

There is one more important Pauline trip to mention, however. In a very real sense it is a fourth missionary trip, as it accomplishes a goal that Paul had for some time—visiting Rome. A trip to Rome is seen by Paul in the book of Romans as the next logical stage in his missionary endeavor (Rom 1:15). In the book of Acts, Paul's life is divided into three periods. The first includes his first appearance as a persecutor, his conversion and his initial training, including extended stays in Arabia, Syria, and Cilicia (probably a total of fifteen years). The second stage is his three missionary trips. Despite their extending the scope of his missionary endeavors as far as Greece, Paul realized—explicitly stated in Romans (e.g., 15:23–28) but directly implied in Acts on the basis of his increasingly westward missionary journeys—that in order to propel his Gentile mission to the next stage he must go to Rome. As the book of Romans indicates, Paul sees Rome as the next important goal in his missionary endeavors, both to evangelize in Rome and to use Rome as a staging ground for a further missionary venture—reaching Spain and the furthest western parts of the Roman Empire. Paul does indeed reach Rome (Acts 28:14), even if it is not according to the plan that he has envisioned, but requires the aid of the Roman army to transport him from Jerusalem and then Caesarea to Rome—a fourth missionary journey (Acts 27:1—28:15). The book of Acts ends with Paul imprisoned, but welcoming visitors (Acts 28:30–31). It is unlikely that there was a third volume written by Luke, or that one was ever intended. However, the way Acts ends points to a further expansion of Paul's missionary endeavors, from Rome to beyond. Tradition has it that Paul was released from prison, and some traditions even say that he made it to Spain (*1 Clem.* 5:7),[27] or at least evangelized further in the Mediterranean (so the Pastoral Epistles; see 1 Tim 1:3, 5; 2 Tim 4:13, 19; Titus 3:12). Regardless of how this turned out, the book of Acts appears to end along a trajectory that points to further expansion of the mission to the Gentiles, from Jerusalem, to Judea, to Samaria, to Caesarea, to Asia Minor, to Illyricum, to Macedonia and Greece, to Rome and beyond, perhaps as far as Spain (see Rom 15:19, 24).

Mission to the Jews First and Then to the Gentiles

The second feature of the missionary strategy of the Paul of Acts captures what distinguishes Paul's missionary intentions. In Rom 1:16, Paul speaks of the gospel as the power of God for salvation, to the Jew first and then to the Greek.[28] The book of Acts, as it continues on from Luke's Gospel, first establishes continuity with Jesus' mission, and then extends

---

27. There has also been discussion of whether Paul knew Latin. William Ramsay believed that he did (*Paul the Traveller*, 225), and he has been followed by some.

28. Some have thought of Paul's connection to the Jewish mission as inconsistent with his statement in Gal 1:16 that he was appointed as one to preach to the Gentiles (see also Gal 2:2). What we are attempting to show is that Paul's preaching to the Gentiles was consistent with and a continuation of the mission to the Jews. Paul himself notes this in Gal 3:8, when he speaks of Scripture foreseeing that God would justify the Gentiles.

this mission to the Jews, but with only occasional forays into evangelization of Gentiles. As we noted above, in Acts 9–11 there is a confluence of the Jewish and Gentile strands of mission, but without integration of them, and without development of the Gentile mission. This integration and development is left to Paul. In Paul, these two strategies come together in his approach. Even though this strategy is not distinctly articulated in his letters, it is implied in his phrase "to the Jew first and then to the Greek," found not only in Rom 1:16 but also in Rom 2:9, 10.

In Acts, Paul's strategy is first to visit a synagogue or the Jews in a city, and begin his proclamation of the gospel from that venue. This is the approach that he uses in the following places according to the explicit references in Acts: Salamis on Cyprus, the first point of contact with the Mediterranean island (Acts 13:5); Pisidian Antioch, where the first of Paul's missionary speeches is given (Acts 13:15); Iconium (Acts 14:1); Philippi, the first significant city in Macedonia that Paul visits, where he visits a place of prayer as there does not appear to have been a synagogue in the city (Acts 16:13);[29] Thessalonica, a city though technically in Macedonia but by the first century thought of as a Greek city,[30] and the first significant one of them that Paul visits (Acts 17:1); Berea (Acts 17:10); Athens, the leading city of Greece, where he gives his third missionary speech (Acts 17:17); Corinth, a major political and economic center (Acts 18:4);[31] Ephesus, on his first, brief visit to this city (Acts 18:19); and Ephesus again when he returns (Acts 19:8). There is a clear pattern here: Paul instigates his mission of evangelizing the Jews in a given location by visiting the synagogue and participating in their worship, taking the opportunity from Scripture to persuade them (even if it includes arguing with them) that Jesus is the Messiah and that the kingdom of God has been inaugurated by him, and to make converts (see Acts 13:16-41, treated below; 14:1; 17:2, 12, 17; 18:4, 19; 19:8). Clearly Paul had not abandoned his own people (cf. Rom 9–11), but began his missionary endeavor in a new city by making connections to the local Jewish community. However, Paul's approach in the synagogue was clearly forceful and direct. He used the Jewish Scriptures to try to persuade and convince them that Jesus was the Messiah, and sometimes he needed to argue this point vigorously.

---

29. See McDonald and Porter, *Early Christianity*, 461-62.
30. See ibid., 415-16.
31. See ibid., 428-32.

In the light of this, it is not surprising that some of those who heard Paul in the synagogue became upset with him. In fact, it is more often the case than not that once Paul began his outreach it resulted in some kind of unrest. However, the transition from synagogue to the larger Gentile world also often constituted the means by which Paul bridged the gap between Jew and Gentile and then proceeded to evangelize the Gentiles. In that sense, the reaction of the Jews was both unfortunate and fortuitous for the Gentile mission. For example, on Cyprus Paul begins in the synagogue and then proceeds to evangelize the rest of the island, but encounters the adversarial Elymas the magician (Acts 13:8–11). This encounter results in the successful evangelization of Sergius Paulus the proconsul (Acts 13:7). In Acts 13:46, after the Jews become filled with jealousy after Paul's successful evangelization in Pisidian Antioch (note his speech, discussed below), Paul tells them that he is going to turn to the Gentiles. When the Gentiles begin to hear Paul's message, Luke says, they begin to rejoice and glorify the word of the Lord, and the word of the Lord is being spread through the whole region—again, Jewish rejection leads to Gentile acceptance, even though the Jews continue their antagonism (Acts 13:48, 49, 50). Another example occurs at Iconium, where, after Paul speaks in the synagogue, the Jewish unbelievers stir up the Gentiles against Paul, who has been successful in evangelizing Jews *and* Gentiles (Acts 14:2). Similarly, in Philippi, after Paul commands the spirit of the Python to come out of the prophetess, Paul is set upon by her masters, and jailed (Acts 16:18, 23). In Thessalonica also, after preaching for three Sabbaths in the synagogue, and having converts, Paul has a number of Jews gather a mob to oppose him (Acts 17:5). This same mob follows him to Berea, so that after he preaches in the synagogue there, a crowd is stirred up against him (Acts 17:13). In Athens, Paul again begins in the synagogue, while also speaking with those in the market place. It is those in the market place, in particular the Epicureans and Stoics, who engage him in further discussion, but are unable to accept the notion of the resurrection of Jesus (Acts 16:17, 32). In Corinth, Paul does not meet with even the same amount of success that he has in synagogues elsewhere, and so he goes to the house of Titius Justus, next to the synagogue, and continues his teaching (Acts 18:6, 7). Finally, in his second trip to Ephesus, Paul again begins in the synagogue, but there are a number who are opposed to the Way, and so this time he continues his teaching in the school of Tyrannus (Acts 19:9).

We must note, however, that it is not invariable that Paul begins his evangelization in the synagogue. In Lystra, for example, there is no mention of Paul starting his mission in the synagogue, but he is confronted upon entry into the city with a lame man, whom he heals. This leads the locals to attempt to venerate Paul and Barnabas as Hermes and Zeus (Acts 14:8, 12). These people are most likely Gentiles, not Jews. However, it is Jews in Antioch and Iconium who come to Lystra to attempt to kill Paul (Acts 14:19). This is a rare instance, however, and perhaps accounted for by the historical facts themselves—that on the way into the city Paul performs the healing that leads directly to the veneration.

There are several observations to make regarding this mission strategy. We note, first, that visiting a synagogue occurs at or near the entrance of Paul into a new area, such as Cyprus or Asia Minor, or even Macedonia or Achaia. Second, there is no mention of Paul visiting a synagogue to instigate his missionary outreach when he returns to a city that he has evangelized previously, apart from Ephesus. This repeat visit can be accounted for on the basis of the circumstances in the city. When Paul returned to Ephesus he found that the people there were confused in their theology, and, even though they were probably believers,[32] he had essentially to begin again with them. Third, it is important to note the consistent pattern of moving from the synagogue to the larger Gentile world. One of the points of transition may have been the Gentile God-fearers (besides Cornelius in Acts 10:2, 22, 35; see Acts 13:16, 26, 43 in Pisidian Antioch; 16:14 in Philippi; 17:4 in Thessalonica; 17:17 in Athens; and 18:7 in Corinth).[33] These devout people, who had respect for Jewish law and practice, may have been the point of transition between the synagogue and the wider Gentile world. These Gentiles would have worshipped at the synagogue, but were not proselytes and so maintained many significant connections to the wider Gentile world. Fourth, despite the fact that this strategy of evangelism is not mentioned elsewhere in Paul's letters, it is entirely consistent with his specified priorities of the Jew first and then the Greek. Fifth, Paul's mission in Acts, as his statements in Romans also indicate, reflects a strategy that maintains the place of the Jews while extending access to the gospel to Gentiles in a systematic and continuative way. Even as Paul's ministry developed, and well into his third missionary journey, he continued to use this

---

32. Porter, *Paul of Acts*, 80–86.
33. See ibid., 56–57; and especially the article by Wilcox, "God-Fearers."

strategy, despite opposition. There is not a developing displacement or supersessionist theology at work here, but a theology on Paul's part that recognizes, endorses, and maintains the place of the Jews in God's missionary plan, while using it as the basis for a mission to the Gentiles. Thus, even in Corinth and Ephesus, Paul began by preaching and teaching in the synagogue despite opposition from within the synagogue itself. His priority for missionary outreach was to go to the Jews first, and then the Gentiles, and he appears to have maintained this pattern virtually invariably. This not only provided a useful strategy in terms of establishing first contact with those of similar religious and ethnic background before moving to the world of the Gentiles, but it maintained his theological priorities—despite rejection by the Jews and acceptance by Gentiles, Paul was not going to forget his own people, because God had not abandoned his people.

Content of the Missionary Preaching of Paul

We have discussed the overall plan of Paul's mission in Acts, and we have treated the mechanism by which he continued the theological pattern of going to the Jew first and then to the Gentile. We have received some hint of what it was that Paul proclaimed when he was in the synagogue, especially as it related to interpreting Scripture in terms of the coming of the Lord Jesus Christ. However, in order to gain a fuller picture of what Paul's missionary message was, and hence how this fit his strategy, we need to turn to his three missionary speeches in Acts. There are a number of types of speeches by Paul in Acts.[34] These include apologetic speeches (such as those delivered to the Jerusalem Jews in Acts 22:1–21, before Felix in Acts 24:10–21, before Agrippa and others in Acts 26:2–23, and to the Roman Jewish leaders in Acts 28:17–20), his farewell speech to the Ephesian elders (Acts 20:18–35), and his missionary speeches. There are three missionary speeches to consider. This paper is not the place to discuss the nature of ancient speeches, or even the speeches in Acts, except to observe that there are a variety of theories regarding the creation and use of speeches in the ancient world. Appeal is often made to Thucydides's statement regarding speeches (1.22.1), but this statement is susceptible to much and varied interpretation.[35] It is clear

---

34. These are treated in Porter, *Paul of Acts*, 151–71 for apologetic speeches, 115–18 for the Miletus speech, and 126–50 for the missionary speeches.

35. The options are discussed in Porter, "Thucydides 1.22.1."

that speeches were used for a variety of purposes. Some of these were primarily theological and some historiographical, and many no doubt both. Even if we believe that the speeches may have been delivered by Paul in circumstances resembling the ones depicted in Acts—and we affirm that this is the case—the speeches are probably in many if not most instances summaries of what was said on the occasion. That may also be their virtue in discussing them here, however, as they were in those circumstances no doubt designed to capture the essence of what was said on the occasion—even if they do not capture everything.

There are three missionary speeches to consider.[36] The first is Paul's speech at Pisidian Antioch (Acts 13:16–41). This is Paul's first significant speech in the book of Acts, and it is addressed to an audience primarily, though not exclusively, Jewish.[37] The speech is given in response to an invitation by the leaders of the synagogue to address the group. There are several features of this speech that indicate the nature of Paul's mission in Acts. The first is that he addresses his remarks to "Israelite men" and "those who fear God" (Acts 13:16). Even though he is in a synagogue, Paul is inclusive in his address, speaking both to Jews[38] and to those attracted to Judaism, the God-fearers. In effect, Paul is "creating a bridge ... between the Jewish origins and original Jewish audience of the gospel and the subsequent presentation of the gospel to Gentiles by the Apostle to the Gentiles."[39] The second is that Paul's message is grounded in God's actions in the past towards Israel.[40] The historical narrative that Paul recounts serves at least two purposes. One is to create a linkage for both Jews and Gentiles to a history of God's actions with his people. Another is to show that it is God who has been at work in the past and is at work in the present.[41] In other words, God's present actions in Jesus Christ are

---

36. So says Schneider, *Apostelgeschichte*, 1:96.

37. Roloff, *Apostelgeschichte*, 202.

38. Paul uses the phrase "Israelite men" also in Acts 21:28. It is used elsewhere in Acts in 2:22, 3:12, and 5:35.

39. Porter, *Paul of Acts*, 133. See also Acts 13:26, 38.

40. Parallels between Paul's historical account here and Stephen's account in Acts 7:2–50 have been noted. On the similarities and differences, see Squires, *Plan of God*, 70–77.

41. The emphasis upon God's role with Israel is indicated by both the historical survey and the syntax of the passage, in which, in nine of ten indicative verbs, God is the one indicated as caring for Israel. See Squires, *Plan of God*, 70. For an even fuller analysis, emphasizing register analysis and person deixis, see Martín-Asensio,

grounded in God's faithful actions in the past, known to the Jews but needing to be known by the Gentiles. A third observation is that Paul does not treat this historical information as simply an accounting of the past, but as the basis for proclamation of the good news in the present (Acts 13:32). Jesus is seen by Paul, and depicted here in Acts, as the fulfillment of the promise made to Abraham in the Old Testament. The fourth observation is that Paul not only grounds his historical account in Scripture, but also marshals a number of scriptural proofs regarding who Jesus is.[42] Paul says that Jesus was raised by God (Acts 13:33, citing Ps 2:7), that he is raised from the dead and will not decay (Acts 13:34, 35, citing Isa 55:3 LXX and Ps 16:10 LXX), and that his words are to be taken seriously (Hab 1:5).[43] Thus, this first missionary speech, though addressed to more than simply Jews, utilizes the Scriptures as the common basis for talking about who Jesus is.

The second speech is that of Barnabas and Paul at Lystra (Acts 14:15–17). This speech occurs in the unusual pattern noted above, where Paul does not first enter a synagogue, but needs to address the crowd when they attempt to venerate him and Barnabas. This speech is thus addressed to a primarily Gentile audience. Though a less self-consciously planned speech than the one at Pisidian Antioch,[44] it merits examination in terms of Paul's missionary teaching. Paul's first major statement after his words of address is to ask the purpose for the Lystran's behavior. This question no doubt grows out of the immediacy of the situation, but it makes a number of important statements. One is that there is a common human nature that is shared by Jew and Gentile alike, a form of natural theological argument.[45] This multiple level appeal includes the implication that all humans share common origins, destiny, and functions,

---

Transitivity-Based Foregrounding, 112–28. Martín-Asensio (113) rightly rejects Jervell's attempt to use the two historical accounts to equate Israel and the church (Jervell, *Theology of the Acts*, 24).

42. Kee (*Good News*, 14) notes the synthesis of what he sees as disparate texts, while Moessner ("'Script' of the Scriptures") sees the passages united around the idea of the will of God, a point emphasized throughout the speech.

43. Several of the quotations are introduced by the perfect tense-form, indicating stative aspect. See Porter, *Verbal Aspect*, 289 n. 16.

44. On the issue of whether it should be treated as a speech or not, see Porter, *Paul of Acts*, 137.

45. See Rackham, *Acts*, 233, on Paul's use of "accommodation" to speak to the Lystrans.

and is designed to form a common bond between Paul the Jew and the Gentiles who are seeking to venerate him and his companions. Once this common foundation is established, Paul can move to the heart of what he wants to say. He wants to ensure that this common element provides a sufficient foundation in natural law to justify his addressing the issue of Jesus Christ. The fact that the Lystrans wanted to venerate Paul and Barnabas as gods gives Paul the entry point for finding common ground. There are thus four elements to Paul's speech in terms of God. He notes God's role in the creation of humanity, the common destiny of humanity, the ignorance of human beings of knowledge of God, and God's not leaving himself without a witness in terms of natural phenomena. We will treat Paul's use of natural theology in the final speech, but he never gets to move beyond this to working out the implications of a common human nature.

The third and final missionary speech is Paul's speech on the Areopagus.[46] This speech is different from the previous two in that it is a missionary speech specifically created for a Gentile audience. As a result, Paul addresses the Athenians directly. This is consistent with his speeches elsewhere, in that Paul usually addresses a specific audience. The second feature is that Paul focuses upon their religiousness or superstitious nature.[47] As with his other speeches, Paul forms a foundation in his address that is suited to his particular audience. In this case, he has observed that his Athenian audience has a significant interest in things religious, including their erecting numerous objects of worship, even to the point of creating a statue to an unknown god.[48] His recognition of their religiosity is a means of establishing a common ground for their discussion (a form of *captatio benevolentiae*, in which a speaker attempted to capture the goodwill of the audience and find a point of common contact from which to address them).[49] Paul uses this point of connection around religiosity, and in particular the monument to the unknown god, as a means of introducing the one true God. The common ground

---

46. The bibliography on this speech is massive. For a summary, see Porter, *Paul of Acts*, 141–42, esp. n. 60.

47. See ibid., 143.

48. Many have disputed the accuracy of this account. However, van der Horst has argued for the accuracy of Luke's language, as well as claiming that the reference may even have been to the God of the Jews ("Altar of the 'Unknown God.'")

49. See Winter, "*Captatio Benevolentiae.*"

of his argument is definitely similar to the type of natural theology argument that Paul uses in Rom 1:18–32. This includes reference to God as creator (Acts 17:24–29; note the citation of Aratus, *Phaen.* 5) and judge (Acts 17:30–32).[50] Paul's argument naturally leads him to the resurrection of Jesus, at which point he is cut off and not able to continue.

We can glean from these three speeches, however, a common pattern regarding the content of Paul's missionary speeches, and hence his mission in Acts. Some of those features include the following: He addresses his comments appropriately to his audience. He speaks to Jews as a Jew and to the Gentiles as a man born and reared in the Gentile world. He addresses them specifically, depending upon his context. The second is that he lays an appropriate foundation for his comments. For the Jews, this involves reference to their past as God's people, led by his servants such as Abraham and Moses. The third is that he does not dismiss, ridicule, or otherwise negate their own particular background, but he uses it to establish who they are and how it is that he relates to them, either ethnically or conceptually. Fourth, Paul uses this established common ground as a means of bridging who they are and the message that he wants to bring. This message is appropriately shaped for the audience, but has in common that it introduces Jesus (Acts 13:23), raised from the dead (Acts 13:30, 34; 17:31), who is the righteous judge of humanity (Acts 17:31) or who brings the good news of salvation to humanity (Acts 13:32). For Jews, this is seen as the fulfillment of prophecy (Acts 13:33, 34, 35, 41). For Gentiles, this is seen as the fulfillment of a nature-based theological argument, in which the creator God (Acts 14:15; 17:24–29) has not left himself without testimony in the world (Acts 14:17; 17:27).

CONCLUSION

We have argued that there is one cord, a crimson thread if you will, that unites the missionary emphasis of the book of Acts. This cord consists of three strands.

The first strand goes back to the very mission of Jesus as depicted by Luke. The second is the Jewish mission, instigated by Jesus for his disciples to carry out. Luke never fully describes the Jewish mission beyond its early years, but provides some evidence that it continued to grow in

---

50. Those who have advocated Paul's use of a natural theology argument here and in Romans include Witherington, *Acts*, 425–26, 511.

tandem with the mission to the Gentiles, while traditional and external sources suggest that Christianity spread throughout the Diaspora at least in part through the efforts of the apostles. Luke's purpose is to show how the Jewish mission provided the basis and justification for Paul's mission to the Gentiles, demonstrating that Paul and his mission were in continuity with not only the mission of Jesus, but the Jewish mission that was centered in Jerusalem.

The third is the Gentile mission, which began with the Twelve, but was quickly taken over by the apostle to the Gentiles, Paul. Though these three strands are united in this single cord, they are not all equally emphasized throughout the book. Instead, there is a progression, from the mission of Jesus, which carries over from Luke's Gospel into the early chapters of Acts, to the mission to the Jews, which is intermixed with various efforts to evangelize the Gentiles, finally to the mission to the Gentiles and its greatest exposition in the story of the mission of the apostle Paul. Through a delicate interweaving of Paul's story with the growing Jewish and Gentile mission, the ground is laid for the emergence of the great proponent and motivator of the Gentile mission. Paul moved far beyond Jerusalem and Judea, and even Samaria and Antioch, to Cyprus, Asia Minor, Greece, and then to Rome, and perhaps even beyond. Throughout his missionary efforts, Paul used the mission strategy of forming ties with the local Jewish community first before turning to the Gentiles, and he proclaimed the same message wherever he went. This message was that the God of the Jews and Gentiles alike, whether known through Scripture or through nature, was at work in redeeming humanity by means of the death and resurrection of Jesus Christ. This was the message that by the end of the book of Acts was well on its way to reaching the end of the earth.

BIBLIOGRAPHY

Baur, F. C. *Paul, the Apostle of Christ*. 2 vols. Vol. 1 trans. E. Zeller, vol. 2 trans. A. Menzies. 2nd ed. Edinburgh: Williams & Norgate, 1876.

Bienert, W. A. "Das Apostelbild in der altchristlichen Uberlieferung." In *Neutestamentliche Apokryphen in deutscher Übersetzung*, edited by W. Schneemelcher, 2:6–28. 2 vols. 6th ed. Tübingen: Mohr Siebeck, 1997.

Brawley, R. L. *Luke–Acts and the Jews: Conflict, Apology, and Conciliation*. SBLMS 33. Atlanta: Scholars, 1987.

———. "Paul in Acts: Lucan Apology and Conciliation." In *Perspectives on Luke–Acts*, edited by C. Talbert, 129–47. Danville, VA: Association of Baptist Professors of Religion, 1978.

Bruce, F. F. *The Book of the Acts*. NICNT. 2nd ed. Grand Rapids: Eerdmans, 1988.
deSilva, D. A. *An Introduction to the New Testament: Contexts, Methods and Ministry Formation*. Downers Grove, IL: InterVarsity, 2004.
Duchesne, L. *Early History of the Christian Church from Its Foundation to the End of the Fifth Century*. 3 vols. London: John Murray, 1909.
Dupont, J. *The Salvation of the Gentiles*. New York: Paulist, 1967.
Fitzmyer, J. A. *Romans: A New Translation with Introduction and Commentary*. AB 33. New York: Doubleday, 1993.
Goulder, M. D. *A Tale of Two Missions*. London: SCM, 1994.
———. *Paul and the Competing Mission in Corinth*. Library of Pauline Studies. Peabody, MA: Hendrickson, 2001.
Haenchen, E. *The Acts of the Apostles*. 14th ed. 1965. Reprint, Philadelphia: Westminster, 1987.
Jervell, J. *The Theology of the Acts of the Apostles*. Cambridge: Cambridge University Press, 1996.
Kee, H. C. *Good News to the End of the Earth: The Theology of Acts*. Philadelphia: Trinity Press International, 1990.
Köstenberger, A. K., and P. T. O'Brien. *Salvation to the Ends of the Earth: A Biblical Theology of Mission*. NSBT 11. Downers Grove, IL: InterVarsity, 2001.
Martín-Asensio, G. *Transitivity-Based Foregrounding in the Acts of the Apostles: A Functional-Grammatical Approach to the Lukan Perspective*. JSNTSup 202. Sheffield: Sheffield Academic Press, 2000.
McDonald, L. M., and S. E. Porter. *Early Christianity and Its Sacred Literature*. Peabody, MA: Hendrickson, 2000.
Moessner, D. P. "The 'Script' of the Scriptures in Acts: Suffering as God's Plan (βουλή) for the World for the 'Release of Sins.'" In *History, Literature and Society in the Book of Acts*, edited by B. Witherington, III, 218-50. Cambridge: Cambridge University Press, 1996.
Porter, S. E. *The Paul of Acts: Essays in Literary Criticism, Rhetoric, and Theology*. WUNT 115. Tübingen: Mohr Siebeck, 1999.
———. "Thucydides 1.22.1 and Speeches in Acts: Is There a Thucydidean View?" *NovT* 32 (1990) 121–42.
———. *Verbal Aspect in the Greek of the New Testament, with Reference to Tense and Mood*. SBG 1. New York: Lang, 1989.
Powell, M. A. *What Are They Saying about Acts?* New York: Paulist, 1991.
Rackham, R. B. *The Acts of the Apostles: An Exposition*. 8th ed. London: Methuen, 1919.
Ramsay, William. *St. Paul the Traveller and the Roman Citizen*. London: Hodder & Stoughton, 1895.
Roloff, J. *Die Apostelgeschichte*. NTD 5. Berlin: Evangelische Verlagsanstalt, 1981.
Sahlin, H. *Der Messias und das Gottesvolk: Studien zur protolukanischen Theologie*. ASNU 12. Uppsala: Seminarium Neotestamenticum Upsaliense, 1945.
Sanders, J. T. *The Jews in Luke–Acts*. Philadelphia: Fortress, 1982.
Schnabel, E. J. *Early Christian Mission*. I. *Jesus and the Twelve*. Downers Grove, IL: InterVarsity 2004.
Schneider, G. *Die Apostelgeschichte*. HTKNT 51.1, 2. 2 vols. Freiburg: Herder, 1980, 1982.
Squires, J. T. *The Plan of God in Luke–Acts*. SNTSMS 76. Cambridge: Cambridge University Press, 1993.

Tannehill, R. C. *The Narrative Unity of Luke–Acts*. 2 vols. Philadelphia: Fortress, 1989.

Thornton, C.-J. *Der Zeuge des Zeugen: Lukas als Historiker der Paulusreisen*. WUNT 56. Tübingen: Mohr Siebeck, 1991.

van der Horst, P. W. "The Altar of the 'Unknown God' in Athens (Acts 17:23) and the Cult of 'Unknown Gods' in the Graeco-Roman World." In his *Hellenism—Judaism—Christianity: Essays on Their Interaction*. 2nd ed. Louvain: Peeters, 1994.

van Unnik, W. C. "The 'Book of Acts': The Confirmation of the Gospel." *NovT* 4 (1960) 26–59.

Wilcox, M. "The 'God-Fearers' in Acts—A Reconsideration." *JSNT* 13 (1981) 102–22.

Winter, B. W. "The Importance of the *Captatio Benevolentiae* in the Speeches of Tertullus and Paul in Acts 24:1–21." *JTS* 42 (1991) 507–15.

Witherington, B. III. *The Acts of the Apostles: A Social-Rhetorical Commentary*. Grand Rapids: Eerdmans, 1998.

6

The Content and Message of Paul's Missionary Teaching

Stanley E. Porter

INTRODUCTION

WHAT WAS THE CONTENT and message of Paul's missionary teaching, that is, what was it that Paul, as reflected in his letters, said to evangelize those he encountered, and that he instructed those he converted to say to others? First, let me clarify some necessary and important issues before I proceed. The first is what I mean by the terms "mission" or "missionary." I take the term "mission" in terms of what is understood by the traditional term "missionary work," that is "the attempt to convert non-Christians to the Christian faith, regardless of any geographical or cultural considerations."[1] I further wholeheartedly endorse Robert Plummer's statement that the notion of mission "is not simply a shorthand for all the expected activities of the Christian church . . . nor is it simply cross-cultural or cross-geographical evangelism."[2] There is too much of the language of both around to suit my liking. Too many Christian churches call themselves missional simply as a smokescreen to describe their continuing to do business as usual. That is certainly not what I have in mind. Similarly, other churches use the terminology only of that which takes place somewhere far away, and all too often out of sight and hence not of immediate concern. Instead, I use

---

1. Plummer, *Paul's Understanding of the Church's Mission*, 1.
2. Ibid., 1–2.

the terms "mission" and "missionary" in terms of "what ways Paul expected the early Christians in scattered communities across the Roman Empire to win any outsiders (whether local persons or those separated by geographical or cultural distance) to the same religious commitment that they espoused."[3]

A second major definitional issue is how Paul's letters relate to the book of Acts in terms of missionary teaching and preaching. We have accounts in the book of Acts that give some idea of what Paul—or at least the Paul of Acts—preached in his various missionary encounters. If one believes that these accounts are consonant with the Paul of the letters,[4] then we have a fairly good idea of what this preaching might have consisted of. We have such speeches as his missionary speech at Pisidian Antioch (Acts 13:16–41), at Lystra (Acts 14:15–17), and in Athens (Acts 17:22–31).[5] We have the good fortune in this volume to have a separate representation of the book of Acts, so I need not raise the question here of the relationship of the Paul of Acts to the Paul of the letters. I will confine my comments to what we find in Paul's letters.

The third issue concerts which letters we wish to consider. Paul's letter corpus can be divided up in any number of ways: the main letters and the others; the main letters, the prison letters and the pastorals; the authentic and the (purportedly) inauthentic; the church letters and the personal letters; and other configurations. Even though I take all of the letters as authentic, some of the factors that I still must weigh are the fact that all of the letters are addressed to communities that are already Christian, that is, none of the letters is evangelistic or missionary in nature. To some extent, a number of these issues are extraneous to consideration, because, no matter how you parse the Pauline epistolary situation, the standard view of most scholars is that, within his letters, Paul does not explicitly state what his missionary teaching or preaching is. Thus, when we turn to the letters, it is usually asserted that we do not have explicit accounts of the content or message of his missionary teaching. He is writing to those who are already converted, so he does not need to write with this consideration in mind. Furthermore, most

---

3. Ibid., 2.
4. As I do. See Porter, *Paul of Acts*, 187–206.
5. See ibid., 126–50, for treatment of these three speeches.

scholars argue that Paul does not instruct or tell his churches to evangelize others.[6]

In this paper, I wish first to offer a brief survey of some of the recent attempts to come to terms with this widespread recognition of the paucity of Pauline epistolary evidence for the content of his missionary teaching. However, I am not so skeptical that we lack such insight. In fact, I believe that we do have (at least) a single passage that offers a way forward in this discussion, because it does offer us an explicit statement by Paul regarding the content of his missionary teaching, and an imperative to his churches in their missionary preaching. Once we have this passage firmly established as reflecting the content of his message, then I believe that we can extrapolate from it to get an idea of the heart of Paul's missionary teaching and preaching, as well as formulate the content of the message that he wishes his churches to proclaim.

A BRIEF OVERVIEW OF RECENT PROPOSALS

Plummer has recently surveyed the various approaches to Paul's missionary teaching. He is concerned with the question of Paul's expectations for his churches' engagement in missions. As a result, he presents a thorough overview of the past one hundred years of research, organized by person and time-period.[7] However, he also notes that "Paul rarely, if ever, commands the recipients of his letters to evangelize."[8] This is certainly true—at least if one takes a narrow view of what constitutes evangelization. On numerous occasions, however, Paul speaks of evangelizing (here referring to passages that use the verb *euangelizō*, εὐαγγελίζω):[9]

> Rom 1:15: "so I am eager to preach the gospel to you also who are in Rome"
>
> Rom 10:15: "And how can anyone preach unless they are sent?"
>
> Rom 15:20: "my ambition to preach the gospel, not where Christ has already been named, lest I build on someone else's foundation"

---

6. See Plummer, *Paul's Understanding of the Church's Mission*, 1.

7. Ibid., 2–42.

8. Ibid., 1.

9. I could include other words and phrases as well, but I restrict myself to this lexeme.

1 Cor 1:17: "For Christ did not send me to baptize but to preach the gospel"

1 Cor 9:16: "For if I preach the gospel, that gives me no ground for boasting"

1 Cor 9:18: "in my preaching I may make the gospel free of charge"

1 Cor 15:1: "Now I would remind you, brothers and sisters, in what terms I preached to you the gospel, which you received, in which you stand"

1 Cor 15:2: "gospel . . . by which you are saved, if you hold it fast—unless you believed in vain"

2 Cor 10:16: "so that we may preach the gospel in lands beyond you"

2 Cor 11:7: "I preached God's gospel without cost to you?"

Gal 1:8, 9: "But even if we, or an angel from heaven, should preach to you a gospel contrary to that which we preached to you, let him be accursed . . . If any one is preaching to you a gospel contrary to that which you received, let him be accursed"

Gal 1:11: "the gospel which was preached by me is not of human origin"

Gal 1:16: "that I might preach him among the Gentiles"

Gal 1:23: "they only heard it said, 'He who once persecuted us is now preaching the faith he once tried to destroy'"

Gal 4:13: "you know it was because of a bodily ailment that I preached the gospel to you at first"

Eph 2:17: "And he came and preached peace to you who were far off and peace to those who were near"

Eph 3:8: "To me . . . this grace was given, to preach to the Gentiles the unsearchable riches of Christ"

Plummer wishes to go beyond this narrow language and see commands to evangelize in several other passages: Phil 1:12–18 as evidence that the church was evangelizing; Eph 6:15 as indicating an expectation of evangelization; 1 Cor 4:16, 11:1 as invoking Paul as an example to be imitated in missionary outreach; 1 Cor 7:12–16 as an example of good behavior; and 1 Cor 14:23–25 as indicating concern for non-believers.[10] In none of them, however, even if one accepts these passages, does he give the content of his evangelistic message or give instruction to his audience as to what they should say in their evangelistic efforts.

Schnabel, in his recent, massive treatment of the topic of early Christian mission, offers a categorization of five possible explanations for this lack.[11] (1) With reference to Rom 15:19–23, some scholars, Schnabel notes, claim "that Paul's missionary program received its profile from the conviction of the imminent return of Jesus Christ and hence did not aim at actively involving the newly founded churches in the mission of the church."[12] (2) Another explanation is that "the new converts would have been motivated by their conversion and by God's Spirit to engage in missionary activity as a matter of course, which made it unnecessary for Paul to challenge them with appeals to be involved in evangelistic outreach."[13] (3) "Some scholars argue that the church is missionary in character, which explains the lack of appeals to engage in missionary outreach."[14] (4) Some scholars would contend that there is a non-transferability between Paul's understanding of mission and other missionary contexts.[15] (5) Finally, Schnabel notes the position that holds that Paul's missionary concept "was still developing" or focused solely on the "spiritual growth of the young churches."[16] All of these, one notes, are negative proposals that give reasons and explanations why we do not find such statements regarding evangelization. When it comes to making a positive statement, Schnabel himself summarizes the message in terms not of Paul but of the early Christian missionaries as a whole. As a result, he offers three statements that, he claims, summarize such missionary teaching: God's redemptive messianic revelation, the new identity, and the promise of paradise restored. However, in supporting

---

10. Plummer, *Paul's Understanding of the Church's Mission*, 72–96. He also notes several "passive" missionary passages (pp. 96–105). Bowers, "Church and Mission in Paul," is opposed to these examples as illustrating a Pauline call to missionary outreach by his churches.

11. I note that most of the scholars treated by Plummer in his chronological survey can be placed within these categories. See also Hahn, *Mission in the New Testament*.

12. Schnabel, *Early Christian Mission*, 2:1452.

13. Ibid.

14. Ibid., 1453.

15. Ibid., 1454.

16. Ibid., 1455, 1456.

these statements, he draws upon much more than simply Paul's letters. He refers in most detail to Acts (including Paul's speeches, such as at Pisidian Antioch, Acts 13:16–41), other epistles such as 1 Peter, and even Revelation.[17] There is little reason to dispute that when taken as a whole there is an evangelistic thrust to the New Testament. However, the question is what was the content of Paul's missionary teaching and preaching.

Köstenberger and O'Brien focus upon what they call the gospel that Paul preached. They draw upon Romans 1 and 3, and isolate these distinguishing features as the content of Paul's gospel: (1) Paul's total commitment to the gospel. This includes being set apart for the gospel of God (Rom 1:1), and being eager to preach the gospel in Rome (Rom 1:15–16). (2) The Old Testament warrant, content, purpose, and saving power of Paul's gospel. This includes its being promised beforehand in the Old Testament (Rom 1:1–2), Jesus Christ as son of David and risen son of God as the content of the gospel (Rom 1:3–4), the purpose of the gospel being the risen Christ's rule over this new people of God (Rom 1:5), and the power of the gospel for salvation (1:16–17; 3:21–26).[18] These statements are a fine summary of the content of the gospel as seen in especially Rom 1 and 3 (granted, a selective interpretation of these chapters, and these only); however, saying that these are an adequate representation of the content of Paul's missionary message (even if they are how he understood the gospel) is a far cry from saying that this is the message that he advocated to others to pass on, since the passage gives no indication of this.

In other words, after surveying some of the recent discussion of the content of Paul's missionary message and teaching, and the message he wished others to pass on, we are admittedly still some distance from discovering the message of Paul's missionary preaching.

THE CONTENT OF PAUL'S MISSIONARY PREACHING

There are a number of factors to consider in attempting to discover the message and content of Paul's missionary teaching. One is to break free of the apparent compulsion to find what might best be characterized as

---

17. Ibid., 1562–68.

18. I quote and paraphrase the headings they use in Köstenberger and O'Brien, *Salvation to the Ends of the Earth*, 173–79. Cf. Plummer, *Paul's Understanding of the Church's Mission*, 51–56, on the power of the gospel.

distinctively evangelistic wording. Plummer has done this to some extent by differentiating between explicit commands, passive commands, and such "incidental evidence" as miracles, prayer, teaching regarding building the church, and Paul's own suffering,[19] but at the end of the day the form may be visionable, but the content is still lacking. Although few explicitly say this, I believe that most scholars are, at least in the first instance, looking for verbs such as "evangelize" and nouns such as "good news" as the focal point of their attempts to find the content of Paul's teaching. In some ways this is understandable, as the failure to find explicit language leaves the question open and more highly debatable. What we need instead is a way of discovering what might have been said or advocated by Paul that his hearers might say in an evangelistic context without necessarily using preconceived evangelistic language. A second factor is to consider the way in which such a missionary message would be formulated, so as to capture the content of Paul's proclamation and to give substance to his transferable missionary message.

2 Corinthians 5:20 as the Content of Paul's Missionary Preaching

I believe, however, that there is (at least) one passage that may indicate a step forward in such discussion, in that it provides a formulation that indicates the substance of Paul's missionary preaching and is formulated in such a way that it indicates the message Paul wished his converts to pass on to others, 2 Cor 5:20.[20] This passage has been discussed a few times before in consideration of Paul's missionary message. For example, Bowers raises the question of how "the ministry of reconciliation," which is the theme of 2 Cor 5:18—6:2, relates to the "we" and "you" of the passage and his relation to his readers. He concludes that the "we" and "you" are kept distinct and that the passage is "directed in the first instance to wayward believers, not to unbelievers."[21] Bowers's explanation is subject

---

19. Plummer, *Paul's Understanding of the Church's Mission*, chs. 3 and 4.

20. There are other potential passages as well that could be examined in a treatment such as this. One would be 1 Thess 1:9–10. A complicating factor for this passage, however, is the widespread belief (whether correct or not) that there is a pre-Pauline insertion in this passage. See, e.g., Holtz, "Euer Glaube an Gott." Some, however, believe that the wording is Paul's, but delivered when he first evangelized the Thessalonians. See Langevin, "Le Seigneur Jésus."

21. Bowers, "Church and Mission in Paul," 95. Bowers's only support for the notion that the passage is directed to "wayward believers" is citation of Martin's commentary *2 Corinthians*, 169–70.

to question at every point, as we will see below, except one—this passage is indeed about the ministry of reconciliation.

The Context of 2 Corinthians 5:11–21

Second Corinthians 5:20–21 is found at the end of one of Paul's four major reconciliation passages, 2 Cor 5:11–21. He opens this section in 2 Cor 5:11 by stating the motivation for his actions. With the prospect of death before him (2 Cor 5:1–10), and hence fearing God (v. 11), Paul states that "we" are in the process of persuading people. There are two questions here. The first is: Who are the "we" of 2 Cor 5:11–21? And the second is: Who are the people Paul is intent on persuading? The "we" of Paul's writings has proved very difficult to decide. The terms of discussion are usually between inclusive and exclusive, but I would suggest that these distinctions should be nuanced by seeing whether "we" is general or particular, and whether it is in opposition to "you."[22] The "we" of 5:11 probably includes Paul and his companions, as he distinguishes between "we" and "you," with "you" including the Corinthians and those beyond. This opposition seems to continue throughout the passage, until v. 18. He is thereby both made known to God and to his audience, the Corinthian believers ("your consciences"). He clarifies his motives, not as self-serving but arising out of the love of God, who died for all people so that they might live for him (5:14–15). Such a person in Christ, Paul says, is a new creation, whose old existence has passed away (5:17). In v. 18, Paul outlines in inclusive terms the reconciling work of God for all humanity. God is the one who reconciles us to himself through Christ and has given us a ministry or service of reconciliation (5:18). Paul then clarifies what this reconciling action of God entails—God was reconciling the world to himself through Christ, not counting their trespasses against them, and committing to us the word of reconciliation—in three parallel participial constructions (5:19). The first participle is part of a periphrastic construction, with the use of the instrumental preposition ἐν (through or by Christ),[23] followed by two further dependent parti-

---

22. See Dick, *Schriftstellerische Plural*, 95–96, 98; Carrez, "Le 'Nous' en 2 Corinthiens," esp. 478; Cranfield, "Changes of Person and Number," esp. 286–87; Bowers, "Church and Mission in Paul," n. 1, for bibliography (however, his statement about the emphatic positioning of "you" in 2 Cor 6:1 needs further thought).

23. On the periphrastic construction, see Porter, Καταλλάσσω, 132–36, against such views as the independent use of the verb "be."

ciples stating what reconciliation entails. The fact that a present and then an aorist participle follows the primary construction is not a problem as the tense-forms are aspectual and not temporal.²⁴ As a result, Paul says, we all—Paul, his followers and Corinthian believers—are ambassadors on behalf of Christ as God entreats through us. The message that Paul says that we are to proclaim to others is this: We beg on behalf of Christ, be reconciled to God (5:20).²⁵ The ground of this reconciliation is the sinless Christ becoming sin on our behalf (5:21). In other words, in this context in which Paul begins from the standpoint of himself and his followers as persuaders of the gospel, he articulates the notion of God's reconciling actions and, then, includes the Corinthian believers as fellow ambassadors of this message to others.

Exegetical Support for Interpretation of 2 Corinthians 5:20

There are a number of issues in 2 Cor 5:20 to be treated.²⁶ These include the role of ambassadors on behalf of Christ (v. 20a), God's entreating through us (v. 20b), the content of what the ambassadors are proclaiming (v. 20cd), and the audience of that entreaty. These issues will be treated together in this section.

1. Ambassadors on Behalf of Christ

Paul states that "we" are ambassadors on behalf of Christ (v. 20a). Bash has noted that the language here is for the most part similar to that found in the ambassadorial inscriptions (e.g., use of the preposition "on behalf of," *hyper*, ὑπέρ), but he has also noted some differences both from inscriptional and from literary usage.²⁷ Ambassadors in the ancient world

---

24. The major objection to this interpretation of the participles has been voiced by Collange, *Énigmes*, esp. 271, followed most recently by Kim, "2 Cor. 5:11–12 and the Origin of Paul's Concept of 'Reconciliation,'" esp. 366 (this article has been reprinted by him in several places, including as: "God Reconciled His Enemy to Himself.") The major objection is the time and kind of action of the verb. On these issues, see Porter, Καταλλάσσω, 136–38, where it is shown that the tense-forms are aspectual and do not refer to time, but are used as discourse markers. For a more detailed response, see Porter, "Paul's Concept of Reconciliation, Twice More," esp. 134–44.

25. Justification for this analysis will be offered below. Note that there is no reference to "you" in the phrase "we beg on behalf of Christ."

26. The following section expands upon what is found in Porter, Καταλλάσσω, 138–43; supplemented by Porter, "Reconciliation and 2 Cor 5,18–21," esp. 702–4. My Καταλλάσσω is drawn upon throughout this article.

27. Bash, *Ambassadors for Christ*, esp. 87–115. E.g., he notes the use of the active voice here, whereas the literary texts typically use the middle voice, as well as the

were those who were sent on behalf of another individual or group to represent or promote the interests of that party.[28] Bash shows that the ambassadorial language of Paul is for the most part consonant with ambassadorial language of the ancient world, which helps us to understand how to understand Paul's formulation of his language of representation here in 2 Cor 5:20. Most commentators interpret v. 20 as Paul's appeal to the Corinthians to be reconciled.[29] Despite attempts to defend this position by various means,[30] this is an odd construal of the Corinthians' salvific situation, and another alternative that makes better sense of both the grammar and the discourse structure is worth considering—this is an appeal not to the Corinthians, but to the unreconciled, and captures Paul's "language of evangelism," to quote Marshall. As Marshall states further, this language "sounds much more like a description of the gospel message proclaimed to the non-Christian" than it does language to those who are already Christians.[31] In vv. 18 and 19, Paul has set this up as a logical progression. He has first noted that God is the one who reconciles us to himself and has given us the ministry of reconciliation.[32] As noted above, this ministry of reconciliation is outlined further in v. 19. Here Paul notes that God was reconciling, not counting trespasses and, finally, committing to us the word of reconciliation. God is the initiator of the reconciling action, and this reconciliation results not in the call to further reconciliation but to a ministry or service that consists of

---

preposition περί (88–89). He also notes the difference in tense-form, but overdraws the temporal distinctions between them (88).

28. Ibid., 40.

29. E.g., Furnish, *II Corinthians*, 349–50; Martin, *2 Corinthians*, 140; Wolff, *2 Korinther*, 131–32, who takes it as not representative of Paul's missionary preaching on the basis of a temporal understanding of the tense-forms; Bowers, "Church and Mission in Paul," 95; Thrall, *2 Corinthians*, 1:437–38, who gets hung up on the meaning of the tense-forms as strictly temporal; Barnett, *2 Corinthians*, 309.

30. E.g., as a recent interpreter, Bash (*Ambassadors for Christ*, 104; following Barclay, *Obeying the Truth*, 225; and Furnish, *Theology and Ethics in Paul*, 224–27; cf. also Furnish, *II Corinthians*, 350) believes that the appeal is to the Corinthians in terms of their becoming what they already are, that is, the indicative-imperative construct. This is based on a misunderstanding of the nature of the indicative-imperative construct (e.g., it uses formal grammatical terms to describe theological notions), besides introducing theological notions that are not found in the passage.

31. Marshall, "Reconciliation," 129. See also Belleville, "Gospel and Kerygma," 149.

32. See Plummer, *2 Corinthians*, 182 with "us Christians" (note that he backs away from this in v. 19); Barrett, *2 Corinthians*, 176.

a message of reconciliation (the genitive indicating the content of the ministry or service). This is what Paul outlines in v. 20. In v. 20, Paul's use of the first person plural verb includes his Christian readers with himself in calling them all ambassadors on behalf of Christ. It is noteworthy that here Paul includes himself with other Christians as ambassadors on behalf of Christ, as Christ's spokespeople in and to the world. Many commentators understand the plural reference to be more limited, that is, to Paul and his fellow apostles,[33] but in the light of the reference to "us" in vv. 18b and 19b and the parallelism with v. 20, a more inclusive reference is probably the best explanation.[34] The particle *oun*, οὖν serves as a suitable connective, linking together vv. 18–19 with vv. 20–21.[35] On the basis of this reconciling action of God, therefore, we all are ambassadors on behalf of Christ.

2. God Entreats through Us

There is contention over the use of the genitive absolute clause introduced by *hōs*, ὡς: "as God entreats through us" (v. 20b). The use of *hōs*, ὡς here probably indicates subjective motivation, and can be rendered "with the assertion that, on the pretext that, with the thought that God appeals through us."[36] Bash is concerned to determine whether God is seen as the sender of the ambassador here. He rejects this because of the double sending that is implied (from God and from Christ), and the fact that reconciliation is to God, even though Christ is clearly the sender.[37] Bash is perhaps pressing the metaphor of ambassadorship too far so as to have conformity with ancient conventions (and he wishes to draw clear distinctions in the natures of God and Christ in this passage).[38] Nevertheless, the understanding might be that "we are ambassadors on behalf of Christ, with the parallel assertion that God too is entreating us."

---

33. E.g., Kijne, "We, Us and Our in 1 and II Corinthians," 178; Furnish, *II Corinthians*, 339; Barnett, *2 Corinthians*, 304.

34. Carrez, "Le 'Nous' en 2 Corinthiens," 478, who sees the term as inclusive in 2 Cor 5:17–21.

35. Contra those who take the "therefore" back to 2 Cor 2:14: Furnish, *II Corinthians*, 338; Barnett, *2 Corinthians*, 309.

36. See Porter, Καταλλάσσω, 140 and n. 66.

37. Bash, *Ambassadors for Christ*, 89. Rejecting the views of such as Bultmann, *2 Corinthians*, 163 n. 174 and Hughes, *2 Corinthians*, 210.

38. Bash, *Ambassadors for Christ*, 92–93. However, some do press the metaphor too far. See Thrall, *2 Corinthians*, 1:437, and others she cites.

The language used of God is not ambassadorial language, but language of exhortation that stands behind the ambassadorial work done on behalf of Christ. The genitive absolute clause utilizes a verb of speaking to introduce direct speech ("we beg on behalf of Christ"),[39] and this direct speech contains indirect speech within it ("be reconciled to God").[40] Rather than being addressed to the readers of the letter, the direct speech in v. 20c is addressed to those to whom the Corinthian believers are ambassadors, that is, those whom they are calling to reconciliation.

3. The Content of the Ambassadorial Proclamation

Paul tells the Corinthians directly that we are all ambassadors on behalf of Christ, along with God too entreating us, to proclaim the following message: we are pleading on behalf of Christ (v. 20c). What they are to plead for is that others, unbelievers, would be reconciled to God (v. 20d). As Windisch has said, reconciliation is the call of the apostle to the still unconverted world.[41] The verb for reconcile used here, in contrast to the previous forms in the passage with their active participial forms (vv. 18, 19), is in the aorist passive imperative form. The aorist grammaticalizes an event as complete,[42] here used to make an appeal to the events encompassed as a whole in God's work through Christ on the cross. This content is briefly itemized in the statement in v. 21, which summarizes the life and death of Christ in terms of one not knowing sin being made sin (or a sin offering?) on behalf of humans.[43] The sense is that sinners did not have their transgressions counted against them, but that Christ, depicted as knowing no sin, was made, appointed, or designated sin, i.e., their transgressions were counted against him. The syntax of καταλλάσ-σω, *katallassō* here is found elsewhere in Paul's use of reconciliation

---

39. Note that there is no use of "you" here to possibly confuse whether Paul is opposing "we" to "you." Belleville ("Gospel and Kerygma," 149) takes this to indicate that it is not a direct appeal to the Corinthians.

40. Cf. Bash, *Ambassadors for Christ*, 89, who takes both as examples of direct speech. This is possible.

41. Windisch, *Der zweite Korintherbrief*, 126. This is a position that seems to have been held by earlier interpreters, such as Meyer, *Epistles to the Corinthians*, 539; Hughes, *2 Corinthians*, 210–11.

42. Not as past (especially in the imperative!), as some would assert, and certainly not punctiliar. Contra Wolff, "True Apostolic Knowledge of Christ," esp. 95; Thrall, *2 Corinthians*, 1:438.

43. See Porter, Καταλλάσσω, 142; Barnett, *2 Corinthians*, 314 n. 65.

language: God is the goal or direction toward which reconciliation is to proceed ("to God" in the dative case). There is no specific phrase of means or instrument linked with the imperative in this instance. In this case, the work of Christ is not unspecified with the verb, since the context makes it clear—especially v. 21—that the means for reconciliation is by his becoming sin.

IMPLICATIONS OF 2 CORINTHIANS 5:20 FOR PAUL'S MISSIONARY PREACHING

There are a number of implications of 2 Cor 5:20 for understanding the content of Paul's missionary preaching, and the message that he wishes his churches to likewise proclaim. These can be discussed in terms of two major sections. One is the substance of the teaching found in this immediate context. The other is the larger implications of this verse as encapsulating Paul's missionary message for others.

The Substance of Paul's Missionary Preaching

As Marshall states, if the analysis above is correct, "the original use of the language of reconciliation is to be found in the proclamation of the kerygma, and what Paul is describing is the gospel of the cross which he preached."[44] If this verse constitutes an accurate encapsulation of Paul revealing the substance of his missionary preaching, there are a number of implications that can be derived from it.

1. RECONCILIATION AT THE HEART OF PAUL'S EVANGELISM

The first is that reconciliation stands at the heart of Paul's evangelistic message.[45] Reconciliation language focuses in Paul around *katallassō*, καταλλάσσω, and its derived cognates. The word-group seems to have been used by Greek writers to describe the exchange of goods or things, and to describe the process by which hostility between parties is eliminated and friendship is created. Thus, the basic sense of the word for exchange can be metaphorically extended to include the exchange of relations, such as the exchange of enmity for friendship, between persons or larger political entities. This usage can be refined further in terms of

---

44. Marshall, "Reconciliation," 129.

45. This section reflects language developed further in Porter, "Paul's Concept of Reconciliation, Twice More," 132–33.

grammatical categories of usage. The following categories are relevant: (a) the subject effects reconciliation between mutually antagonistic parties (any voice form may be used); (b) the subject effects reconciliation by persuading a hostile party to give up its anger against the subject (active voice); (c) the subject is reconciled or effects reconciliation by persuading a hostile party to give up its anger, usually against the subject (middle or passive voice form); (d) the subject effects reconciliation by giving up its own anger against another party (passive voice form); (e) the subject effects reconciliation by giving up its own anger against another party (active voice form). Apart from a possible instance in Sophocles (*Ajax* 743–744), the first significant religious usage of *katallassō*, καταλλάσσω-based reconciliation language is in 2 Maccabees (1:5; 7:33; 8:29). In none of these is the active voice form of the verb (e) used. The context of 2 Cor 5:18-20 makes clear that God is the initiator of reconciliation. In both vv. 18 and 19, it is God who is the agent who effects reconciliation. This usage was apparently formulated by Paul, who saw God, the offended party in the reconciliation process, as the instigator of reconciliation. Paul says that it was God who reconciled us to himself and that God was reconciling the world to himself. Further, God is both the initiator of reconciliation and the one toward whom reconciliation is directed. As Paul says in both vv. 18 and 19, God was reconciling to himself. The object of God's reconciliation was, according to v. 18, "us," and according to v. 19, "the world." Some scholars have thought that this suggests that the entire world of humankind is within the sphere of reconciliation.[46] The use of "world" is not necessarily so inclusive. Its parallel use with "us" suggests that it refers to those of the fallen world who are reconciled, without reference to what the percentage is or what role the human plays (cf. v. 20), further reinforced by the following participial clause referring to their sins not being counted against them. There is no limit stated of the extent of God's reconciling action, implying that it applies to both Jew and Gentile alike, just as might have been found in a multicultural city such as Corinth.[47] Finally, the means of this action is the mediation of Christ. Christ constitutes the channel or the instrument by which God is at work in the action of reconciliation.

---

46. E.g., Allmen, "Réconciliation du monde."

47. Some of these issues are explored in Murphy-O'Connor, *St. Paul's Corinth*, 78–80.

That this is the content of the message to be proclaimed might come as a surprise. Though an important Pauline concept, reconciliation does not have the same theological status as some other concepts. However, many important Pauline theological notions cohere with it in this context. (1) It is linked to the concept of "new creation" (2 Cor 5:17; cf. Gal 6:15). The act of reconciliation creates a new creation in the sense that those who were estranged from God can now, through his action, be reconciled to him and be at peace with him. (2) Reconciliation is not simply a concept in itself but is one that generates its own call to service and a message to proclaim (2 Cor 5:18, 19). Paul says that we have a ministry or service of reconciliation and that one of the results of this reconciliation is to have a proclamation or word of reconciliation instilled within us. (3) God's concern, as expressed by reconciliation, goes far beyond a single ethnic group to reach the entire world of those who are in some way redeemed. God is concerned to reconcile the entire world, that is, those who respond to the call to be reconciled. (4) The message is a simple and yet profound one, and one that merits beseeching or begging one's audience to accept. Paul uses language of pleading, including prayer, to encapsulate what he expects the Corinthians to say when they make their appeal on behalf of Christ.

2. Widening the Call

The second implication is that there is a clear transferral of responsibility taking place. Christ is the one who sends Paul and his followers as mediators of reconciliation to the Corinthians. Paul is the ambassador. The Corinthians have received this ministry or word of reconciliation. Now, Paul says, their responsibility is for them to become ambassadors on behalf of the cause of God's reconciling activity. There is no question that Paul does not see himself as the sender of the ambassadors. He notes that they are to plead on behalf of Christ; they are not Paul's emissaries. Christ is still the sender of the ambassadors on his behalf, but now Paul is in partnership with all of those who believe in begging others to be reconciled to God.

Other Reconciliation Passages

Reconciliation is the heart of Paul's missionary preaching, and the heart of the message he instructs Christians in his churches to proclaim. This has a number of implications for our conceptualization of his missionary endeavors, including how we understand what he says elsewhere, especially in other reconciliation passages. What is immediately worth noting is that, though reconciliation has semantic overlap with language of justification and salvation, it is not justification that is at the heart of Paul's missionary message. Some of these implications bear further exploration.

1. Reconciliation and Judgment Language

Reconciliation is language that addresses the human predicament as being sinners deserving of God's wrath. All reconciliation passages assume a situation of enmity between contending parties—the result of the dissolution of friendship and demonstrating the need for reconciliation. In Rom 5:9–11, Paul points out that while human beings were still God's enemies, reconciliation occurred, and that this saves us from the coming divine wrath. One of the themes of Romans is that the wrath of God is going to be meted out against all sorts of ungodliness and unrighteousness (1:18).[48] Rather than be an enemy of God and deserve such punishment, Paul states that one can enjoy peace with God (5:1; cf. Col 1:20),[49] that is, reconciliation as that condition where enmity is overcome and peace is restored between parties. Peace in this context is a relational word, indicating a state of well-being that leads to harmonious relations between people groups.[50]

2. Reconciliation and Sacrificial Language

Reconciliation language is also the language of sacrifice on behalf of the forgiveness of sins. There are numerous references to the work of Christ or the blood of Christ in various reconciliation passages (e.g., Rom 5:1, 11, 21). Colossians 1:20 and 22, however, seems to be formulated around sacrifice language. Verse 20 refers explicitly to the blood of Jesus' cross as providing the means for peace to be established between God and

---

48. For discussion of what is meant by the wrath of God, see Porter, Καταλλάσσω, 158.

49. I take the subjunctive reading in Rom 5:1, ἔχωμεν. For defense of this position, see Porter, "Argument of Romans 5," followed by Jewett, *Romans*, 344–45. The use of the subjunctive does not call into question the effectiveness of the work of Christ (so Wolter, *Rechtfertigung und zukünftiges Heil*, 91–94). To the contrary, the use of the hortatory subjunctive exhorts the reader to possess what is (see Porter, *Verbal Aspect*, chs. 4 and 7).

50. See Porter, Καταλλάσσω, 154.

humanity (cf. Rom 5:9). Once one has been reconciled, v. 22 states, one is in the proper condition to be presented to God in the same way that a sacrifice would be presented in the temple.[51] The temple sacrifices were to be pure and holy, and here Paul talks of those who are reconciled being presented to God as holy, blameless, and beyond reproach.

3. Reconciliation and Inclusive Language

The inclusive language of reconciliation revolves around the explicit reference in Eph 2:16 to the reconciliation of Jews and Gentiles. In Ephesians 2, Paul says that groups that were formerly at odds with each other, especially over the issue of circumcision, can be brought near to each other through the blood of Christ. To use metaphorical language, Paul says that Christ is "our peace" (Eph 2:14), making the two into one organism by breaking down the barrier that separated Jews and Gentiles. He tore down the barrier or wall that was dividing them—a probable allusion to the walls of the temple that kept Gentiles out[52]—and made both Jews and Gentiles to be part of a single body. It is this single reconciled body that now has access to God through reconciliation. The reconciliation of humanity allows for reconciliation with God.

There is no doubt that Paul's teaching on reconciliation—even if it is the heart of his missionary message and illustrates the message he instructs his churches to proclaim—does not include a full-orbed view of Paul's gospel. To get that one must go back to his letters. However, in a missionary context, when Paul was concerned to reach those who were not believers in Jesus Christ, he apparently preached a message of reconciliation. This message, while not inclusive of all the gospel, at least promoted the heart of that gospel. It taught about restoring peace with God, and with it creating peace between Jew and Gentile, having sins forgiven through the sacrifice of Jesus Christ, and overcoming the wrath of God.

CONCLUSION

Scholars have selected a few key passages in Paul's writings to exemplify what they believe is the heart of Paul's missionary preaching and teaching. There is no doubt that some of these are very important and

---

51. See Ibid., 179.
52. For options on the choices, see Barth, *Ephesians*, 1:183–87.

meaningful passages. The question is whether anyone of them actually captures the content of Paul's missionary teaching, or whether the passage is just a reflection of the more general notion of the content of the gospel. Most scholars recognize that the difficulty is in determining if any passage in Paul's writings actually expresses his clear evangelistic message as he perhaps would have preached it. More than that, most scholars see very little evidence for Paul instructing his congregations corporately or individually to be involved in evangelism. Even though there may have been some reasons—some of them even plausible—why Paul may not have instructed his congregations in this, this is inevitably unsatisfactory as it leaves us at a remove from the heart of Paul's missionary endeavors. I believe, however, that there is at least one passage that, in its very formulation, indicates that this is the heart of the content of Paul's missionary teaching, and that it offers an encapsulation of what it was that he instructed his congregations to proclaim as well. If this analysis is correct, I believe that we have two important ways forward. One is to explore the implications of this particular passage and those related to it in order to fully appreciate the content of Paul's missionary teaching. Another is to continue to examine Paul's letters for further insight into passages that have a similar formulation and offer a similar window into the heart of his missionary teaching and preaching.

BIBLIOGRAPHY

Allmen, D. von "Réconciliation du monde et christologie cosmique de II Cor 5:14–21 à Col 1:15–23." *RHPR* 1 (1968) 36–38.

Barclay, J. M. G. *Obeying the Truth*. Edinburgh: T. & T. Clark, 1988.

Barnett, P. *The Second Epistle to the Corinthians*. NICNT. Grand Rapids: Eerdmans, 1997.

Barrett, C. K. *A Commentary on the Second Epistle to the Corinthians*. HNTC. New York: Harper & Row, 1973.

Barth, M. *Ephesians*. AB 34, 34A. New York: Doubleday, 1974.

Bash, A. *Ambassadors for Christ: An Exploration of Ambassadorial Language in the New Testament*. WUNT 2.92. Tübingen: Mohr Siebeck, 1997.

Belleville, L. L. "Gospel and Kerygma in 2 Corinthians." In *Gospel in Paul: Studies on Corinthians, Galatians and Romans for Richard N. Longenecker*, edited by L. A. Jervis and P. Richardson, 134–64. JSNTSup 108. Sheffield: Sheffield Academic, 1994.

Bowers, W. P. "Church and Mission in Paul." *JSNT* 44 (1991) 89–111.

Bultmann, R. *The Second Letter to the Corinthians*. Edited by E. Dinkler. Minneapolis: Augsburg, 1985.

Carrez, M. "Le 'Nous' en 2 Corinthiens." *NTS* 26 (1980) 474–86.

Collange J.-F. *Énigmes de la deuxième épître de Paul aux Corinthiens: Étude exegetique de 2 Cor. 2:14—7:4*. SNTSMS 18. Cambridge: Cambridge University Press, 1972.

Cranfield, C. E. B. "Changes of Person and Number in Paul's Epistles." In *Paul and Paulinism: Essays in Honour of C. K. Barrett*, edited by M. D. Hooker and S. G. Wilson, 280–89. London: SPCK, 1980.

Dick, K. *Der Schriftstellerische Plural bei Paulus*. Halle: Niemeyer, 1900.

Furnish, V. P. *II Corinthians*. AB 32A; New York: Doubleday, 1984.

———. *Theology and Ethics in Paul*. London: SCM, 1968.

Hahn, F. *Mission in the New Testament*. SBT 47. London: SCM, 1965.

Holtz T. "'Euer Glaube an Gott': Zu Form und Inhalt von 1 Thess 1,9f." In *Die Kirche des Anfangs: Festschrift für Heinz Schürmann*, edited by R. Schnackenburg, J. Ernst, and J. Wanke, 459–88. Freiburg: Herder, 1978.

Hughes, P. E. *Paul's Second Epistle to the Corinthians*. NICNT. Grand Rapids: Eerdmans, 1962.

Jewett, R. *Romans*. Hermeneia. Minneapolis: Fortress, 2007.

Kijne, J. J. "We, Us and Our in I and II Corinthians." *NovT* 8 (1965–1966), 171–79.

Kim, S. "God Reconciled His Enemy to Himself: The Origin of Paul's Concept of Reconciliation." In *The Road from Damascus: The Impact of Paul's Conversion on His Life, Thought, and Ministry*, edited by R. N. Longenecker, 102–24. MNTS. Grand Rapids: Eerdmans, 1996.

———. "2 Cor. 5:11–12 and the Origin of Paul's Concept of 'Reconciliation.'" *NovT* 39 (1997) 360–84.

Köstenberger, A. J., and P. T. O'Brien. *Salvation to the Ends of the Earth: A Biblical Theology of Mission*. NSBT 11. Downers Grove, IL: InterVarsity, 2001.

Langevin, P.-E. "Le Seigneur Jésus selon un texte prépaulinien, 1 Thess 1,9–10." *Sciences ecclésiastiques* 17 (1965) 263–82, 473–512.

Marshall, I. H. "Meaning of 'Reconciliation.'" In *Unity and Diversity in New Testament Theology: Essays in Honor of George E. Ladd*, edited by R. A. Guelich, 117–32. Grand Rapids: Eerdmans, 1978.

Martin, Ralph. *2 Corinthians*. WBC 40. Waco, TX: Word, 1986.

Meyer, H. A. W. *Critical and Exegetical Hand-Book to the Epistles to the Corinthians*. New York: Funk and Wagnalls, 1884.

Murphy-O'Connor, J. *St. Paul's Corinth*. Collegeville, MN: Liturgical, 2002.

Plummer, A. *A Critical and Exegetical Commentary on the Second Epistle of St. Paul to the Corinthians*. ICC. Edinburgh: T. & T. Clark, n.d.

Plummer, R. L. *Paul's Understanding of the Church's Mission: Did the Apostle Paul Expect the Early Christian Communities to Evangelize?* PBM. Carlisle: Paternoster, 2006.

Porter, S. E. "The Argument of Romans 5: Can a Rhetorical Question Make a Difference?" *JBL* 110 (1991) 655–77.

———. Καταλλάσσω *in Ancient Greek Literature, with Reference to the Pauline Writings*. Córdoba: Ediciones El Almendro, 1994.

———. "Paul's Concept of Reconciliation, Twice More." In *Paul and His Theology*, edited by S. E. Porter, 131–52. PAST 3. Leiden: Brill, 2006.

———. *The Paul of Acts: Essays in Literary Criticism, Rhetoric, and Theology*. WUNT 15. Tübingen: Mohr Siebeck, 1999.

———. "Reconciliation and 2 Cor 5,18–21." In *The Corinthian Correspondence*, edited by R. Bieringer, 693–705. BETL 125. Louvain: University Press/Peeters, 1996.

———. *Verbal Aspect in the Greek of the New Testament, with Reference to Tense and Mood*. SBG 1. New York: Lang, 1989.

Schnabel, E. J. *Early Christian Mission*. II. *Paul and the Early Church*. Downers Grove, IL: InterVarsity, 2004.

Thrall, M. *A Critical and Exegetical Commentary on the Second Epistle to the Corinthians*. 2 vols. ICC. Edinburgh: T. & T. Clark, 1994–2000.

Windisch, H. *Der zweite Korintherbrief*. 9th ed. Göttingen: Vandenhoeck & Ruprecht, 1924.

Wolff, C. "True Apostolic Knowledge of Christ: Exegetical Reflections on 2 Cor 5:12ff." In *Paul and Jesus: Collected Essays*, edited by A. J. M. Wedderburn, 92–97. JSNTSup 37. Sheffield: Sheffield Academic, 1989.

———. *Der zweite Brief des Paulus an die Korinther*. THNT 8. Berlin: Evangelische, 1989.

Wolter, M. *Rechtfertigung und zukünftiges Heil: Untersuchungen zu Röm 5:1–11*. BZNW. Berlin: de Gruyter, 1978.

7

Paul's Missionary Strategy

Goals, Methods, and Realities

ECKHARD J. SCHNABEL

THE EARLY CHRISTIAN MISSION began with Jesus of Nazareth.[1] The record provided by Luke in the Book of Acts indicates that the Twelve initiated missionary outreach after Easter as commissioned by the risen Lord, both in Judea and beyond, to both Jews and Gentiles.[2] The notion that Paul was the most influential missionary among Gentiles in the first century is based on three facts. First, numerous writings of Paul survive, which allow us to describe his theological convictions in which the mission to the Gentiles is repeatedly mentioned. Second, we have a historical record of Paul's missionary work for the years AD 42–60 in the second part of the Book of Acts. Third, we have much less information about John and Peter and no information whatsoever on the missionary work of the other apostles. It is the last point that suggests that the view that the Apostle Paul was the greatest missionary is true less by comparison and evaluation than by default. In the following survey of the goals, the methods, and the realities of Paul's missionary strategy, I will treat the information provided by the book of Acts as a primary source as much as Paul's letters.[3]

---

1. Cf. Schnabel, *Early Christian Mission*, 1:207–62.
2. Ibid., 1:389–913.
3. For the relevant arguments see ibid., 1:20–35. On the historical reliability of the Book of Acts see Hemer, *Acts in the Setting of Hellenistic History*; Thornton, *Zeuge des Zeugen*; Winter and Clarke, eds., *Acts in Its Ancient Literary Setting*. For a critique

PAUL'S MISSIONARY STRATEGY: THE GOALS OF PROCLAIMING THE GOSPEL

The strategy that informed and controlled Paul's work as a missionary is best described on the basis of passages in Paul's letters where he refers to his self-understanding. Relevant passages are 1 Cor 3:10–15; 9:19–23; 15:1–11; 2 Cor 2:14–16; 4:7–15; Rom 1:14; 10:14–21; 15:15–21; Col 1:24–29. The following comments summarize the most pertinent aspects that arise from these descriptions.

1 Corinthians 3:10–15

In this text Paul describes his role as founder of the church in Corinth. He had to do this because of the activities of teachers in the Corinthian congregation who denigrated his ministry on the basis of contemporary rhetorical criteria, which they used to evaluate the apostles and the teachers of the church.[4] Paul emphasizes the following facts.

(1) The apostles and teachers are "servants" (διάκονοι, *diakonoi*, 3:5), i.e., people who get something done at the behest of a superior, assistants who attend to the tasks at hand. This designation implies that all high-handedness and all self-interest concerning successful missionary and pastoral work are rendered impossible. Paul uses metaphors from agriculture and house construction to describe the work of missionaries, preachers, and teachers: they plant, they water, they build (3:6–9), tasks and activities that are no cause for boasting.

(2) God is the "Lord" (κύριος, *kyrios*) of missionary and of pastoral work (3:5). He is the superior at whose behest the missionaries, preachers, and teachers serve. Missionary ministry and church ministry are both tasks that God has given, work that God has assigned, commissions that God has granted.

(3) The servant relationship between the missionaries and teachers and the Lord establishes the unity of the ministry of all missionaries and

---

of the unhistorical treatment of the Book of Acts in New Testament scholarship, see Botermann, *Judenedikt*, 17–49.

4. Cf. Pogoloff, *Logos and Sophia*; Litfin, *St. Paul's Theology of Proclamation*; Winter, *Philo and Paul*.

teachers who serve the church: they are "one" (3:8), i.e., they have a common purpose. This reality renders all notions of superiority moot.

(4) Paul understands his task to be that of a missionary called by God to "plant" (3:6) and to "lay the foundation" as a "skilled master builder" (σοφὸς ἀρχιτέκτων, *sophos architektōn*, 3:10), i.e., to establish new congregations.[5] In other words, Paul is a pioneer missionary who travels from city to city proclaiming the message of Jesus Messiah, Savior, and Lord, before audiences who had never heard that message before. He helps them to find faith in the revelation of Israel's God in Jesus Christ who died on the cross and who rose from the dead on the third day. And he gathers the new believers in a new community of people who meet regularly, representing God's presence in the world as his "temple" (3:16). The fact that Paul was active in Corinth for over one and a half years (Acts 18:2, 11, 12) demonstrates that Paul did not regard pioneer missionary work as an evangelistic *blitz* whose results needed to be consolidated by other preachers and teachers. For Paul, "laying the foundation" included the instruction of the new believers in the fundamental content of faith in Jesus Christ and in the basic teachings of Scripture (i.e., the Old Testament).

(5) The foundation that Paul lays is Jesus Christ himself (3:11), specifically the message of Jesus the crucified Messiah (1:23; 2:2). The content of the missionary proclamation is focused on the crucified and risen Jesus Christ.

(6) Missionary success comes from God. This is true both for pioneer missionaries and for preachers and teachers in local congregations: it is God who gives growth (3:6, 7). The decisive factor of missionary work is not the missionary, but God himself: it is only the power of God who convinces people of the truth of the gospel, which otherwise appears to Jewish audiences as a stumbling block and to pagan audiences as nonsense (1:18—2:5). The effectiveness of Paul's missionary work does not depend on grand strategies and specific tactics. It does not depend on rhetorical techniques or methods of accommodation. It is dependent on God's activity alone. Missionaries and preachers are "nothing" (3:7a), "a nothing from which only a creative act of God can make something.

---

5. Cf. Shanor, "Paul as Master Builder."

Genuine preachers of the gospel can understand themselves and their work only on the basis of a *creatio ex nihilo*."[6]

(7) The churches that are established as the result of missionary work do not belong to Paul or to other teachers: the church is "God's field, God's building" (3:9b). Since both the establishment and the growth of the church are the effective result of God's power, the church is neither the work nor the possession of the apostle: the church belongs to God.

(8) Paul states that "each will receive wages according to the labor of each" (3:8b). This sentence clarifies two matters: the missionaries and the teachers of the church are accountable to God, and it is God alone who decides what constitutes success or failure of missionary and pastoral work. As regards the "wages" that missionaries and teachers receive, Paul does not specify what he means in 1 Cor 3. Later he speaks of "the prize" (τὸ βραβεῖον, *to brabeion*, 9:24), of an "imperishable wreath" (ἄφθαρτον στέφανον, *aphtharton stephanon*, 9:25), and of "the crown" (στέφανος, *stephanos*) of righteousness (2 Tim 4:8). Paul asserts in 1 Cor 3:12–15 that there is missionary work and that there is preaching and teaching that will be rejected by God in the Last Judgment because the message of the crucified and risen Jesus Messiah was misconstrued and misrepresented. Missionary and pastoral work will "remain" on Judgment Day if and when Jesus, the crucified and risen Messiah and Savior, was at the center of the proclamation and of the behavior of the missionaries, preachers, and teachers.

1 Corinthians 9:19–23

In the context of a discussion about the "right" that some Corinthian Christians claim to have as regards dining in pagan temples, Paul formulates the rule of his life as a missionary.[7]

(1) The basic rule of missionary existence requires the missionary to take the listener seriously in a fully consistent manner: "For though I am free with respect to all, I have made myself a slave to all, so that I might win more of them" (9:19). The behavior of the missionary is subordinated to the preaching of the gospel. Paul is prepared to relinquish his freedom,

---

6. Schrage, *Der erste Brief an die Korinther*, 1:292.
7. Cf. Schnabel, *Early Christian Mission*, 2:953–60.

which he has in Christ, if he can win people for faith in Jesus Christ. Paul makes himself dependent upon his non-Christian audiences; he becomes their "slave", i.e., the listeners decide how the missionary lives and how the gospel is proclaimed, since it is the listeners who need to understand the gospel.

(2) Paul does not exclude anyone from his preaching, he is sent to "all." Despite the differentiation of Jewish and pagan audiences and despite his specialized commission as a missionary to Gentiles, Paul always preaches to the "people under the Torah" (9:20).

(3) Paul asserts that missionary accommodation formulates no limitations in advance: he becomes "all things" to all people (9:22). Even though Paul is no longer controlled by the stipulations of the Torah, he does not impede the potential conversion of his Jewish listeners by provocative "lawlessness": ministering to Jewish people, he can live like a Jewish person (9:20) because he wants to win Jews for faith in Jesus Christ. At the same time, when he preaches among pagans, he becomes "as one outside the law" (9:21); he eats what they eat, even if it includes meat that pious Jews would not eat.

(4) Paul states that the goal of his missionary work is to "win" people (9:19, 20a, 20b, 21, 22). To "win" (κερδαίνω, *kerdainō*) a person means to "rescue" him or her (9:22); the person who has a "gain" is not the missionary but the convert. Paul asserts that he seeks to win "more" people (τοὺς πλείονας, *tous pleionas*, 9:19). The unusual Greek phrase does not mean "the majority" or "most," as Paul knows that only some people from any given city come to faith (9:22). In the context of 1 Cor 8–10 Paul asserts, perhaps, that he would win fewer people if he behaved differently, for example if he always displayed the full scope of his freedom.

(5) The normative center of missionary accommodation is the gospel, not the pragmatic motif of effectiveness: "I do it all for the sake of the gospel, so that I may share in its blessings" (9:23). The phrase "for the sake of the gospel" clarifies that Paul promotes cultural relevance rather than cultural relativism. The central content of Paul's missionary proclamation is "the gospel." It is the gospel of Jesus Christ that controls both Paul's preaching and Paul's behavior.

2 Corinthians 4:7–15

When Paul describes the realities of his missionary work in 2 Cor 4, he emphasizes several factors that inform his missionary strategy.

(1) The gospel is a "treasure" contained in "clay jars (ὀστρακίνοις σκεύεσιν, *ostrakinois skeuesin*), i.e., the missionaries who proclaim the gospel are, like pottery made of clay, weak and fragile and quite insignificant in themselves.[8] Christians should not take offense if some people regard the missionary or the rhetoric of his preaching as not very impressive: clay jars that contain a valuable treasure are undeserving of specific attention.

(2) The unimpressive nature of Paul's missionary proclamation underlines the fact that the extraordinary power that can be observed in the work of the missionaries comes from God (4:7b). The redemptive effectiveness of missionary preaching derives neither from the dynamic personality of the missionary nor from the strategies that he employs, but from the truth of the gospel and the power of the Spirit.

(3) As Paul lists some of the difficulties and the suffering that he encounters in his missionary work, he describes his life as a paradox: he experiences in his body the death of Jesus Christ (4:10). This means at the same time that the power of God that supports him in the midst of the trials is evidence for the present reality of the resurrection of Jesus Christ.

(4) This is the reason why Paul never abandons the hope that the gospel may be accepted by "more and more people" (4:15).

Romans 10:14–21

In the context of his discussion of the reality of the righteousness of God in salvation history, Paul describes the missionary work of the apostles and thus his own ministry.

(1) Authentic missionary work involves the proclamation of the gospel by messengers who have been sent by the Lord (10:14–15). This is the central reality of missions, as Paul's argumentation demonstrates, an argumentation that consists of four parallel questions that form a logical chain and of a quotation from Isa 52:7. Missionaries do not preach on

---

8. Thrall, *2 Corinthians*, 1:322–24.

their own authority, and they do not preach a message that they have themselves created. They are ambassadors sent by God and empowered by the Spirit, messengers who proclaim the saving word of God. The primacy of the proclamation of the word is repeated in 10:17: faith comes from the message that is heard and in which the word of the crucified and risen Jesus Christ is manifested.

(2) The missionary work of the apostles and of Paul represents the fulfillment of messianic promises. The quotation of Isa 52:7 emphasizes that the proclamation of the messengers of the gospel brings the salvation that God had promised. By omitting the phrase "on the mountains," which focused the message of the messengers of joy on Mount Zion, Paul highlights his conviction that the mission of the messengers of the gospel is a universal mission. At the same time the "lone herald of the LXX" is transformed into "multiple preachers of the good news."[9] In 10:18, Paul uses the language of Ps 19:5 to describe the universal scope of the proclamation of the gospel: the voice of the gospel can be heard in "all the earth," the word of the gospel goes out "to the ends of the world."

(3) Paul knows at the same time that "only very few" (οὐ πάντες, *ou pantes*; litotes) become obedient to the gospel: the proclamation of the gospel of Jesus Christ has been largely rejected in Israel (10:16). The reason for this rejection is not a lack of messengers, but a lack of faith on the part of those who hear the preaching of the gospel. Paul quotes Isa 53:1 to explain that a word sent by God or a message authorized by God is not always accepted nor accepted by everybody, not even by all the Jewish people.

Romans 15:15–21

In this passage Paul describes his work as an apostle to the Gentiles in the context of his plans for visiting Rome. He speaks of the grace that God has extended to him so that he may be a servant of Jesus Christ for the nations.

(1) Paul describes himself as pioneer missionary: "I make it my ambition to proclaim the good news, not where Christ has already been named,

---

9. Wagner, *Heralds of the Good News*, 173.

so that I do not build on someone else's foundation" (15:20–21). As an *architektōn* moved from city to city working on major building projects, Paul travels to regions in which the gospel had not been preached and to cities in which no church had yet been established.[10]

(2) The oral proclamation of the gospel is the primary activity of missionary work. The goal of missionary work is to reach people who have not heard the good news of Jesus Christ "by word and deed" (λόγῳ καὶ ἔργῳ, *logō kai ergō*, 15:18). Missionaries proclaim the good news of Jesus Christ (εὐαγγελίζεσθαι, *euangelizesthai*, 15:20). The "word" (λόγος, *logos*) is the message that the missionaries convey: the proclamation of the good news of Jesus Messiah, the crucified and risen Savior.

(3) The reality of Paul's life is an integral part of his missionary work. When Paul states in 15:17 that he boasts of his "work for God," the term "work" (ἔργον, *ergon*) refers to the entire scope of his ministry and experience as well as to his behavior in everyday life as a missionary.

METHODS OF PAUL'S MISSIONARY WORK: TARGET AUDIENCES

Geographic strategies

Some scholars suggest that the geographic scope of Paul's apostolic ministry can be explained with the help of Old Testament prophecies or in the context of Old Testament and Jewish geography. Rainer Riesner argues that Paul interpreted his calling in terms of the mission of the Servant of the Lord that the prophet Isaiah expected for the last days: the mission of the Servant of the Lord reaches the "end of the earth" (Isa 49:6); the "survivors of the nations" that the prophets mention in Isa 66:19 are messengers who are sent to the nations; they first go to Tarshish (Tarsus) and they reach in a semicircular movement in a northwesterly direction Put (Cilicia), Lud (Lydia), Meshech (Mysia), Tubal (Bithynia), Javan (Greece, Macedonia), and the distant coastlands (the regions in the far west, Spain).[11] Riesner suggests that the geographical framework of Isa 66:19 explains why Paul planned a mission to Spain, but not a mission to Gaul.

10. Cf. Derrett, "Paul as Master-Builder."
11. Riesner, *Paul's Early Period*, 245–53.

This explanation is attractive as it acknowledges the significance of Israel's Scriptures for Paul's theology. However, it cannot ultimately explain the geographical movements of Paul. First, the two geographical endpoints that Paul mentions in Rom 15:19 (Jerusalem and Illyricum) cannot be connected with Isa 66:19. Second, the envoys of Isa 66:19 are Gentiles who have survived God's judgment, a notion that can hardly be applied to Paul who is a Diaspora Jew. Third, the geographical identifications in Isa 66:19 do not fit Paul's movements: Tarshish is usually identified with Tarsus, and Put with Libya or with Cyrene in North Africa. It seems unlikely that Paul abandoned this tradition and adopted the identification found in the Book of Judith which links "Put and Lud" with Cilicia (Jdt 2:23). Riesner's identification of Meshech with Mysia and of Tubal with Bithynia, two areas in which Paul planned missionary work that he was eventually not able to carry out, is selective: in contemporary Jewish traditions, Tubal is identified not only with Bithynia but sometimes with Iberia/Spain (Josephus) and with Europe from Bulgaria to France (*Jubilees*); and Meshech is identified not only with Mysia but also with Cappadocia (Josephus), with Spain and France (*Jubilees*), and with Illyricum (Hippolytus).[12] Also, the first fifteen years or so of Paul's missionary work in Nabatea, in Syria, and in Cilicia between AD 32/33 and 45 remain without explanation if Isa 66:19 provides the blueprint for Paul's mission.

James Scott suggests that the apostles divided the world in terms of the regions in which the descendants of Noah lived, as they are listed in the Table of Nations in Gen 10, and that Paul saw himself as a missionary to the territory of Japhet. Scott argues that this is the reason why Paul preached the gospel "from Jerusalem to Illyricum" (Rom 15:19) and why he wanted to go to Spain (Rom 15:22–24, 28–29): he engaged in missionary work in Asia Minor and in Europe, the territory in which Japhet and his descendants settled.[13]

The diverse geographical identifications in Jewish (and in early patristic) traditions, and the details of Paul's actual missionary work, render it doubtful whether his missionary strategy was informed by the tradition of the Table of Nations. First, this explanation ignores the first fifteen years of Paul's missionary work in Nabatea, in Syria, and in Cilicia. Paul's "independent" mission did *not* begin after the Apostles'

---

12. Scott, *Paul and the Nations*, 48–49 (Table 3).
13. Ibid., 135–80.

Council in AD 48, but in AD 32/33, immediately after his conversion when he went to Arabia/Nabatea and to Syria and Cilicia (cf. Gal 1:17; 2 Cor 11:32). Arabia belongs not to the territory of Japhet, but to the descendants of Mizraim, i.e., to the territory of Ham. Second, Paul's plan to preach the gospel in the "province of Asia" (Acts 16:6), i.e., in the geographical region of Lydia, is a problem for Scott since Lud was a son of Shem (Gen 10:22). Since Paul was prevented from preaching the gospel in the Province of Asia (Acts 16:6), the hypothesis survives in terms of Paul's actual movement at this point, but not in terms of Paul's intention. When Paul at a later stage reaches the Province of Asia (Acts 19), planting a church in the city of Ephesus, Scott defends his "Japhet" hypothesis by connecting the city of Ephesus, which was established by Ionian colonists, with Javan, one of the sons of Japhet. He maintains that Paul's missionary work in the Province of Asia, i.e., in the territory that the Greeks called Lydia, was a more indirect ministry. This explanation is not convincing. Paul's statement in Col 1:7 ("Epaphras . . . is a faithful minister of Christ on our[14] behalf") suggests that he regarded Epaphras's missionary work in the Lykos Valley (in the eastern part of the Province of Asia) as his responsibility. Third, the only identifications of Japhet's descendants that are not controversial in Jewish and in the patristic traditions are the identification of Javan with Ionia (or the Greeks) and the identification of Madai with the Medes. Paul did go to "Javan" (Athens, Corinth), but he did not go to Media. The suggestion that Paul understood his missionary work as "Japhet mission" is not convincing.

It appears that Henri Clavier is correct when he suggests that if Paul followed a plan that controlled his missionary travels, such a plan was born, developed, specified, and adapted in the course of the events as they unfolded.[15]

The strategy of Paul was simple: he wanted to proclaim the message of God's saving revelation in Jesus Christ to Jewish audiences and to Gentile audiences, particularly in areas in which it had never been proclaimed (Gal 2:7; Rom 15:14–21). The planning for the implementation of this goal was also relatively simple: he traveled on the major Roman

---

14. For the text-critical problem, see the commentaries. Commentators such as Lightfoot, Abbott, Lohse, Gnilka, Schweizer, O'Brien, Pokorný, Wolter, Barth/Blanke, Dunn, and Hübner agree that the reading ἡμῶν "on our behalf" is to be preferred. The Greek editions of the New Testament continue to prefer the reading ὑμῶν "on your behalf."

15. Cf. Clavier, "Méthode et inspiration," 177.

roads as well as on smaller local roads from city to city, preaching the message of Jesus the Messiah and Savior in synagogues, in market places, and in lecture halls, and gathering the new converts in local communities of followers of Jesus. This is what he did in Arabia, in Syria (Antioch), in Cilicia (Tarsus), on Cyprus (Paphos), in the Provinces of Galatia (Pisidian Antioch, Iconium, Lystra, Derbe), Asia (Ephesus), Macedonia (Philippi, Thessalonica, Berea) and Achaia (Athens, Corinth), and, if he was released from the (first) Roman imprisonment,[16] presumably in Spain (cf. Rom 15:23–28) and on Crete (Titus 1:5). When it proved impossible to reach a certain region in which he had planned missionary outreach, as was the case with the project of a mission to the Provinces of Asia, Bithynia, and Mysia (Acts 16:7–8), Paul's strategy did not break down: there were other cities in other regions whose citizens needed to hear the gospel. It appears that Paul plannned his missionary travels, targeting cities of neighboring provinces: he moved from Antioch in Syria to Salamis and Paphos on Cyprus, a region immediately east of Syria; then he moved from Cyprus to southern Galatia, a region north of Cyprus; then he targeted the Province of Asia, presumably Ephesus, which was the next "logical" step after having reached the cities of southern Galatia. At the same time he was prepared to leave the "tactical selection" of locations for missionary work to God's sovereignty if his initial plans did not work out: when he was not able to reach the Province of Asia, he targeted the Province of Pontus and Bithynia, and when this plan could not be realized, he moved to Europe. The transition to Europe was not part of his missionary plans at the time (cf. Acts 16:9), and yet he spent three years in Macedonia and Achaia.

Since we have no reliable information about the location of the missionary activity of the other apostles, we need to humbly accept the fact that we do not know whether Paul sought to implement a grand strategy of "missionary geography" with regard to his own convictions or with regard to the coordination of his missionary work with that of the other apostles.

Urban Strategies

Roland Allen suggests that Paul's missionary strategy focused on cities—the centers of Roman administration, of Greek culture, and of Jewish

---

16. *1 Clement* 5:5–7; *Muratori Canon* 35–39; *Acts of Peter* 1; cf. Ellis, *Making of the New Testament Documents*, 278–82.

presence—with the hope that the churches in the cities would eventually evangelize the rural areas.[17] Paul indeed preached in the centers of several Roman provinces: in Antioch in Syria, presumably in Tarsus in Cilicia, in Paphos on Cyprus, in Perga in Pamphylia, in Thessalonica in Macedonia, in Corinth in Achaia, and in Ephesus in the Province of Asia.

Since Paul always sought to preach to Jewish audiences, this list of cities is not surprising: in the Diaspora, Jews tended to live in the major cities, not in rural areas. There are other considerations that suggest that the case for describing Paul's mission in terms of a "metropolis mission" is not as strong as some think. First, we have hardly any information about the first fifteen years of Paul's missionary work in Arabia, Syria, and Cilicia to prove or disprove such a strategy for the years between AD 32 and 45. Second, as regards the thirteen years of Paul's missionary work between AD 45 and 57, we should note that Paul apparently bypassed important cities that were situated on the roads that he travelled: Side in Pamphylia, Termessos and Sagalassos in Pisidia, Cybistra in Lycaonia. Third, Luke's brief comment in Acts 13:48–49 suggests that Paul's missionary work was not limited to cities but also reached rural areas: "When the Gentiles heard this, they were glad and praised the word of the Lord; and as many as had been destined for eternal life became believers. Thus the word of the Lord spread throughout the region." The term χώρα (*chōra*) refers here to the people living in the towns and villages that Pisidian Antioch controlled. When Harvie Conn asserts that "the book of Acts deals almost entirely with cities; missionary work is almost limited to them,"[18] we need to remember that Luke's narrative is highly selective, which makes comments such as Acts 13:49 all the more intriguing. Luke has much more information than he records; asides such as Acts 13:49 indicate that Paul's mission reached smaller towns and villages as well.

Social Strategies

Paul had contacts with members of the ruling elite, some of whom were converted to faith in Jesus Christ, while others were friendly towards him. Examples include Sergius Paulus the proconsul of Cyprus (Acts 13:6–12); the "prominent women" in Thessalonica and in Berea (Acts

---

17. Allen, *Missionary Methods*, 13.
18. Conn, "Lucan Perspectives."

17:4, 12); and the Asiarchs in Ephesus (Acts 18:31).[19] Luke's reference to the high social position of these people does not serve some political agenda: he reports the hostile actions of "the God-fearing women of high standing and the leading men" in Pisidian Antioch (Acts 13:50), and he mentions governors who keep Paul in custody despite the fact that they know Paul to be innocent (Acts 24:27; 25:9). The high social position of the people with whom Paul has positive encounters is a function of Luke's description of the progress of the early Christian mission. Several factors are relevant. First, persons of a high social status have houses in which the new communities of believers can meet. Second, aristocrats with whom Paul maintains friendly contacts are able to protect Paul and the local Christians in politically critical situations. Third, and perhaps most importantly, the gospel evidently reached not only the lower classes and the poor, but also the upper classes and the rich.

Did Paul intentionally aim at reaching members of the elite with the gospel? The fact that Paul traveled from Paphos on Cyprus to Pisidian Antioch, a small Roman colony in the Anatolian highlands, suggests that he did. When Paul engaged in missionary work in Paphos, he encountered Sergius Paulus, the proconsul (governor) of the senatorial Province of Cyprus, who, according to Luke's report in Acts 13:12, was converted to faith in the Lord Jesus Christ. This Sergius Paulus is possibly identical with Lucius Sergius Paullus who is mentioned in an inscription from Rome where he is described as one of five curators of the Tiber River (*curatores riparum et alvei Tiberis*) who were responsible for regulating the flow of the Tiber during the principate of Claudius between AD 41 and 47.[20] The conversion of Sergius Paulus in Paphos could help explain why Paul and Barnabas traveled from Paphos straight to Pisidian Antioch, bypassing the cities of Perga and Attalia: inscriptions[21] indicate that the family of the Sergii owned estates in southern Galatia and had contact with Pisidian Antioch in the Julio-Claudian period (assuming that the identification with the Sergii Paulli of the Tiber inscription and of the Antioch inscription is correct).[22] It is entirely plausible to assume

---

19. Gill, "Acts and the Urban Elites," 108–9.
20. Cf. Mitchell, *Anatolia*, 6–7; Nobbs, "Cyprus," 284–85.
21. *MAMA* VII 486; *MAMA* VII 319; *MAMA* II 321.
22. Mitchell, "Population and the Land in Roman Galatia," 1073–74 n. 134; Riesner, *Paul's Early Period*, 276; Halfmann, *Senatoren*, 30, 55–56, 101–2, 105; cf. Fox, *Pagans and Christians*, 293–94.

that Paul received letters of introduction from Sergius Paulus to the governor's relatives in southern Galatia. This does not necessarily contradict W. M. Ramsay, who suggested in connection with Gal 4:13 ("you know that it was because of a physical infirmity that I first announced the gospel to you") that Paul had contracted malaria in Pamphylia and that this was the reason why he traveled to southern Galatia with its higher elevations.[23]

As Luke narrates Paul's mission to Antioch, he mentions the "leading men of the city" (τοὺς πρώτους τῆς πόλεως, *tous prōtous tēs poleōs*, Acts 13:50), i.e., the members of the local elite in the municipal aristocracy, people who controlled public life in Antioch on account of their social standing and their wealth that came from their estates. If Paul came to Pisidian Antioch as a result of his encounter with Sergius Paulus, hoping that he could find similar access to the aristocracy of this Roman colony in the border region of Phrygia and Pisidia, the Jews of Antioch thwarted the potential of this plan according to Acts 13:50.[24]

Ethnic Strategies

In his brief comment on his self-understanding as a missionary in the introduction to his letter to the Christians in Rome, Paul asserts: "I am a debtor both to Greeks and to barbarians, both to the wise and to the foolish" (Rom 1:14). Paul states that God has commissioned him to proclaim the gospel to all people without any distinction. Paul seeks to reach the "Greeks" (Ἕλληνες, *Hellēnes*), i.e., the elites of the Greco-Roman world. But he also seeks to reach the "foreigners" (βάρβαροι, *barbaroi*), i.e., the people who have no Greek culture and whom the elites exclude from the decision-making processes. He preaches to the "wise" (σοφοί, *sophoi*), i.e., to the people who are educated. But he also preaches to the "foolish" (ἀνόητοι, *anoētoi*), i.e., to the uneducated. This programmatic list suggests that Paul deliberately disregards the traditional social and cultural categories and classifications, which were defined and drawn up by the elites. Paul sees himself obligated, in the words of U. Wilckens, "to exclude neither the Greek because he belongs as educated person to the ruling elite, nor the barbarian because he has no culture and is of no

---

23. Ramsay, *St. Paul the Traveller*, 92.
24. Cf. Breytenbach, *Paulus und Barnabas*, 48.

significance (cf. 1 Cor 1:26ff.). The gospel concerns everybody without regard to who he or she is, as it makes everybody *coram deo* equal."[25]

Paul generally began his missionary preaching in a city in which he had newly arrived in the local synagogue. Paul always understood himself as a Jew, even and especially as a missionary among the Gentiles. He accepted the Jewish jurisdiction of the synagogues for himself, as is demonstrated by the fact that he was punished five times with the "forty minus one" lashes (2 Cor 11:24). As Paul had been trained as a rabbi, he would quickly be invited to preach in synagogue services. As a missionary who sought to reach pagans with the gospel, he would find Gentiles in the synagogues: proselytes, i.e., Gentiles who had converted to Judaism, God-fearers, i.e., Gentiles who acknowledged Israel's God and who attended synagogue services, and other sympathizers. Seen from a tactical point of view, Gentiles who believed in Israel's God were the best candidates for successful evangelism. This alone suggested that a Jewish Christian missionary to the Gentiles should begin missionary work in the local synagogue where he would encounter not only Jews but also Gentiles.

Many Gentiles who converted to faith in Jesus Christ, perhaps the majority of the non-Jewish believers, were God-fearers and sympathizers with the Jewish faith. This can be inferred from the fact that Paul could presuppose as a matter of course that the believers in the churches that he had established, at least the leading teachers, were familiar with Israel's holy Scriptures and with Jewish traditions and customs. Stephen Mitchell surmises correctly that "the transformation of the pagan world to Christian monotheism" is hardly conceivable without the pagan God-fearers in the synagogues who had a monotheistic notion of God.[26]

Simultaneous to preaching in the local synagogue, Paul established contact with the citizens in the agora, i.e., in the commercial and political center of the city. The evidence for Paul preaching in the marketplaces of cities is not very extensive, but unambiguous: Luke reports in Acts 17:17 that Paul went "every day" to the marketplace and spoke "with those who happened to be there."[27] The Greek construction (present

---

25. Wilckens, *Der Brief an die Römer*, 1:81.
26. Mitchell, "Wer waren die Gottesfürchtigen," 64.
27. Reinbold, *Propaganda und Mission*, 200, asserts that Acts 17:17 is a stylized picture of Paul used by the author who allegedly wanted to allude to Socrates, the Athenian philosopher. Reinbold believes that Paul's ministry took place in small settings, "in

participle παρατυγχάνοντας, *paratyngchanontas*) implies that going to the agora and speaking with passers-by was a routine that the apostle followed regularly.

There is no evidence that Paul visited pagan temples with the purpose of proclaiming the gospel before worshipers present in the temple precinct. As Paul was familiar with the political, social, and religious power structures of Greek and Roman cities, such a strategy is not likely. The Christian missionaries and the small Christian communities who were repeatedly threatened by local opponents had to abstain from provocative actions if they wanted to be tolerated in the Greek and Roman cities. Paul's assertion in Rom 2:22 that there are Jews who rob temples has been interpreted in terms of Jews illegally removing objects from temples of pagan shrines,[28] or in terms of trading in objects that have been stolen from pagan temples.[29] As the context in Romans 2 is critical of such behavior, it is plausible to conclude that Paul would have disagreed with the early medieval missionaries who profaned images of pagan deities, altars, and sacred groves, destroying temples and shrines.[30] Paul would never have used force in order to advance the gospel among pagans. Nor did Paul emulate pagan customs in organizing processions and carrying objects with him that could have enhanced the acceptance of himself or of his message. And we hear nothing of prayers or hymns recited and sung in public that may have impressed pagans.[31]

---

families, houses, small groups, (small) *ekklesiai* etc." (104); he concludes: "The mission of the historical Paul was characterized by micro-communication, not by public or semi-public speeches, sermons or similar appearances" (205). This interpretation cannot explain the public accusations, the legal proceedings, and the personal attacks that Paul endured in cities both in Asia Minor and in Greece.

28. Cf. Dunn, *Romans*, 1:114–15.

29. Käsemann, *Romans*, 71. Many interpret Rom 2:22 as a metaphorical reference to Jews robbing God of things that belong to him; cf. Cranfield, *Romans*, 1:169–70.

30. Cf. von Padberg, *Mission und Christianisierung.*, 146–51; cf. ibid. for the following note.

31. The early medieval missionaries carried with them mobile altars, containers for consecrated oil, crosses, pictorial representations of Christ on boards, relics, and priestly garments. They often entered pagan territories with supplicatory processions during which hymns of confession, hymns of praise, and petitions were sung.

Local strategies

The early Christian mission was closely connected with private houses. In the ancient world, the term "house" (οἶκος, *oikos*; Lat. *familia*) described the "house as living space and familial domestic household." J. Becker is correct when he points out that the private house became the "base of missionary work, the foundational center of a local church, the location of the assembly for worship, the lodging for the missionaries and envoys and at the same time the primary and decisive place of Christian life and formation."[32] There are several reasons why the early missionaries chose private homes as meeting places of the new Christian communities. First, attempts to meet in the local synagogue repeatedly failed as the local Jewish leadership opposed Paul. Second, the houses of converted Jews and Gentiles were immediately available as meeting places. They did not have to be remodeled or refurbished since the meetings of Christian believers did not require any special architectural features. Third, Jews were accustomed to meet in private houses, both in Palestine and in the Diaspora. Jews, proselytes, and God-fearers who converted to faith in Jesus Christ would thus not have been surprised about the choice of private homes as meeting places for religious activities. Fourth, a private home provided excellent conditions for important elements of the meetings of Christian believers such as familial fellowship and common meals during which the Lord's Supper was celebrated. Fifth, private houses allowed the Christians to meet in a relatively inconspicuous manner, which became a pressing necessity as soon as the local synagogues no longer tolerated the believers in Jesus Messiah.

REALITIES OF PAUL'S MISSIONARY WORK: THE COMMUNICATION OF THE GOSPEL

Establishing Contact

Paul spoke very deliberately of the "entrance" (εἴσοδος, *eisodos*) to the people who heard his proclamation of the gospel (1 Thess 1:9). Paul obviously reflected upon the factors and the conditions that come into play during the process of establishing first contacts with Jewish and Gentile listeners.[33] Paul first visited the local synagogue, presenting himself as

---

32. Becker, "Paulus und seine Gemeinden," 125. On this subject see now Gehring, *House Church and Mission*.

33. Cf. 1 Thess 1:9; 1 Cor 2:1–2; 16:8–9; 2 Cor 2:12; Gal 4:14; Col 4:3.

an experienced interpreter of Scripture. He used the customary readings from the Torah and the Prophets in his synagogue sermons as opportunities to proclaim Jesus of Nazareth as Messiah. With only one exception (Acts 20:7), all Sabbath passages of Acts are related to Paul preaching in synagogues.[34] At the same time, as the brief remark in Acts 17:17 indicates, Paul sought to get in contact with the general population of a city in the agora, i.e., the central, public place where he could reach a numerous and diverse audience, including the decision makers of the city.

It appears that Paul's behavior as an "orator" surprised educated Gentiles both at the point of initial contact and afterwards. In 1 Cor 2:1, Paul reminds the Christians in Corinth of the events that took place when he first visited the city: "When I came to you, brothers and sisters, I did not come proclaiming the mystery of God to you in lofty words or wisdom." Paul's forceful remarks in the context of this passage (1 Cor 1:18—2:5) can most appropriately be understood against the background of Greco-Roman orators. Bruce Winter suggests that an analysis of the orators of the Second Sophistic helps us to understand this passage.[35] The first visit of a sophist in a city gave him the opportunity to provide the citizens with a taste of his oratory. When Aristides visited Smyrna for the first time (in AD 176), the citizens came out to greet him. The most gifted young people offered themselves as students, a date for a lecture by Aristides was set, and an invitation formulated. Before the day on which the lecture was to take place, Aristides had a "dream" in which he was told to declaim in the council chamber at ten o'clock that very day. He was able to arrange this impromptu appearance at very short notice. Even though hardly anybody had heard of this turn of events, the council chamber was so packed "that it was impossible to see anything except men's heads, and there was not even room to shove your hand between the people." Aristides delivered the preliminary speech sitting down, the following declamation was presented standing up. The excited audience was spellbound throughout his delivery, so much so that "every man counted it his gain, if he should bestow some very great compliment on me." Aristides's "dream" was probably prompted by a rival sophist, "an Egyptian" who happened to present a declamation in the odeion on that particular day at two days' notice. Aristides was thus able to carry off a complete victory over the Egyptian, whose event at-

34. Cf. Acts 13:14-15; 16:13; 17:2; 18:4.
35. Winter, *Philo and Paul*, 147-65.

tracted only seventeen people.[36] This story confirms what other sources tell us: the sophist orators wanted to impress their audiences with their declamations, both the young men of the leading families of the city and invited guests and other people who would pay for the experience of listening to the oratory. The first "coming" of an orator to a city evidently followed certain conventions, as he sought to establish his reputation as an orator. If he was successful and found acceptance, he could profit socially and financially.

In the eyes of the pagan citizens of a city, Paul was an orator who was looking for an audience. Compared with the conventions of the contemporary orators, however, Paul's conduct was unconventional. Paul asserts that his behavior was deliberate: "When I came to you, brothers and sisters, I did not come proclaiming the mystery of God to you in lofty words or wisdom. For I decided to know nothing among you except Jesus Christ, and him crucified. And I came to you in weakness and in fear and in much trembling. My speech and my proclamation were not with plausible words of wisdom, but with a demonstration of the Spirit and of power, so that your faith might rest not on human wisdom but on the power of God" (1 Cor 2:1–5). The term πίστις (*pistis*) in 1 Cor 2:5 takes up a rhetorical term: Paul specifically addresses the expectations of his listeners in terms of his rhetorical abilities. Aristotle links πίστις ("confidence", "conviction") with the combined application of three proofs: τὸ ἔθος (*to ethos*), τὰ πάθη (*ta pathē*), and ἀπόδειξις (*apodeixis*; Aristotle, *Rhet.* 1.1.1356a). The orator persuades by *ethos* when he delivers his speech in a manner that demonstrates that he is worthy to be trusted. For Aristotle, this was the most effective means of proof. In order to be believed, the orator needs to convey a sympathetic picture of himself as a credible and likable person. The term *pathos* describes the feelings of the listeners that can be utilized strategically in order to guarantee the effectiveness of the oration. The term *apodeixis* describes the method by which an orator can prove what is not certain by referring to what is certain, i.e., to specific arguments. Paul uses in 1 Cor 2:4 not only the term *apodeixis*, but also δύναμις (*dynamis*, "power"), a term that is used by Isocrates and Aristotle in their definition of rhetoric: rhetoric is the "power" to detect the means of persuasion, rhetoric is the "power of speaking" (δύναμις τοῦ λέγειν, *dynamis tou legein*). In 1 Cor 2:4 Paul

---

36. Aristides, *Or.* 51.29–34.

uses the verb πείθω (*peithō*; Lat. *persuadere*, "persuade"), which is often used in definitions of rhetoric. Quintilian speaks of *vis persuadendi*.

When Paul writes in 1 Cor 2:1, "When I came to you, brothers and sisters, I did not come proclaiming the mystery of God to you in lofty words or wisdom," he emphasizes the fact that he intentionally dispenses with the traditional contemporary conventions of rhetoric when he preaches the gospel before Jewish and pagan audiences. He has no interest in being the center of attention or in being praised by others. He does not want to gain in prestige, he does not compete with other orators, nor does he have any financial interests. And, more importantly, he knows that the character of the gospel of Jesus Christ makes it impossible to rely on the strategies of traditional rhetoric as described by Aristotle, Cicero, or Quintilian, to mention only three of the more well-known rhetorical theorists. The message of a crucified Messiah is a "stumbling block" for Jewish listeners and "nonsense" for pagan listeners (1 Cor 1:23). The "proof" (ἀπόδειξις, *apodeixis*) for the validity of the gospel of Jesus Christ is not to be found through the application of logical inference or deduction. The "proof" for the truth of the gospel is to be found in the power of the Holy Spirit. When Paul proclaims the gospel (ὁ λόγος μου καὶ τὸ κήρυγμά μου, *ho logos mou kai to kērygma mou*, 1 Cor 2:4), he speaks "not with plausible words of wisdom" (οὐκ ἐν πειθοῖς σοφίας λόγοις, *ouk en peithois sophias logois*). Rather, he relies "on the demonstration of the Spirit and of power ἐν ἀποδείξει πνεύματος καὶ δυνάμεως (*en apodeixei pneumatos kai dynameōs*)" (1 Cor 2:4). This genitive construction is to be understood as a subjective genitive: the preaching of the gospel is not a demonstration concerning the Spirit or concerning the power of the preacher; rather, it is a demonstration effected by the Spirit and by "power," i.e., by God himself. The powerful Spirit of God "proves" the truth of the proclamation of God's redemptive revelation in Jesus Christ's death and resurrection.[37] This "proof" is the fact that Jews and pagans living in Corinth are being persuaded to accept the message of Jesus the crucified and risen Messiah. The supernatural proof for the validity of Paul's missionary proclamation is the conversion of Jews and pagans to faith in Jesus, the crucified Messiah and Lord.

In 1 Cor 2:5, Paul explains why he renounces traditional rhetorical methods: "so that your faith (ἡ πίστις ὑμῶν, *hē pistis hymōn*) might rest not on human wisdom but on the power of God." Paul knows that

---

37. Cf. Voss, *Das Wort vom Kreuz*, 131; Kammler, *Kreuz und Weisheit*, 171.

the message of the cross cannot be adapted to the theological, rhetorical, or aesthetic expectations of his audiences. It was impossible, in the first century, to speak in a rhetorically alluring manner about a man who had been executed on a cross.[38] The reality of crucifixion was too gruesome, and needed too much explanation, for rhetorical competence and brilliance to be of much help. When Paul taught new converts, he described Jesus as "new Adam"[39] and as the "savior of mankind,"[40] as the "Son of God"[41] and as the "firstborn of the dead."[42] These are terms and categories that could be packaged as attractive religious content when introducing the message about Jesus to Jewish and pagan audiences. Paul asserts, however, that he never dispensed with preaching Jesus the crucified Savior in his missionary proclamation (1 Cor 2:2). The preaching of a crucified Savior makes it impossible to employ the traditional rhetorical methods with their strategies of persuasion. Paul continues to preach a crucified and risen Savior because this is the message that has been given to him to pass on to those who have not heard the gospel, and because he knows that it is the almighty Lord himself, the Creator of the world, who causes Jews and pagans to come to faith.

Standard communication models help us to illustrate the situation in which Paul finds himself as a pioneer missionary.[43] The model of mass communication developed by B. H. Westley and M. S. MacLean distinguishes five elements.[44] The "source" or the communicator (A) focuses on a "universe" of possible objects or events in the environment ($X_{1-\infty}$) and formulates a message (X^*) which is transmitted via a gatekeeper or opinion leader (C) to a receiver or audience (B). The gatekeeper (e.g., a spokesperson or a journalist) sends the message in connection with his or her knowledge of reality (X_{3c}) to the audience (X^{**}). The audience or receiver sends feedback (f_{BA}) to the source of the communication. At the same time there is feedback from the gatekeeper to the source (f_{CA}) and from the receiver to the gatekeeper (f_{BC}). In the communication model of C. E. Shannon and W. Weaver, a further element plays a role: noise (D).

38. Cf. Hengel, *Crucifixion*, on the shame connected with crucifixion.
39. Cf. Kreitzer, "Adam and Christ"; Hofius, "Adam-Christus-Antithese."
40. Cf. Gill, "Saviour for the Cities of Crete," 220–30.
41. Hurtado, "Son of God"; Hurtado, *Lord Jesus Christ*, 101–8.
42. Hofius, "Erstgeborener."
43. Cf. Reck, *Kommunikation*.
44. Cf. Burgoon et al., *Human Communication*.

The transmission of a message is generally accompanied by disturbances, unwanted stimuli that can influence the accuracy of the message, e.g., static interference during a phone conversation, called "noise" in human communication.

God, the Primary Communicator

When we apply this model of communication to Paul's mission and to Paul's description of his mission, it becomes quickly evident that Paul regards God and Jesus Christ as the "source" or the "communicator," and that he understands himself and the other apostles as messengers (or "gatekeepers") of the gospel, who have been called, sent and empowered by God and Jesus Christ.[45] The basic texts in which Paul clearly expresses this conviction are 1 Thess 2:13, 2 Cor 5:18–20, and Rom 10:14–17. Paul asserts in 1 Thess 2:13: "We also constantly give thanks to God for this, that when you received the word of God that you heard from us, you accepted it not as a human word but as what it really is, God's word, which is also at work in you believers." The message that Paul conveys in his missionary work is not his own message, but "the word of God," i.e., the saving word that God himself speaks. Similarly, in Rom 10:17 Paul asserts that the message that he preaches in his missionary work is "the word of Christ." In 2 Cor 5:20, Paul declares that he and the other apostles are "ambassadors for Christ, since God is making his appeal through us." When Paul challenges both Jews and Gentiles to believe in God's redemptive salvation in Jesus Christ, it is God the Almighty himself who appeals to sinners to be reconciled to him through faith in Jesus Christ.[46]

The Message

When Paul describes in 1 Cor 2:1–5 his missionary preaching in the city of Corinth, emphasizing that he dispenses intentionally with the art of rhetoric when he proclaims the gospel of Jesus the crucified Messiah and Savior, he implies that this message required neither an *enkomion* on the greatness of the city of Corinth nor a *dialexis* aiming at putting

---

45. Reck, *Kommunikation*, 180–83.

46. Thrall, *2 Corinthians*, 1:437 asserts, quoting Barrett, *2 Corinthians*, 178: "This means, on the one hand, that the message is not Paul's own, but, on the other hand, that 'where Paul speaks, God speaks.'"

his listeners in a good mood. He did not depend on a critical audience suggesting a subject for a public declamation, expecting a demonstration of rhetorical expertise. The subject-matter of his public discourses had been determined long before he arrived in the city. Paul emphasizes that his public speaking as a missionary always focused on Jesus, the crucified Messiah and Savior: "I decided to know nothing among you except Jesus Christ, and him crucified" (1 Cor 2:2). He did not allow himself to be distracted by any other subject when he initiated contact with the citizens of Corinth. Passages such as 1 Thess 1:9–10 and Rom 15:20–21 confirm Luke's account in the book of Acts: Paul's missionary discourses included an explanation of the necessity to turn from idols to the true and living God, of the death and resurrection of Jesus, of the identity of Jesus as Messiah and *Kyrios* and Savior, of the coming day of judgment, and of the expected return of Jesus.

The Messenger

The "gatekeeper" of missionary communication is the apostle. Paul was very much aware of the fact that personal credibility is an important factor when an orator visits a city for the first time, seeking to establish contact with the citizens. In the local synagogue, Paul had credibility on account of his training as a rabbi in Jerusalem under Gamaliel (Acts 22:3), and on account of his competence in interpreting Scripture.[47] In the public agora, Greek and Roman citizens would have been impressed by his Roman citizenship[48] if they were aware of it, by his international travel experience,[49] and by miracles (2 Cor 12:11–12; Acts 13:12; 19:12).[50] To assert his personal credibility, Paul refers to his behavior and ministry: his travels, his homelessness, and his economic independence (1 Thess 2:9; 1 Cor 4:11–12; 9:6–18; 2 Cor 6:5; 11:7–10, 23–29). He refers to his personal relationship with the people who have come to faith in Jesus Christ through his preaching (1 Thess 1:4—3:10). He rejects recommendations by others, including letters of recommendation (2 Cor 3:1–3).

---

47. Cf. Hays, *Echoes of Scripture*; Stanley, *Paul and the Language of Scripture*.

48. Cf. Acts 16:37–38; 22:25–29; 23:27; cf. 25:10–11; 28:19; see the discussion in Riesner, *Paul's Early Period*, 147–56; Hengel and Schwemer, *Paul between Damascus and Antioch*, 16, 160.

49. Cf. Schnabel, *Early Christian Mission*, 2:1030–1292; see also Rapske, "Acts, Travel and Shipwreck."

50. Cf. Schreiber, *Paulus als Wundertäter*; Twelftree, "Signs, Wonders, Miracles."

Paul is concerned that at least the Christians know that his missionary work is no money-making business (1 Thess 2:2; 1 Cor 2:17; 5).

The Audience

The encounter with Jewish audiences in the local synagogues was initially unproblematic. Since there were no comparable models for traveling missionaries in Second Temple Judaism, the one notable factor concerning Paul, a rabbi trained in Jerusalem, was the fact that he was a teacher who visited synagogues in the Diaspora without having been sanctioned by the Sanhedrin. The Jews in the local synagogues were presumably surprised about Paul's initiative and commitment to the message that he proclaimed. The fact that Jewish teachers championed divergent doctrines was not a fundamentally novel experience for Paul's audiences, however. Jewish exegesis of the Second Temple Period was used to diverging opinions, the discourse of the rabbis proceeded in controversial discussions.

Paul's audiences in the synagogues must have regarded at least four aspects of his teaching as extraordinary: (1) his conviction that the long-awaited Messiah had arrived, fulfilling the prophets' promises of salvation; (2) his insistence that Jesus Messiah had been sentenced to death by crucifixion, that he died, and that he rose from the dead; (3) his assertion that faith in Jesus Messiah was now the only valid condition and criterion for receiving God's forgiveness and redemption at the Last Judgment; (4) his emphasis that the messianic era of salvation had dawned and that Gentiles come to faith in Israel's God and in Jesus and that they are incorporated into God's people without being circumcised and without keeping the Torah's purity and food laws. The first two points provided good topics for robust discussion. The third emphasis questioned the Jewish listeners' status as God's elect people, and it tied salvation to a human being. Here everything depended on the question whether Jesus was indeed the promised Messiah as the heavenly Son of Man and Son of God. The fourth emphasis jolted the traditional social structure of the Jewish people: the notion that God granted salvation to large numbers of pagans, apart from circumcision and observance of the dietary laws, was surprising in view of the expectation that the nations would come to Zion and worship the one true God in the context of Israel.

The patterns of reaction that Luke reports in the book of Acts cover the entire range from neutral listening to positive acceptance and emphatic rejection.[51] These various reactions can be explained with the mentality of the Jewish listeners. When Jews become convinced by Paul's preaching that Jesus is the Messiah, they join him and the new community of believers in Jesus, and they are willing to endure opposition. When they reject Paul's message, they have hardly any other option than to take action against Paul and to try to silence him, following the rules of Scripture concerning the handling of false prophets, seducers of the people, and blasphemers.

As regards pagan audiences, Paul's discourse about pagan religion would not have caused much protest during the initial contact—pagans would have heard similar evaluations of their religious convictions from the local Jews and from some philosophers who questioned the existence of the Olympian gods. They would have been familiar with the claim of Jewish teachers that their gods were nothing compared to the reality of the God of Abraham. Gentile listeners would have regarded at least four emphases of Paul's teaching as extraordinary: (1) the exhortation to believe not only in the one true God of the Jews, but also to accept the offer of grace by one single mediator of salvation; (2) the message that this mediator of salvation was a crucified man from provincial Judea; (3) the claim that this Jesus came back from the dead; (4) the expectation that they would gather in a new community that was being established in the city in which neither ethnic origins nor social status played any role. The claim that there is only one single mediator of salvation was extraordinary: neither the gods, nor the emperors or the heroes whom people worshiped demanded exclusive loyalty, although the notion of exclusive salvation would have reminded them of the religious convictions and praxis of the Jews. The information that the mediator of salvation was a human being would not have been curious for Gentile listeners, as they worshiped heroes and gods with human traits. But the emphasis that salvation is tied to faith in a person who had been executed by crucifixion and who was said to have risen from the dead was sensational or, rather, nonsensical.

Luke reports the following patterns of reaction by Gentile audiences:[52] (1) god-fearing Gentiles who sympathized with the Jewish faith listen willingly and attentively (Acts 16:14); (2) pagans are prepared

---

51. Cf. Tyson, *Images of Judaism*, 132–45; Setzer, *Jewish Responses to Early Christians*; Schnabel, *Early Christian Mission*, 2:1349–51.

52. Schnabel, *Early Christian Mission*, 2:1352–53.

to listen to what Paul and his fellow missionaries have to say (Acts 13:7; 24:24); (3) pagan philosophers take the initiative to dialogue with Paul about his teaching (Acts 17:18–20, 32); (4) pagan officials of provincial administrations and of city magistrates acknowledge that Paul does not teach subversive beliefs (Acts 18:14–16; 19:35–40; 25:25, 31); (5) pagans are deeply affected by miracles that happen in the course of the missionaries' ministry (Acts 13:12; 19:17); (6) pagans are so impressed by the miracles that they want to honor the missionaries as gods in human form (Acts 14:11–13); (7) pagans are stunned on account of the content and the claims of the Christian message (Acts 24:25); (8) god-fearing pagans who sympathize with the Jewish faith come to faith in Jesus, including aristocratic women and men (Acts 13:43, 48, 49; 14:1, 21; 16:14; 17:4, 12; 18:4, 7); (9) pagans come to faith in Jesus, including a Roman governor and a member of the "Council for education and science" in Athens (Acts 13:12; 14:21; 16:33–34; 17:34; 18:8; 19:18); (10) pagans who have come to faith in Jesus rejoice in the preaching of the missionaries and are filled with joy (Acts 13:48, 52; 16:34); (11) God-fearers who attend the synagogue service reject the teaching of the missionaries and their offer of salvation (Acts 13:48); (12) pagan philosophers make fun of the message that the missionaries proclaim (Acts 17:32); (13) pagans ridicule and reject the proclamation of Jesus the crucified Savior (1 Cor 1:23); (14) pagans initiate legal proceedings against Paul, accusing him of disturbing the peace and of illegal introduction of alien Jewish customs (Acts 16:20–21); (15) on some occasions pagans are motivated by the financial loss that the activities of the missionaries have caused (Acts 16:16–19; 19:23–27); (16) pagans organize a protest meeting against the missionaries (Acts 19:29–34); (17) praetors have Paul and Silas flogged by the lictors and throw the missionaries into prison (Acts 16:22–23).

These patterns of reaction can also be explained with the mentality of the Gentiles, e.g., with the curiosity of Athens' philosophers or with the religious excitement of the citizens of Lystra after the astounding miracle that the missionaries caused. It is plausible that economic losses became the cause for actions of Gentiles against the missionaries. It is striking to note that the sources do not report plans of pagans to eliminate Paul. This fits the tolerant attitude concerning religious affairs both of the Roman authorities and of the local populations. People with particular spiritual needs could worship any deity or hero who appeared useful and helpful. As long as the authorities knew that Paul did not endanger the public order, they could leave Paul alone.

The Obstacles

What communication models describe as "noise" are the obstacles that make missionary proclamation difficult. The offer of salvation as liberation from guilt and sin, the offer of hope for a perfect existence after death, the offer of fellowship with people from all walks of life and all classes of society, were attractive convictions that Paul could emphasize. Despite the attractiveness of these important elements of the early Christian preaching, the central emphasis of Paul's proclamation of a crucified Savior was difficult if not impossible to grasp for Jewish and Greek audiences (1 Cor 1:18–23; 2:14; 3:19).

For Jewish audiences, Paul's insistence that the crucified Jesus of Nazareth was the Messiah and that faith in this crucified Messiah was necessary for salvation was utterly startling, indeed bizarre and scandalous (σκάνδαλον, *skandalon*, 1 Cor 1:23). This emphasis, as well as the teaching that pagans who believe in Jesus Messiah are incorporated into God's people without circumcision, repeatedly provoked massive disagreement that disturbed the communication process to the point of complete collapse, forcing Paul to leave the synagogue. The message that God's messianic revelation and salvation no longer took place along the traditional fault-line between Jews and Gentiles, but within both Jews and Gentiles, was extraordinary indeed.[53] Paul's letters indicate that Paul was persecuted by his fellow Jews for the following reasons:[54] (1) he preached faith in Jesus the crucified and risen Messiah as necessary for salvation; (2) he argued for a radical re-evaluation of the privileges of the chosen people of God that fundamentally defined and described the identity of pious Jews; (3) he encouraged, indeed exhorted, Jewish believers to ignore important parts of the Torah, for example the purity laws and the food laws; (4) he did not teach the necessity of circumcision as prerequisite for membership in the people of God; (5) he allegedly abrogated all ethical norms and standards since the Torah no longer played a central role.

---

53. Stenschke, *Luke's Portrait of Gentiles*, 287.
54. Kruse, "Apostle," with reference to 1 Thess 2:15–16; Gal 1:13–24; 2:15–21; 4:29; 5:11; 2 Cor 11:24, 26, 30–33; Rom 3:7–8; Phil 3:4–8.

As regards contacts with pagan audiences, the insistence that Jesus, the exclusive mediator of salvation, was a Jew must have been provocative. More importantly, pagans regarded Paul's emphasis that Jesus was executed by crucifixion and that it was precisely this death that reveals and procures salvation as nonsense (μωρίαν, *mōrian*, 1 Cor 1:23). Also, the proclamation of Jesus' resurrection was regarded as extraordinarily strange: Gentiles might have been able to theoretically acquiesce to a hero coming back from the dead. But to suggest a glorious resurrection for a prophet and teacher who had been rejected by his own people and who had been executed by the governor of a Roman province who sentenced him to death by crucifixion was unbelievable.

Conversion

The goal of missionary proclamation is the conversion of Jews and pagans to faith in Jesus Messiah, Savior, and Lord, the transformation of traditional patterns of religious, ethical, and social behavior, and integration into the community of fellow believers. Paul interprets conversion and its consequences as "demonstration of the Spirit and power" (1 Cor 2:4; cf. 1 Thess 1:5). Turning to the true and living God and to Jesus the crucified Messiah presupposes acknowledging God's salvific revelation in sending Jesus into the world and to the cross. According to Rom 10:9, conversion happens through the confession by which individuals turn to and submit to God and his Messiah. The "confession" (*homologia*) consists in "the acknowledgment that the believer stands before God as transgressor who can win his salvation not by his own ability but only through God's grace and through the help of the *Kyrios* (cf. Gal 2:16; 1 Cor 1:26–30)."[55]

Paul asserts that when Jews turn to the Lord and believe in Jesus Christ, God removes "the veil" that has prevented them from understanding the Scriptures as pointing to Jesus the Messiah (2 Cor 3:16). Paul understands his mission as to help Gentiles to turn (ἐπιστρέφω, *epistrephō*) "from darkness to light and from the power of Satan to God" (Acts 26:18). When pagan polytheists are converted, they "turn to God from idols, to serve a living and true God" (1 Thess 1:9), they turn away from "the weak and beggarly elemental spirits" (Gal 4:9). Luke refers in his account of Paul's missionary work to the "conversion" (ἐπιστροφή, *epistrophē*) of individuals and families (Acts 13:38; 17:30; 20:21; 26:18, 20).

---

55. Stuhlmacher, *Biblische Theologie des Neuen Testaments*, 1:344.

Paul's exhortation of the Corinthian believers in 1 Cor 6:9–11 helps us to understand Paul's understanding of the conversion of Gentiles: "Do you not know that wrongdoers will not inherit the kingdom of God? Do not be deceived! Fornicators, idolaters, adulterers, male prostitutes, sodomites, thieves, the greedy, drunkards, revilers, robbers—none of these will inherit the kingdom of God. And this is what some of you used to be. But you were washed, you were sanctified, you were justified in the name of the Lord Jesus Christ and in the Spirit of our God." The "vices" that Paul mentions represent, in part, accepted behavior of pagans: visiting prostitutes, worshipping various Greek, Roman, and Egyptian gods, indulging in homosexual activity, being greedy, and getting drunk during banquets represents behavior that did not raise eyebrows. Paul's missionary preaching did not present a solution to a moral crisis that his pagan listeners would have perceived as such. Rather, Paul's preaching revealed that their moral contentment was the result of their failure to recognize the consequences of their behavior on the Day of Judgment. In the words of Stephen Chester, Paul seeks to move his pagan listeners "from false contentment to crisis to security in Christ."[56] The transformation that conversion to faith in the true and living God and to faith in Jesus Christ brings is both "an inward affair of the conscience" and "a radical change of moral and social identity." This transformation results from the repentance of unrecognized sin. It involves a break with many of the traditional values of contemporary pagan society. And it entails obedience to Scripture, to the word of Jesus Christ and to the teaching of the apostles. Another important result of conversion is joy (1 Thess 1:5–6), a gift of God's Spirit that transcends the grievances of human existence (Rom 8:18, 22), a joy that proves its worth in the midst of suffering (Rom 8:31–39). This joy was a reality that was a new experience for the Gentiles (Acts 13:48, 52; 16:34).[57]

Paul's missionary work did not end with the oral proclamation of the good news of Jesus Christ and with the conversion of individuals. Paul established churches, communities of men and women who had come to faith in Jesus the Messiah and Savior, and who came together to study the Scriptures, to learn what Jesus Christ had done and taught, and to live according to the will of the living God.

---

56. Chester, *Conversion at Corinth*, 147; the following quotation ibid.

57. Cf. Hawthorne, "Joy"; see Michel, "Freude," on the concept of joy in Greco-Roman literature.

BIBLIOGRAPHY

Allen, Roland. *Missionary Methods: St. Paul's or Ours?* 1912. Reprint, Grand Rapids: Eerdmans, 1993.

Barrett, C. K. *A Commentary on the Second Epistle to the Corinthians.* BNTC. London: Black, 1973.

Becker, Jürgen. "Paulus und seine Gemeinden." In *Die Anfänge des Christentums: Alte Welt und neue Hoffnung*, edited by J. Becker, 102–59. Stuttgart: Kohlhammer, 1987.

Botermann, Helga. *Das Judenedikt des Kaisers Claudius: Römischer Staat und Christiani im 1. Jahrhundert.* Hermes Einzelschriften 71. Stuttgart: Steiner, 1996.

Breytenbach, Cilliers. *Paulus und Barnabas in der Provinz Galatien: Studien zu Apostelgeschichte 13f. 16,6. 18,23 und den Adressaten des Galaterbriefes.* AGJU 38. Leiden: Brill, 1996.

Burgoon, Michael, et al. *Human Communication.* 3rd ed. London: Sage, 1994.

Chester, Stephen J. *Conversion at Corinth: Perspectives on Conversion in Paul's Theology and the Corinthian Church.* Studies of the New Testament and its World. Edinburgh: T. & T. Clark, 2003.

Clavier, Henri. "Méthode et inspiration dans la mission de Paul." In *Verborum Veritas.* FS G. Stählin. Edited by O. Böcher and K. Haacker, 171–87. Wuppertal: Brockhaus, 1970.

Conn, Harvie M. "Lucan Perspectives and the City." *Missiology* 13 (1985) 409–28.

Cranfield, C. E. B. *The Epistle to the Romans.* 2 vols. ICC. Edinburgh: T. & T. Clark, 1975–1979.

Derrett, J. Duncan M. "Paul as Master-Builder." *EQ* 69 (1997) 129–37.

Dunn, James D. G. *Romans.* 2 vols. WBC 38A–B. Dallas: Word, 1988.

Ellis, Earle E. *The Making of the New Testament Documents.* 1999. Reprint, Leiden: Brill, 2002.

Fox, Robin Lane. *Pagans and Christians in the Mediterranean World from the Second Century A.D. to the Conversion of Constantine.* 1986. London: Penguin, 1988.

Gehring, Roger W. *House Church and Mission: The Importance of Household Structures in Early Christianity.* Peabody, MA: Hendrickson, 2004.

Gill, David W. J. "Acts and the Urban Elites." In *The Book of Acts in Its Graeco-Roman Setting*, edited by D. W. J. Gill and C. Gempf, 105–18. Vol. 2 of *The Book of Acts in Its First-Century Setting.* Exeter: Paternoster, 1994.

———. "A Saviour for the Cities of Crete: The Roman Background to the Epistle to Titus." In *The New Testament in its First Century Setting: Essays on Context and Background.* FS Bruce W. Winter. Edited by P. J. Williams, 220–30. Grand Rapids: Eerdmans, 2004.

Halfmann, Helmut. *Die Senatoren aus dem östlichen Teil des Imperium Romanum bis zum Ende des 2. Jahrhunderts n. Chr.* Hypomnemata 58. Göttingen: Vandenhoeck & Ruprecht, 1979.

Hawthorne, Gerald F. "Joy." In *Dictionary of the Later New Testament*, edited by P. H. Davids and R. P. Martin, 600–605. Downers Grove, IL: InterVarsity, 1997.

Hays, Richard B. *Echoes of Scripture in the Letters of Paul.* New Haven: Yale University Press, 1989.

Hemer, Colin J. *The Book of Acts in the Setting of Hellenistic History.* Edited by C. H. Gempf. WUNT 49. Tübingen: Mohr Siebeck, 1989.

Hengel, Martin, and Anna Maria Schwemer. *Paul between Damascus and Antioch: The Unknown Years.* London: SCM; Louisville: Westminster John Knox, 1997.

Hengel, Martin. *Crucifixion in the Ancient World and the Folly of the Message of the Cross.* Philadelphia: Fortress, 1978.

Hofius, Otfried. "Die Adam-Christus-Antithese und das Gesetz. Erwägungen zu Röm 5,12–21." In *Paul and the Mosaic Law,* edited by J. D. G. Dunn, 165–206. WUNT 89. Tübingen: Mohr Siebeck, 1996.

———. "'Erstgeborener vor aller Schöpfung'—'Erstgeborener aus den Toten'. Der Christushymnus Kol 1,15–20." In *Auferstehung-Resurrection,* edited by F. Avemarie and H. Lichtenberger, 185–203. WUNT 135. Tübingen: Mohr Siebeck, 2001.

Hurtado, Larry W. *Lord Jesus Christ: Devotion to Jesus in Earliest Christianity.* Grand Rapids: Eerdmans, 2003.

———. "Son of God." In *Dictionary of Paul and his Letters,* edited by G. F. Hawthorne et al., 900–906. Downers Grove, IL: InterVarsity, 1993.

Kammler, Hans-Christian. *Kreuz und Weisheit: Eine exegetische Untersuchung zu 1 Kor 1,10—3,4.* WUNT 159. Tübingen: Mohr Siebeck, 2003.

Käsemann, Ernst. *Commentary on Romans.* Grand Rapids: Eerdmans, 1980.

Kreitzer, Larry J. "Adam and Christ." In *Dictionary of Paul and his Letters,* edited by G. F. Hawthorne et al., 9–15. Downers Grove, IL: InterVarsity, 1993.

Kruse, Colin G. "Apostle." In *Dictionary of Jesus and the Gospels,* edited by J. B. Green et al., 27–33. Downers Grove, IL: InterVarsity, 1992.

Litfin, Duane. *St. Paul's Theology of Proclamation. 1 Corinthians 1:4 and Greco-Roman Rhetoric.* SNTSMS 79. Cambridge: Cambridge University Press, 1994.

Michel, O. "Freude." *RAC* VIII, 348–418.

Mitchell, Stephen. *Anatolia: Land, Men, and Gods in Asia Minor. II. The Rise of the Church.* 1993. Reprint, Oxford: Oxford University Press, 1995.

———. "Population and the Land in Roman Galatia." *ANRW* II/7.2 (1980) 1053–81.

———. "Wer waren die Gottesfürchtigen?" *Chiron* 28 (1998) 55–64.

Nobbs, Alanna. "Cyprus." In *The Book of Acts in Its Graeco-Roman Setting,* edited by David W. J. Gill and Conrad Gempf, 279–89. Vol. 2 of *The Book of Acts in Its First-Century Setting.* Carlisle: Paternoster, 1994.

Padberg, Lutz E. von. *Mission und Christianisierung: Formen und Folgen bei Angelsachsen und Franken im 7. und 8. Jahrhundert.* Stuttgart: Steiner, 1995.

Pogoloff, Stephen M. *Logos and Sophia: The Rhetorical Situation of 1 Corinthians.* SBLDS 134. Atlanta: Scholars, 1992.

Ramsay, William M. *St. Paul the Traveler and the Roman Citizen.* Edited by Mark Wilson. Grand Rapids: Baker, 2001.

Rapske, Brian M. "Acts, Travel and Shipwreck." In *The Book of Acts in Its Graeco-Roman Setting,* edited by D. W. J. Gill and C. Gempf, 1–47. Vol. 2 of *The Book of Acts in Its First-Century Setting.* Carlisle: Paternoster, 1994.

Reck, Reinhold. *Kommunikation und Gemeindeaufbau: Eine Studie zu Entstehung, Leben und Wachstum paulinischer Gemeinden in den Kommunikationsstrukturen der Antike.* SBB 22. Stuttgart: Katholisches Bibelwerk, 1991.

Reinbold, Wolfgang. *Propaganda und Mission im ältesten Christentum: Eine Untersuchung zu den Modalitäten der Ausbreitung der frühen Kirche.* FRLANT 188. Göttingen: Vandenhoeck & Ruprecht, 2000.

Riesner, Rainer. *Paul's Early Period: Chronology, Mission Strategy, Theology.* Grand Rapids: Eerdmans, 1998.

Schnabel, Eckhard J. *Early Christian Mission.* 2 vols. Downers Grove, IL: InterVarsity, 2004.

Schrage, Wolfgang. *Der erste Brief an die Korinther.* 4 vols. EKK 7. Zürich: Benziger; Neukirchen-Vluyn: Neukirchener Verlag, 1991–2001.

Schreiber, Stefan. *Paulus als Wundertäter: Redaktionsgeschichtliche Untersuchungen zur Apostelgeschichte und den authentischen Paulusbriefen.* BZNW 79. Berlin: de Gruyter, 1996.

Scott, James M. *Paul and the Nations: The Old Testament and Early Jewish Background of Paul's Mission to the Nations with Special Reference to the Destination of Galatians.* 1995. Reprint, WUNT 84. Tübingen: Mohr Siebeck, 2002.

Setzer, Claudia J. *Jewish Responses to Early Christians. History and Polemics, 30–150 C.E.* Minneapolis: Fortress, 1994.

Shanor, Jay. "Paul as Master Builder: Construction Terms in First Corinthians." NTS 34 (1988) 461–71.

Stanley, Christopher D. *Paul and the Language of Scripture: Citation Technique in the Pauline Epistles and Contemporary Literature.* SNTSMS 69. Cambridge: Cambridge University Press, 1992.

Stenschke, Christoph W. *Luke's Portrait of Gentiles Prior to Their Coming to Faith.* WUNT 2/108. Tübingen: Mohr Siebeck, 1999.

Stuhlmacher, Peter. *Biblische Theologie des Neuen Testaments.* 3 vols. Göttingen: Vandenhoeck & Ruprecht, 1992–1999.

Thornton, Claus-Jürgen. *Der Zeuge des Zeugen: Lukas als Historiker der Paulusreisen.* WUNT 56. Tübingen: Mohr Siebeck, 1991.

Thrall, Margaret E. *A Critical and Exegetical Commentary on the Second Epistle to the Corinthians.* 2 vols. ICC. Edinburgh: T. & T. Clark, 1994–2000.

Twelftree, Graham H. "Signs, Wonders, Miracles." In *Dictionary of Paul and his Letters*, edited by G. F. Hawthorne et al., 875–77. Downers Grove, IL: InterVarsity, 1993.

Tyson, Joseph B. *Images of Judaism in Luke–Acts.* Columbia: University of South Carolina Press, 1992.

Voss, Florian. *Das Wort vom Kreuz und die menschliche Vernunft: Eine Untersuchung zur Soteriologie des 1. Korintherbriefes.* FRLANT 199. Göttingen: Vandenhoeck & Ruprecht, 2002.

Wagner, J. Ross. *Heralds of the Good News: Isaiah and Paul "In Concert" in the Letter to the Romans.* NovTSup 101. Leiden: Brill, 2002.

Wilckens, Ulrich. *Der Brief an die Römer.* 3 vols. EKK 6/1–3. Neukirchen-Vluyn/Einsiedeln: Neukirchener Verlag/Benziger, 1978–1982.

Winter, Bruce W. *Philo and Paul among the Sophists.* SNTSMS 96. Cambridge: Cambridge University Press, 1997.

Winter, Bruce W., and Andrew D. Clarke, eds. *The Book of Acts in Its Ancient Literary Setting.* Vol. 1 of *The Book of Acts in Its First-Century Setting.* Edited by Bruce W. Winter. Exeter: Paternoster, 1993.

8

The Hebrew Mission

Voices from the Margin?

Cynthia Long Westfall

INTRODUCTION

Currently, the term "mission" is a buzz word and writing a personal mission statement is a common practice in business. For business consultants, *mission* is an organization's pragmatic intention, which enables an enterprise to stay true to its *identity*. It is the reason the entity exists—it is "the sole reason for being." Mission is inextricably linked with *vision* (the view for the future, which inspires an enterprise to move forward), and *values* (the beliefs that govern behavior). Mission, vision, and values are combined together in a *strategic plan* that establishes the needs that are addressed, and the goals and objectives. It answers the questions: Why do we exist? What are we planning to do? How do we plan to get there? Who do we want to become? This terminology both gives helpful focus to the discussion of Christian mission and broadens what is relevant to the discussion. The concept of mission may be viewed as a constellation that includes the concepts of identity, values, and vision, as well as a strategic plan.[1]

While such an approach could be condemned as anachronistic, it is rather a question of definition and level of approach. The current

---

1. See, for example, "DIY Committee Guide: Vision, Mission, and Values," n. p. Accessed 5 May 2006. Online: http://www.diycommitteeguide.org/index.cfm/section/news/key/SCTN3_DIYGUIDE_2.

discussion and definition of mission parallels statements of mission in Scripture. A dominant metaphor in Scripture similar to mission according to this definition is membership in and expansion of the kingdom of God. It involves our participation in the transfer of the kingdom of the world to the rule of God with the goal stated in Rev 11:15:

> The kingdom of the world has become
> the kingdom of our Lord and of his Christ
> And he will reign for ever and ever.

An eloquent Pauline statement in Scripture that couches Christian mission in a manner that encompasses identity, vision, values, and strategy is Paul's statement about the "ministry of reconciliation" in 2 Cor 5:18–21:

> All this is from God who reconciled us to himself through Christ and gave us the ministry of reconciliation: that God was reconciling the world to himself in Christ, not counting people's sins against them. And he has committed to us the message of reconciliation. We are therefore Christ's ambassadors, as though God were making his appeal through us. We implore you on Christ's behalf: Be reconciled to God. God made him who had no sin to be sin for us, so that in him we might become the righteousness of God.

Yet, much of the discussion of Christian mission starts with a more narrow definition of mission, such as a "conscious, deliberate, organized, and extensive effort to convert others to one's religion by way of evangelization or proselytization."[2] Such definitions are concerned with a legitimate element in the church's strategic plan, but tend to limit the definition of mission to direct explicit proclamation. Consequently, some fail to find "mission consciousness" in the Hebrew Christian literature, which is understood to be merely strengthening believers and/or addressing intercommunity matters.[3] However, in agreement with John Dickerson, I believe that investigation into mission "must take into account the full range of activities which intentionally contribute to the

---

2. Köstenberger and O'Brien, *Salvation to the Ends of the Earth*, 254.

3. However, while Köstenberger and O'Brien say there was no mission in Second Temple Judaism based on their definition, they find more material on mission in the texts under consideration than most other treatments (Köstenberger and O'Brien, *Salvation to the Ends of the Earth*, 223–50). But for a discussion on mission in Second Temple Judaism, see Dickson, *Mission-Commitment*, 11–85.

goal of mission—the conversion of non-believers,"[4] which is, of course, an integral part of the reconciliation of the world to God and the transfer of the kingdom of the world to his lordship. The documents that represent Jewish Christianity in the early church offer significant developments in the areas of identity, vision, and values, which made a lasting contribution to mission, and reveal a different approach to strategy that may reflect mission in the context of persecution and crisis.

WHAT CONSTITUTES THE HEBREW MISSION IN TERMS OF IDENTITY, GEOGRAPHY, LEADERSHIP, AND CANON?

In the beginning, the earliest Christians in Jerusalem did not appear to see themselves as distinct from Judaism. They regarded themselves as the climax of Judaism and apparently continued to observe the law. They attended the temple and their faith in Jesus as the Messiah and his imminent *parousia* was within the framework of Jewish eschatological hope. At first, they had little concern for the Gentiles, except perhaps for the hope that the nations would flock to Mount Zion (Matt 10:5–6, 23; 15:24; and Matt 8:11–12; Luke 13:29; Mark 11:17; cf. Isa 56:7).

The first converts to early Christianity were Jews, both Hebrews and Hellenists, in Jerusalem. The stoning of Stephen and the subsequent persecution (Acts 7:59—8:8) shifted the margins of the early church growth to the Jews in the Diaspora. The subsequent encounters and successes with the Samaritans (Acts 8:4–8), the Ethiopian eunuch (Acts 8:26–40), Cornelius (Acts 10), and the Gentiles in Antioch (11:19–30) caught the apostles in Jerusalem by surprise.[5] Nevertheless, these allegedly accidental successes may be taken as paradigmatic in Luke's view for at least some of the Hebrew mission in the second half of the first century. That is, whatever is meant by Paul's distinction between Peter's gospel to the circumcised and Paul's gospel to the uncircumcised (Gal 2:7), Luke did not depict the Hebrew mission as restricted from reaching Gentiles.

---

4. Dickson's definition of mission is "the range of activities by which members of a religious community desirous of the conversion of outsiders seek to promote their religion to non-adherents." He includes "ethical or verbal apologetic, financial assistance of missionaries and prayer for the conversion of humankind." Dickson, *Mission-Commitment*, 10, 51.

5. Andrew Chester examines the early Christian movement in Judea and Galilee and states, "It is not clear that it ever set out to be a large, popular movement: the crowds simply came." See Chester, "Jews of Judaea and Galilee," 24.

In Acts, the Hebrew mission continued to be centered in Jerusalem and initially was led by the "pillar apostles" (Gal 1:19; 2:9). At first, Peter spearheaded the Jerusalem leadership, but also traveled and engaged in missionary activity in Samaria and the coastal regions (Acts 8:14–25; 9:32—10:48).[6] However, in AD 41, after the persecution in which James, John's brother, was killed, Peter was arrested, escaped, and then "left for another place" (Acts 12:3-17). At that time, Peter recognized James, the brother of Jesus, as the point man of the Jerusalem church who should be informed of Peter's activities. During the next nine years, Peter could well have been involved in missionary activity in areas outside of Jerusalem such as northern Asia Minor as the early traditions suggest, which includes the areas mentioned in 1 Pet 1:1.[7] Luke places Peter in Jerusalem in AD 50 as a key player in the Jerusalem Council, but that does not preclude him from traveling and returning to Jerusalem as a home base. In the Jerusalem Council, which was directly concerned with mission, James suggested the policy that accepted Gentiles into the faith without requiring them to become Jews, largely on the basis of Paul's success and Peter's application of Cornelius's conversion to the issue (Acts 15). According to Paul, Peter and "the other apostles and the Lord's brothers" customarily went on missionary journeys just as Paul did, but they had the added bonus of taking wives with them (1 Cor 9:5). With the exception of the book of Hebrews, this group of missionaries whom Paul describes was credited by the early church with writing the Jewish Christian canon, and early church tradition preserved stories about this group's subsequent outreach, ultimately placing Peter in Rome and John in Ephesus. The documents would have been understood as shaped in this context of mission.

Besides the Gospel of Matthew, the Hebrew Christian corpus consists of Hebrews, the Johannine literature including Revelation, and the rest of the general epistles, all of which have traditional apostolic associations with the exception of Hebrews. Dunn suggests that the Jewish Christian texts represent a spectrum of diversity within Jewish Christianity, ranging from the book of James, as the most Jewish Christian document, to John's Gospel, which is in dialogue with the

---

6. See E. J. Schnabel's detailed description of Peter's activity before AD 41 in Schnabel, *Early Christian Mission*, 1:703–18.

7. Ibid., 1:723–28.

Hellenistic Gnostic discussion.[8] In addition to the diversity represented in the texts, the churches in Palestine had a legalistic right wing, which had an association with James's leadership in Jerusalem (Gal 2:12), but went beyond James and opposed freedom from the law for the Gentiles. Dunn suggests that this group probably evolved into the Ebionites, who were declared heretical by the second- and third-century church. They closely resembled Jewish Christianity in its primitive stage, except for the early church's close relationship to the temple, which the Ebionites did not continue. The Ebionites appear to have "petrified and hardened" a tradition that was fluid and developing, so that eventually, "heretical Christianity was a form of stunted, underdeveloped Christianity."[9]

WHAT WERE THE CIRCUMSTANCES SURROUNDING THE HEBREW MISSION?

Lieu's description of the general situation of the second-century church is also an apt description of the context of the Hebrew Christian corpus. It was "a beleaguered church forced into an interpretation of the suffering they were enduring; opposition and persecution encourage tighter self-definition, a self-definition which is often expressed in terms which reverse the judgment made by the oppressors."[10] Each document in the Hebrew Christian corpus is shaped in the context of conflict and opposition.

The book of James reveals internal and external conflict—2:14–26 most likely reflects a conflict with Paul or some of Paul's followers,[11] but the author also addressed harsh realities that included poverty and class conflict in the community reflected in their assembly, and general suffering (2:1–17; 5:1–6, 7–11). The references to the context of suffering and persecution in 1 Peter are dominant and distinctive (1:6; 3:13–17,

---

8. See Dunn's chart in *Unity and Diversity* on p. 265. However, he discusses the Johannine literature and Jude under Hellenistic Christianity, he would place Revelation in a special apocalyptic category, and he asserts that 2 Peter represents institutionalization in the early church. Furthermore, he gives 1 Peter a special unifying status. See ibid., 265, 282–83, 303–4, 331–34, 351, 384–85.

9. Ibid., 244–45.

10. Lieu, *Neither Jew nor Greek*, 52, gives this as a general principle in the context of discussing the martyrdom of Polycarp.

11. See, for example, the range of suggestions as to how James engages with Paul in McDonald and Porter, *Early Christianity*, 532–33.

4:12–19; 5:9), so that as Goppelt suggests, the readers' situation is "characterized decisively by conflict with society."[12]

Second Peter and Jude are strident in the face of the adversity of the infiltration of false prophets and teachers into the readers' community. While the adversity can be characterized as internal, the authors are drawing the boundaries of faith in such a way as to exclude the adversaries and so characterize the problems as conflict with outsiders.

There are many hypotheses about the recipients and context of the book of Hebrews, but there is growing consensus that it addresses a community in crisis that has suffered past persecution and faces a present threat ranging from social ostracism to life-threatening persecution (2:14–15; 10:32–35; 12:1–4; 13:3, 11–13).[13] The concern is the community's failure to thrive and temptation to abandon the core of their confession. The distinctive Christology is not produced as a correction of adversaries, but rather as a vision and vehicle for spiritual perseverance and growth.[14]

The context of the Johannine literature has a similar range. While no specific context is given widespread approval for the Gospel of John, there is a consensus that the author addresses the threat of persecution (probably from the larger Jewish community), as well as the docetic heresy and a conflict over authority.[15] Similarly, 1, 2, and 3 John reflect possibly Gnostic or docetic disputes in the church concerning the genuine humanity of Christ (1 John 1:1–3; 4:2–3; 5:6; 2 John 7),[16] portraying the adversaries as outsiders, even "antichrists" who "went out from us" (1 John 2:18–19). The references to antichrists who are in anticipation of *the* antichrist indicate an emphasis on persecution as it relates to eschatology (1 John 2:18–28; 2 John 7). Finally, the book of Revelation reflects persecution of the church by the Roman government and conflict with the Jewish community (2:9). The conflict with the Roman government includes resistance of emperor worship (13:4,

---

12. Goppelt, *1 Peter*, 36.

13. See Lane, *Hebrews 1–8*, lxi–ii. See the selection of the examples of faith in ch. 11, where the theme of sojourning is accompanied by an unusual number of references to death.

14. Westfall, *Discourse Analysis of Hebrews*, 300.

15. McDonald and Porter, *Early Christianity*, 307.

16. See Marshall, *The Epistles of John*, 14–22.

15–16; 14:9–11; 15:2; 16:2; 19:20; 20:4), imprisonment (2:10), and martyrdom (2:13; 6:9; 17:6; 18:24; 19:2).

If there is a common thread in the readers' situations or in the *Sitz im Leben* of the authors, it includes the throes of the period of the "parting of the ways" with Judaism.[17] The Hebrew Christians were caught in a vise of persecution and suffering that grew tighter as the first century drew near to an end. Before 70 CE, the Hebrew mission experienced a combination of support and widespread opposition from the authorities in Jerusalem and the leaders of the synagogue. During the first war against Rome (66–74 CE), the upsurge of Jewish nationalism and the messianic associations would have driven a wedge between Jewish Christians in Palestine and their neighbors. Nevertheless, the Jewish Christians participated in the upheaval and suffering experienced by all Jews during and after the war. They were common targets of the systematic oppression of the Diaspora Jews by Roman policy and officials after the war.[18] After the destruction of the temple, Rabbinic Judaism emerged as a sect that systematically marginalized and excluded Jewish Christians from the community of Israel.[19]

Dunn accentuates the diversity in the forms of proclamation in Christian literature and attributes the differences to contextualization. He states, "These differences were often *integral* to the gospels in their different situations; it would not have been possible to abandon them in the situation which called forth that particular form of proclamation without altering its character as good news to that situation."[20] The Hebrew Christian corpus has been branded by some as so anti-Semitic that a Jew cannot read it. However, as Hereford suggests, the statements about the Jews "have meaning and relevance only when connected with controversy; they are part of the conflict which ended when the Christian church finally separated from Judaism."[21]

---

17. R. T. Herford said the separation came to a head in about 80 CE with the declaration against the Minim (Jewish Christians) officially made by the assembly of the rabbis at Jabneh and was effected in fifty years, though it is more likely that the declaration at Jabneh was the writing on the wall rather than a clear point of separation. See Herford, "Separation," 361.

18. Goodman, "Diaspora Reactions."

19. Alexander, "Parting of the Ways," 23–25.

20. Dunn, *Unity and Diversity*, 32.

21. Herford, "Separation," 367.

WHAT WAS THE TARGET GROUP(S) OF THE HEBREW MISSION?

The Hebrew mission in Judea and Galilee started with a core of converts drawn from the crowds of pilgrims at Pentecost in Jerusalem (Acts 2) and those who were in Jerusalem during the early apostolic ministry (Acts 3–5). The Hebrew mission would have had further success with the crowds that were eyewitnesses of Jesus' ministry and followers of John the Baptist.[22] According to the Gospel of John, the Samaritans responded to the gospel during Jesus' ministry (John 4:1–42), so the first racial boundary that the early Hebrew mission crossed had a precedent in Jesus' mission.

Paul spoke of the existence of three gospels in the Diaspora in Galatians: the gospel for the Gentiles or the uncircumcision (Gal 2:7), the gospel for the Jews or the circumcision (Gal 2:7), and the third gospel of the "Judaizers," which Paul attacks (Gal 1:6–9).[23] The second and third gospels are contained in the diversity of the Hebrew mission. While there is clearly tension and conflict between the proponents of the first two gospels (e.g., Gal 2:11–14), the proponents of the first two gospels are presented as recognizing the validity of the other, while the third gospel opposed the Gentile mission, and demanded that Gentiles be circumcised and keep the law.[24] Luke states that this group belonged to the party of the Pharisees (Acts 15:5). But even before Paul, the Hebrew mission was characterized by a diversity of attitude towards both Jewish tradition and the incorporation of Samaritans and Gentiles into membership. Jesus himself was more radical in his attitude towards tradition than the earliest Christian leadership, and certain Hellenists (including but not exclusively Paul) began to break away from that conservatism.[25]

Michael Goulder suggests that Judaizers, whom Paul characterizes as the third gospel, targeted Gentile Christians who were God-fearers

---

22. McHugh, "In Him was Life," 130.

23. The conflict in 2 Corinthians sounds similar, but is centered in the concept and claim of apostleship and conflict between personalities and leadership styles.

24. See Dunn, *Unity and Diversity*, 23.

25. Dunn states that they "reacted against" the conservatism (Dunn, *Unity and Diversity*, 60–65). However, it is not clear that their behavior was in reaction to the Hebrew Christians as much as a response to situations, circumstances, and opportunities they encountered in the Hellenist synagogues (such as Stephen's interaction with the opposition in Acts 6:8–10) and the forced scattering after Stephen's stoning (Acts 8:4).

who responded to the Pauline mission that served as a bridge to make them more receptive.[26] The standard view of God-fearers is based on descriptions of Cornelius and Paul's address to Gentiles in the synagogue in Psidian Antioch (Acts 10:2, 22, 35; 13:16, 26). It is believed that they were attracted by Jewish monotheism and ethics, they attended the synagogue, but balked at becoming "full members" because of the social and physical disadvantages of the crucial step of circumcision.[27] If this identity of the God-fearers is correct,[28] why would they later respond to the demand of circumcision if that was the former sticking point? It is unlikely that they would abandon Pauline Christianity in order to conform to the very practice that they were avoiding in the first place. It hardly follows that Pauline Christianity would serve as a bridge to their acceptance of circumcision. It may be more likely that Pauline Christianity provided the first exposure to Judaism, and from that they could be persuaded by Hebrew Christians to adopt a life "under the law."[29]

Acts depicts early Gentile conversions as either divinely appointed or as a by-product of the proclamation of a gospel contextualized for the Jews and/or primarily informed by and oriented to Judaism.[30] If 1 Peter is accepted as a document of the Hebrew mission, the text indicates that the recipients were largely converted Gentiles (1:14, 18; 2:9–10, 25; 3:6; 4:3–4). The characterization of the recipients in 4:3 as having left behind them a life of "doing what the Gentiles like to do" does not depict a group of God-fearers that was attracted to Jewish ethics before conversion.

26. Goulder, "Visionaries of Macedonia," see 25 and n. 1.

27. See Finn, "Godfearers Reconsidered." The attested uses of the term as specifically adherents to Judaism as opposed to full members of the synagogue are confined to two participial phrases in Acts and an early third-century inscription from Aphrodisias, which has 52 names under the heading "such as God-fearers," which differentiates the list from the full members. See Reynolds and Tannenbaum, *Jews and Godfearers at Aphrodisias*.

28. Lieu maintains that the term "God-fearers" cannot be understood "exclusively or even primarily as a religious term" where groups of God-fearers soaked in the culture of the synagogue and familiarized themselves with the Septuagint and Jewish exegesis. Rather, they may be primarily benefactors participating in a political and a primarily social act rather than a religious commitment (Lieu, "Do God-fearers Make Good Christians," 334). See also Rajak, "Jewish Community and Its Boundaries," 24.

29. Justin, *Dial.* 47.4.

30. According to Dunn, *Unity and Diversity*, 23, who accentuates the diversity of the early Christian literature, Paul's perception of gospel to the circumcision indicates that in content it was not so very different from Paul's gospel, but was appropriately contextualized for the Jews (Gal 2:2, 6–9).

Instead of understanding Paul's gospel for the Gentiles or the uncircumcision (Gal 2:7) and the gospel for the Jews or the circumcision (Gal 2:7) as involving a strict line of demarcation, the combined evidence in Acts, the Pauline corpus, and the Hebrew Christian corpus would suggest that the difference was one of approach and contextualization, and that the Hebrew mission converted Gentiles as well as Jews and the Pauline mission converted Jews as well as Gentiles.[31]

WHAT CHARACTERIZED THE GOSPEL? THE MESSAGE OF THE HEBREW MISSION

While Dunn speaks of the individuality of the proclamations and the distinctiveness of their emphases, he claims that Acts, Paul, and John share a core kerygma that is an abstraction: a risen, exalted Jesus, a call to faith, and the promise held out to faith.[32] All of these elements may not be repeated in every Hebrew Christian document, but the documents' occasional nature and purpose might account for the omissions.

Documents that mention the need for Christ see it as universal. Though John depicts Jesus as a prophet who speaks on behalf of God to the Jewish people,[33] he speaks of God's love for the entire world (John 3:16) and characterizes the situation of the world as darkness (John 1:4–5; 3:19–21; 8:12; 9:4–5; 11:9–10; 12:35–36, 46) and the absence of eternal life (John 3:36; 5:24). In 2 Pet 3:9, it says that God does not want anyone to perish but for all to come to repentance. Though the 144,000 that are sealed in Rev 7:1–8 are from all the tribes of Israel, Revelation depicts the faithful who have come out of the great tribulation, who "washed their robes and made them white in the blood of the lamb," as a great multitude from every tribe, people, and language (Rev 7:9–16). In the

---

31. Note that in Acts, the explicit reference to the conversion of the followers of John the Baptist is a story from the Pauline mission in Acts 19:1–7, and Paul's missionary strategy of entering new territory by starting with the synagogue and preaching to the Jews before turning to the Gentiles is well-documented. For a recent discussion of the understanding of Paul's theological treatment of the priority of Israel and his relationship with the Jewish people, see Das, *Paul and the Jews*, 187–96. However, in Acts, Luke depicts Paul as also contextualizing his message to Gentile interests and literature (Acts 17:16–33), whereas the Hebrew Christian mission stories and documents are steeped in the Old Testament.

32. Dunn, *Unity and Diversity*, 29–31.

33. Marshall, *New Testament Theology*, 517.

New Jerusalem, the nations will walk by the light of the glory of God and the kings of the earth will "bring their splendor into it" (21:24).

The identification of Jesus as the Messiah and the development of the implications in terms of royalty, the temple, and the *parousia* is a particular emphasis of the Hebrew Christian texts.[34] Furthermore, a primary continuity between Jesus and the Hebrew mission is "the basic association of messiahship with suffering."[35]

Bultmann claims that "faith" is the term that most clearly distinguishes earliest Christianity rather than "orthodoxy."[36] If a suggested dating of the Hebrew Christian corpus ranges from the earliest document as James to the later documents of Johannine literature, there appears to be a progression. The earlier literature shows a concern with faith that is better expressed by action than profession (Jas 2:14–26); this progresses to a growing concern with the content of belief and the identity of the people of God.[37] With the activity of proclamation, the evangelists put the central element(s) of the new faith in a concise and explicit form in a particular context. The Hebrew mission makes the most serious effort in its proclamation to maintain the oneness of God without detracting from Jesus' Lordship, primarily in John's Gospel, and to a lesser extent in Hebrews. In John's Gospel, rather than repentance as a key component, it is believing that leads to life, and the promise of life is a sharp "either-or," as opposed to Paul's depiction of life as a process with an "already-not yet" dimension. However, as Dunn suggests, these may be broadly equivalent, and the apparent diversity is probably more due to the personal preferences and language choices of the proclaimers.[38]

---

34. Westfall, "Messianic Themes." Dunn asserts, "Where the confrontation between Judaism and Christianity remained a factor of importance in the development of confessional Christianity, the confession 'Jesus is the Christ' retained its significance and importance . . . ; but almost nowhere else" (Dunn, *Unity and Diversity*, 44–45).

35. Dunn, *Unity and Diversity*, 43.

36. Bultmann, *Theology of the New Testament*, 2:30, 370.

37. According to Dunn, the two documents that most clearly express the Jewish Christian understanding of the kerygma are Matthew and James. Though Dunn treats Luke and Matthew as unified in the kerygma, he suggests, "It is doubtful whether Paul could have ever given wholehearted approval to the two NT documents which most clearly express the Jewish Christian understanding of kerygma—Matthew and James" (Dunn, *Unity and Diversity*, 26).

38. Ibid., 28–29.

HOW DID THE HEBREW MISSION CONTRIBUTE TO THE EARLY CHURCH'S IDENTITY?

The Hebrew Christian documents develop elements of identity concerning Jesus and the people of God that draw heavily from the Old Testament and the Maccabean and apocryphal traditions.[39] The development of Christology is the greatest theological contribution of the Hebrew corpus and defines the circle of membership. The Christology of the book of Hebrews concerning his exalted position, particularly in ch. 1, appeals for exclusive allegiance to Christ. The author makes a primary contribution to the crucial understanding of Jesus' atoning work by teaching about his high priesthood and his self-sacrifice with a once-for-all offering of sin, explained in terms of the Jewish priesthood and sacrificial system.

The forging of Johannine Christology took place in the context of missiological and apologetic Jewish challenges and controversies about the person of Jesus. Marshall summarizes the description of Jesus in the Gospel of John:

> Jesus is presented unequivocally as the incarnate Word, through whom God created the world and communicates with it, and more personally as his Son who was with the Father before he came into the world and will return to him. His place within the divine identity is clearly depicted. This Christology is also expressed in terms of his being Messiah and Son of Man. Jesus acts as God's messenger and his mission establishes the possibility of salvation. In so doing he brings glory to God.[40]

At the same time as he clarifies Jesus' divinity, John places an increased emphasis on Jesus' humanity, most likely to counter emerging gnosticism in the form of docetism. As a result, John delivers what Chester calls the most highly developed Christology in the New Testament.[41] His emphasis on belief complements his content concerning the identity of

---

39. Concerning John, D. Moody Smith writes, "It is in the interest of the evangelist not to destroy or negate Judaism, but to remain in dialogue with it . . . John holds traditional Jewish messianism and his own distinctive Christology in creative tension" (Smith, "John," 109).

40. Marshall, *New Testament Theology*, 525. As Dunn observes, John overlapped the exalted Jesus with the historic Jesus so that "the glory that was to be his by virtue of his death, resurrection and ascension" was "already visible in his earthly life" (Dunn, *Unity and Diversity*, 27).

41. Chester, "Parting of the Ways, 305.

Christ. John is concerned with a central mission tenant: that the readers share this understanding of the identity of Jesus and believe in him.

The three Johannine epistles also share a central concern with Jesus' identity forged in response to a docetic challenge. They are concerned with the importance of correct belief about Jesus and make a strong statement that "Christian salvation is jeopardized if there is a false belief about Jesus."[42] The most important content of the belief includes that he is the Christ (1 John 2:22; 3:23; 4:2; 5:1), he is the Son of God (1 John 4:15; 5:5, 10, 12), and he "came in the flesh" (1 John 4:2; 2 John 7). There is a missiological concern for the content of faith that is central for proclamation, and for membership.

The identity of group membership developed in this corpus beyond the circle of belief defined by Christology. Certainly in the Johannine literature, the statement that love is the "mark of the Christian" (John 13:34–35; 15:12–13, 17; 1 John 3:10–24; 4:7–21) is a dominant and distinctive theme for the group's identity. However, it is interesting to see how the Hebrew corpus relates the Gentiles to the Jews and brings forward terminology that formerly described Israel to define the church. Jesus in John states that he has other sheep that are not in "this sheep pen," and that they will listen to him and "there shall be one flock and one shepherd" (John 10:16). Both Hebrews and 1 Peter demonstrate continuity between Israel and the church. This argument permeates Hebrews, but comes to a climax in ch. 12, where the examples of faith in ch. 11 are made perfect together with believers and are joined together in a festal assembly.[43] Old Testament imagery for Israel is utilized in the description of the church as God's flock (1 Pet 5:2–4) and the house of God (1 Pet 4:17). However, it is 1 Pet 2:1–10 that is particularly marked in applying to the church a number of phrases that describe Jews in the Old Testament, particularly in v. 9: "a chosen people, a royal priesthood, a holy nation, God's special possession." As Marshall states,

> We have one of the most powerful statements in the New Testament identifying the company of believers as the people of God; language used to describe the privileged position of the Jews as the people of God in the Old Testament is now deliberately applied to the readers so that they are identified as this people.[44]

---

42. Marshall, *New Testament Theology*, 540.
43. Westfall, *Discourse Analysis of Hebrews*, 275.
44. Marshall, *New Testament Theology*, 654.

Such terminology was possibly meant to motivate the Jews to recognize that the church was the real Israel and to join the church, but it was addressed to an audience that explicitly included Gentiles.

WHAT WAS THE CONTRIBUTION OF THE HEBREW MISSION TO THE CHURCH'S VISION?

The Hebrew texts that are most concerned with the vision of the mission in the New Testament corpus are Hebrews, 2 Peter, and Revelation. They are concerned with the future, and inspiring believers to move forward. The vision of Hebrews is significant because it utilizes and applies Jewish history, imagery, and institutions to Christianity. It demonstrates continuity and ties between Israel and the church, not only in terms of the institutions of temple, covenant, sacrifice, and priesthood (Heb 8–10), and the examples of "the ancients of old" in Hebrews 11, but also in terms of the opportunity of entering the rest (Heb 3–4) and the readers' location and goal of heavenly Jerusalem on Mount Zion (Heb 12:18–29). The believers are urged to move forward to enter the rest (4:1, 11), to grow to maturity (6:1–2), to stimulate each other ethically (10:24–25), and to view their lives as a race in a festal assembly in heavenly Jerusalem with the goal of righteousness and peace (12:1–17).[45] Some suggest that Hebrews is written to convert a particular Jewish community. While the author's primary target is a Hebrew Christian community in crisis and in danger of failing to grow and leaving the faith (Heb 6:1–12; 10:26–39), there is an implicit appeal to the larger Jewish community.

Rowland notes that apocalyptic writing has "frequently been a spur for those engaged in movements of change where visions of hope have fuelled powerful societal forces demanding change in the existing order." He concludes that this is exactly the function it performed for Christians: "The Elect were offered conviction of their identity and certainty to engage in that struggle to actualize their visions of the eschatological reign of God."[46] Apocalyptic was a popular form of literature, particularly among the Diaspora Jews, possibly because of its controversial subversive political nature that confronted the oppressors of Israel covertly. Therefore, though Revelation is directed to the churches, there is a popular appeal and within the vision there is an evangelistic appeal

---

45. Westfall, *Discourse Analysis of Hebrews*, 295–300.
46. Rowland, "Parting of the Ways," 235.

to "hear it and take it to heart because the time is near" (Rev 1:3). Note the final invitation: "The Spirit and the bride say, 'Come!' And let those who hear say, 'Come!' Let those who are thirsty come, and let all who wish take the free gift of the water of life" (Rev 22:17).

WHAT WAS THE CONTRIBUTION OF THE HEBREW MISSION TO THE EARLY CHURCH'S VALUES?

The Hebrew Christian corpus considered holiness and reverence to be integral to the proclamation of the mission. Pleas and exhortations for believers to be holy are so prevalent in the texts that for our purposes only a few will be highlighted. For James, faithful righteous actions speak louder than orthodox confessions (Jas 2:18–19). In 1 Peter, purity and reverence are powerful behavior that can result in conversion without proclamation (1 Pet 3:1–2). In 1 John, the author insists that a sinless life is essential for living in the light (1 John 1:5–10; 3:4–10). Jude's attack on false teachers is particularly directed at ungodliness and immorality (Jude 4). Revelation's indictment of ungodly behavior (e.g., Rev 22:15), and plea for no compromise regarding immorality, materialism, and false teaching (e.g., chs. 2–3) characterize the entire text. The Hebrew Christian literature consistently sees an integral relationship between mission and values and places a high priority on communicating those values in community and in proclamation. A formulation of the Christian mission in terms of its values is in 1 Pet 1:15–16: "But just as he who called you is holy, so be holy in all you do, for it is written: 'Be holy, because I am holy.'"

WHAT WAS THE STRATEGY OF THE HEBREW MISSION?

It is important to note that both Luke and Paul describe the Hebrew Christian apostles and the brothers of Jesus as going on mission trips in the same way as Paul, and show Peter and John involved in extensive proclamation in a number of different contexts, so that the Hebrew Christian models for strategy in mission and proclamation are depicted as being similar to Paul's. However, in the Hebrew Christian canon, there are strategies other than explicit and direct proclamation that are mission, and there is an overriding conviction that God is responsible for the conversion of unbelievers.

In 1 Peter, unjust suffering for Christ combined with blameless righteous behavior is a mission strategy (e.g., 1 Pet 3:13–18). The participation in Christ's sufferings brings others to God in the same way that Christ's suffering brought us to God (1 Pet 3:18; 4:13). There are three desired outcomes: questions, shame, and faith. People who view our unjust suffering should be motivated to ask questions and we should always be prepared to give an answer about our hope (1 Pet 3:15). If we answer with gentleness and respect, with a clear conscience, the people who slander us will be put to shame (1 Pet 3:15–16). The goal of playing our part in suffering and being the recipients of abuse because of our faith is to bring others to life (1 Pet 4:6).[47] The Jewish sense of being a race or a people that proclaims a sense of identity in the face of adversity and possible annihilation was evident in the Maccabean period. The strategy of proclamation takes an additional twist in 1 Peter when he urges the wives of unbelievers to submit to their husbands as a mission strategy so that they "may be won over without words by the behavior of their wives, when they see the purity and reverence of your lives" (1 Pet 3:1–2). The suffering and righteous behavior in Peter is seen to be a proof of identity of the people of God and a testimony that sometimes works without words.

In Revelation, the seven churches addressed are described as golden lampstands, which are symbols of their witness to the world (Rev 1:12–13). The author's vision views suffering and martyrdom as having a crucial role in the witness of the seven churches it addresses (Rev 2:3, 9–10, 13) and in the programmatic visions (Rev 6:9–11; 7:9–17; 11:7–12; 13:5–10; 20:4). As in 1 Peter, the people of God carry the mission forward through the combination of suffering and righteousness (e.g., Rev 14:1–5). Explicit proclamation is a property of the book itself, which is a prophecy from Jesus (Rev 1:3; 22:6–19), and of the testimony of the two witnesses that are appointed to prophecy and work miracles for 1,260 days (Rev 11:3–12). However, those who hear a reading of Revelation are

---

47. Compare the model of suffering in 1 Peter with the *Martyrdom of Polycarp*, which describes Jesus' passion and Polycarp's martyrdom and compelled the whole crowd to be amazed at the difference between the unbelievers and the elect (16:1). Was this intended for believers to encourage a tighter self-definition or directed to a pagan audience? Lieu suggests that since Polycarp refused to defend himself to the crowd (persuade the people) because they were not worthy of any explanation (10:2) that it was directed to believers. Lieu, *Neither Jew nor Greek*, 52.

to respond together with Jesus, the prophecy, the Spirit, and the entire church (the bride) with issuing the invitation: "Come!" (Rev 22:17).

The activity of God in mission is a distinctive thread of the Hebrew Christian canon. According to Köstenberger and O'Brien, the Gospel of John is far more concerned with defining and describing the mission of Jesus than it is with the mission of the disciples.[48] Furthermore, John develops the role of the Spirit in conversion in a distinctive way, so that the Spirit convicts the world of sin, righteousness, and judgment (John 16:8–11). In the Petrine literature, the sufferings of Christ bring us to God (1 Pet 3:18) and he is patient and giving time for repentance (1 Pet 3:9). As in the closing of Revelation, the church and individual believers have the privilege, opportunity, and responsibility to join and participate in the salvation that belongs to God (Rev 7:10). He is responsible for the program in which he will reign and be worshipped by the nations (Rev 15:3–4).

The mission of suffering is complementary to Paul's personal testimony of participating in Christ's sufferings (Phil 3:10) and filling up "what is still lacking in regards to Christ's afflictions" (Col 1:24). Still, there are a few differences. Paul presents this kind of suffering as his personal experience and the vindication of his ministry (2 Cor 6:3–10). He encourages mature believers to have the same point of view as if it were their choice (Phil 3:15). However, the Hebrew Christians are participating in the sufferings of Christ as a group and as a normal experience (1 Pet 4:12). This is reflective of the peculiar stress and persecution that the Hebrew Christians are facing as Jews in the Roman Empire and/or as Christians in the Jewish community.

DID THE HEBREW MISSION FAIL?

Alexander claims that "Jewish Christianity was finally destroyed between the upper and nether millstone of triumphant Gentile Christianity and triumphant Rabbinism."[49] This is certainly true of the Ebionites. The Ebionites appear to be the heirs of early Jewish Christianity in that they upheld the law.[50] They professed adoptionism regarding the sonship of

---

48. Köstenberger and O'Brien, *Salvation to the Ends of the Earth*, 203.

49. Alexander, "Parting of the Ways," 24.

50. David Bosch asserts, "It was clear that the Jerusalem party's concern was not mission, but consolidation; not grace, but law; not crossing frontiers, but fixing them; not life, but doctrine; not movement, but institution" (Bosch, *Transforming Mission*, 51).

Christ, and they gave James prominence while they denigrated Paul.⁵¹ This conservative wing within Jewish Christianity lost: their adoptionist view of Christ was considered heretical, they lost the competition for preeminence to Paul, the practice of circumcision of Gentiles was eventually considered heretical, and was even suspect among Christians of Jewish heritage, and they lost the bid for the control of Judaism.⁵² Rabbinic Judaism emerged victorious in the competition for the definition of Judaism,⁵³ and Gentile Christianity claimed to be the true Israel, and so claimed to replace Hebrew Christianity.⁵⁴

However, by the same token, one may say that a similar trajectory from Gentile Christianity failed. There was a tendency to dismiss Judaism and negate the value of the Mosaic law.⁵⁵ This trajectory culminated in Marcion who wanted a Judaism-free Christianity and attempted to eliminate the Hebrew Christian documents from the canon. In the same way,

---

This is an apt description of the Ebionites and the trajectory that produced them. It is not as clear that Bosch is interpreting James and his actions at the Jerusalem Council correctly.

51. Hostility toward Paul was evident in Jewish Christianity. There was tension, confrontation, and competition between Paul and Jewish-Christian leaders including James and Peter that is evidenced in Acts 15 and 21, Galatians, 1–2 Corinthians, and James. Acts 21 indicates that at the time of Paul's arrest, hostile reports about Paul were being circulated in the Jerusalem church, and were taken seriously by James.

52. Bosch writes, "It proved unable, in the long run, to make Jews feel at home. Beginning as a religious movement that worked exclusively among Jews, it changed, in the forties of the first century to a movement for Jews and Gentiles alike, but wound up proclaiming its message to Gentiles only." See Bosch, *Transforming Mission*, 51. Herford states, "Christianity did not begin to move in the same direction as that in which Judaism had moved hitherto; Judaism continued to move on in the same direction as it had formerly done, and Christianity, from its point of origin, moved in a quite different direction. Judaism did not give up its momentum to Christianity and remain motionless. Christianity started by reason of a fresh impulse, otherwise there would be no Christianity." Herford, "Separation," 363.

53. Patzia, *Emergence of the Church*, 151, writes, "Rabbinic Judaism triumphed within the Palestinian Jewish communities." Bosch suggests, "After the war Pharisaic Judaism became far too xenophobic to tolerate anything but a hard-line, exclusive Jewish approach. Jewish Christians were forced to choose between the church and the synagogue, and it appears that many chose the latter" (Bosch, *Transforming Mission*, 51).

54. Patzia claims that Jewish Christianity "was largely replaced by the Gentile-Christian church, which now claimed to be the true Israel" (Patzia, *Emergence of the Church*, 151).

55. Das claims that this was already occurring in Rome and was addressed by Paul in Romans (Das, *Paul and the Jews*, 191).

Marcion was declared heretical, and the Hebrew Scripture continued to be authoritative for the church.

As Dunn suggests, the parting of the ways between Judaism and Christianity really occurred within Jewish Christianity first.[56] It was the Hebrew Christian canon that countered adoptionism with the high Christology that alienated the Jews in the Gospel of John, the Johannine epistles, and Hebrews.[57] If there was conflict between Paul and the apostolic leadership, there is also evidence of conflict between John and Peter in the Gospel of John—these are the kinds of personality clashes that characterize relationships within church leadership and argue for the historicity of the documents. The decision of the Jerusalem Council not to require the circumcision of Gentiles was momentous and certainly provided a stumbling block for the future conversion of Jews to the church, but this was not a compromise, a concession, a trick, or a coup, but rather a mutual decision in which Peter and James played a key role. There is no evidence in the Hebrew Christian corpus that they considered it their vision, goal, expectation, or responsibility to dominate or convert all of Judaism. Rather, the experience of suffering, ostracism, and persecution is portrayed not only as expected but as part of the mission strategy in 1 Peter. Hebrews portrayed the life of faith as sojourning (Heb 11) and exhorted believers to go to Christ outside of the camp and bear the disgrace that he bore (Heb 13:12). If Gentile Christianity claimed to be the true Israel, it is because the Petrine epistles, the Johannine literature, and the author of Hebrews provided the primary justification to use the title. The unity between Jew and Gentile in the church that was forged in the first century, and the application of the status of Israel to the uncircumcised, were prohibitive for the attraction of the majority of Jews to the gospel, but that was not the immediate goal or expectation of the Hebrew Christian canon. Therefore, the recent research that tends to restrict the meaning of the term Jewish Christianity to "the enforced maintenance of Jewish practice among Christians everywhere in the church"[58] or presents the

---

56. Dunn, *Unity and Diversity*, 261.

57. Chester stipulates, "It can of course be claimed that it is precisely the high Christology of the Fourth Gospel, and the nature of the claims made about Jesus, that forces the division between Judaism and Christianity, and there is surely some truth in that; but we have also to ask to what extent the formulation of a Christology of this kind was meant to work retrospectively, to justify the situation in which the Johannine community found itself" (Chester, "Parting of the Ways," 305).

58. Vallée, *Shaping of Christianity*, 35.

goal of Jewish Christianity as winning the heart of Israel misrepresents the diversity within Jewish Christianity and particularly ignores the theology and mission of the Hebrew Christian corpus. To call the Hebrew mission a failure is to judge it by a triumphalistic standard that its canon does not support, and to fail to appreciate that "The blood of the martyrs is the seed of the church" (Tertullian), which was at least one of its explicit strategies.

BIBLIOGRAPHY

Alexander, P. S. "'The Parting of the Ways' from the Perspective of Rabbinic Judaism." In *Jews and Christians: The Parting of the Ways A.D. 70 to 135*, edited by J. D. G. Dunn, 1–25. Tübingen: Mohr, 1992.

Bosch, David J. *Transforming Mission: Paradigm Shifts in Theology of Mission*. American Society of Missiology Series 16. Maryknoll, NY: Orbis, 1991.

Bultmann, R. *Theology of the New Testament*. Vol. 2. ET. London: SCM, 1955.

Chester, Andrew. "The Jews of Judaea and Galilee." In *Early Christian Thought in Its Jewish Context*, edited by J. Barclay and J. Sweet, 9–26. Cambridge: Cambridge University Press, 1996.

———. "The Parting of the Ways: Eschatology and Messianic Hope." In *Jews and Christians: The Parting of the Ways A.D. 70 to 135*, edited by J. D. G. Dunn, 239–306. Tübingen: Mohr, 1992.

Das, A. A. *Paul and the Jews*. Peabody, MA: Hendrickson, 2003.

Dickson, J. P. *Mission-Commitment in Ancient Judaism and in the Pauline Communities: The Shape, Extent and Background of Early Christian Mission*. WUNT 159. Tübingen: Mohr Siebeck, 2003.

Dunn, J. D. G. *Unity and Diversity in the New Testament: An Inquiry into the Character of Earliest Christianity*. 2nd ed. Harrisberg, PA: Trinity Press International, 1990.

Finn, T. "The Godfearers Reconsidered." *CBQ* 47 (1985) 75–84.

Goodman, M. "Diaspora Reactions to the Destruction of the Temple." In *Jews and Christians: The Parting of the Ways A.D. 70 to 135*, edited by J. D. G. Dunn, 27–38. Tübingen: Mohr, 1992.

Goppelt, L. A. *A Commentary on 1 Peter*. Ed. F. Hahn. Trans. J. E. Alsup. Grand Rapids: Eerdmans, 1988.

Goulder, M. "The Visionaries of Macedonia." *JSNT* 43 (1991) 15–39.

Herford, R. T. "The Separation of Christianity from Judaism." In *Origins of Judaism: Religion, History and Literature in Late Antiquity: A Twenty-Volume Collection of Essays and Articles*, edited by J. Neusner and W. S. Green, 3.1: 359–70. New York: Garland Publishing, 1990.

Köstenberger, A. J., and P. T. O'Brien. *Salvation to the Ends of the Earth: A Biblical Theology of Mission*. NSBT 11. Downers Grove, IL: InterVarsity, 2001.

Lane, W. L. *Hebrews 1–8*. WBC 47A–B. Dallas: Word, 1991.

Lieu, J. M. "Do God-fearers Make Good Christians?" In *Crossing the Boundaries: Essays in Biblical Interpretation in Honour of Michael D. Goulder*, edited by S. E. Porter, P. Joyce, and D. E. Orton, 329–45. BIS 8. Leiden: Brill, 1994.

———. *Neither Jew nor Greek? Constructing Early Christianity*. London: T. & T. Clark, 2002.

Marshall, I. H. *The Epistles of John*. NICNT. Grand Rapids: Eerdmans, 1978.

———. *New Testament Theology: Many Witnesses, One Gospel*. Downers Grove, IL: InterVarsity, 2004.

McDonald, L. M., and S. E. Porter. *Early Christianity and Its Sacred Literature*. Peabody, MA: Hendrikson, 2000.

McHugh, J. "In Him Was Life." In *Jews and Christians: The Parting of the Ways A.D. 70 to 135*, edited by J. D. G. Dunn, 123–58. Tübingen: Mohr, 1992.

Patzia, A. G. *The Emergence of the Church: Context, Growth, Leadership and Worship*. Downers Grove, IL: InterVarsity, 2001.

Rajak, T. "The Jewish Community and Its Boundaries." In *The Jews among Pagans and Christians*, edited by J. Lieu, J. North, and T. Rajak, 9–28. London: Routledge, 1992.

Reynolds, J., and R. Tannenbaum. *Jews and Godfearers at Aphrodisias*. Cambridge Philological Society Supplement 12. Cambridge: Cambridge University Press, 1987.

Rowland, C. "The Parting of the Ways: The Evidence of Jewish and Christian Apocalyptic and Mystical Material." In *Jews and Christians: The Parting of the Ways A.D. 70 to 135*, edited by J. D. G. Dunn, 213–37. Tübingen: Mohr, 1992.

Schnabel, E. J. *Early Christian Mission. I. Jesus and the Twelve*. Downers Grove, IL: InterVarsity, 2004.

Smith, D. Moody. "John." In *Early Christian Thought in Its Jewish Context*, edited by J. Barclay and J. Sweet, 96–111. Cambridge: Cambridge University Press, 1996.

Vallée, G. *The Shaping of Christianity: The History and Literature of Its Formative Centuries (100–800)*. New York: Paulist, 1999.

Westfall, C. L. *A Discourse Analysis of Hebrews: Relationship between Form and Meaning*. London: T. & T. Clark, 2006.

———. "Messianic Themes of Temple, Enthronement and Victory in Hebrews and the General Epistles." In *The Messiah in the Old and New Testaments*, edited by S. E. Porter, 210–29. MNTS. Grand Rapids: Eerdmans, 2007.

9

Bible and Mission

Missiology and Biblical Scholarship in Dialogue

MICHAEL W. GOHEEN

INTRODUCTION

I REMEMBER WELL MY first course on biblical foundations for mission.[1] We moved rather quickly through the Old Testament since there was not much missionary gold to be mined there—or so we believed. Somehow the extermination of the Canaanites just did not seem to fit our view of mission. We dealt with Jonah, Ruth, and Isaiah 40–66 since they fit more readily. The New Testament more promptly yielded its missionary gold but there were still favorites—"go and make disciples," "you will be my witnesses to the ends of the earth," and so forth. The problem was that, sitting in that evangelical Bible college, situated as it was in the revivalist tradition of the early twentieth century, we all knew what mission was. All we needed was a biblical foundation to justify it. Our point of departure was an already existing missionary enterprise, to which we all joyfully offered our commitment. Through this lens we looked for missionary texts and found those that fit our paradigm, that is, a geographical expansionist understanding of mission that highlights sending from one (Christian) place to another (pagan) place. It did not matter that on closer scrutiny Jonah did not really fit in any other way

---

1. See Bosch, "Reflections on Biblical Models of Mission."

beyond crossing the water or that the "go" of the Great Commission was not an imperative at all.

These comments are not meant in the least to be disparaging. My point is simply that when we examined the Bible's teaching on mission, our pre-existing understanding or our anticipatory fore-structures of mission dictated what we saw in the Scripture. Thus we did not bring our missionary practice to the Bible to be critiqued, shaped, and developed. Rather endeavors familiar to all of us were legitimized by divine authority. I want to make clear I am not interested in joining the bandwagon that bashes the modern missionary movement of the nineteenth and twentieth centuries. I am grateful for what was accomplished and believe there was much that was biblical about it. My purpose is to raise at the beginning of this paper the hermeneutical issue that "where we stand helps to direct our gaze and influences what we see in Scripture."[2]

Interestingly, if mission advocates saw a unidirectional, geographical mission enterprise, it seems that many in the guild of New Testament studies saw nothing, or very little, about mission in the Bible. At least, that is what Elisabeth Schüssler Fiorenza observed thirty years ago:

> Exegetical inquiry often depends upon the theological and cultural presuppositions with which it approaches its texts. Historical scholarship therefore judges the past from the perspective of its own concepts and values. Since for various reasons religious propaganda, mission and apologetics are not very fashionable topics in the contemporary religious scene, these issues have also been widely neglected in New Testament scholarship.[3]

However, things are changing today. Throughout the twentieth century numerous factors have challenged this view of mission. Perhaps the two most important factors are the dramatic rise, growth, and vitality of the Majority World church with its various expressions of the gospel, alongside the parallel marginalization of the church in the West. In the International Missionary Council world conferences between Tambaram (1938) and Willingen (1952), each of the fundamental assumptions that undergirded a colonialist view of mission broke down. The separation of mission and church was challenged; it was advocated that the church is missionary by its very nature. The division of the world between the Christian West and the pagan Third World dissolved; the West is as much

2. Green, "Recovering Mission-Church."
3. Schüssler Fiorenza, "Miracles, Mission, and Apologetics," 1.

a mission field as the Third World—mission is in all six continents; mission as geographical expansion gave way to an understanding of mission as the task of the whole church wherever it was to witness to the whole gospel in the whole world.

With these changes, it is not surprising to see the importance of a return to Scripture to inquire anew about what the Bible says about mission. This book is part of a growing recognition of the need to return to Scripture afresh to bring our thinking and practice of mission under the authority of God's Word. Can our new situation enable us to see dimensions of mission in Scripture we have not seen before? Nicholas Lash has suggested that

> If the questions to which ancient authors sought to respond in terms available to them within their cultural horizons are to be "heard" today with something like their original force and urgency, they have first to be "heard" as questions that challenge us with comparable seriousness. And if they are to be thus heard, they must first be articulated in terms available to us within *our* cultural horizons. There is thus a sense in which the articulation of what the text might "mean" today is a necessary condition of hearing what that text "originally meant."[4]

Our interpretation of the past is made possible by anticipatory forestructures that are oriented to present concerns. This orientation opens up interpretive categories that allow us to interpret the text, and understand the original concern of the author who is likewise engaged with the self-same matter at hand. Perhaps with our "raised consciousness of mission"[5] we can see themes in the biblical text we did not see before. Joel Green speaks of a "missional reframing." What he asks about Luke–Acts can be asked about the whole of Scripture:

> With the image of "reframing" I want to call to our attention the way picture frames draw out different emphases in the pictures they hold. Similarly, even if the essential nature of the church has not changed, new frames bring to the forefront of our thinking and practices fresh emphases. If we take seriously the missional orientation of the work of Jesus and his followers as these are

---

4. Lash, "What Might Martyrdom Mean," 17–18.
5. LeGrand, *Unity and Plurality*, xiv.

narrated in the Gospel of Luke and Acts of the Apostles, what do we see?[6]

With an older understanding of mission inadequate, and a growing awareness of our missionary calling in our own culture, what do we see?

This paper will engage the preceding chapters in this book on Bible and mission. I will dialogue with key themes mentioned in the papers that are important in missiological discussion.

PARTICIPATING IN THE *MISSIO DEI*

Perhaps the first question that we need to ask is: What do we mean by mission? The word itself does not appear in the Bible. In fact, the Jesuits were the first to use the word in its Latin form (*missio*) to describe the work of spreading the Christian faith among people (and this included Protestants!) who were not part of the Roman Catholic Church. From that point on the word became primarily associated with the spread of the Christian faith from the Western world to the non-West. By the early nineteenth century, this kind of "foreign missions had become the new orthodoxy."[7] Under the weight of the factors mentioned above—growth of the Third World church, the decline of the Western church, the fall of colonialism—this view of mission has come under attack. From the 1950s on, coinciding with this attack, has come a striking increase in the use of the term "mission," and a broadening of its meaning. We might well ask if the word is useful.

Recognising the dangers of anachronism, Cynthia Westfall asks in her chapter whether or not the current use of the term "mission," found in the contemporary language of "mission statements," language that speaks of purpose and identity, might not be a helpful starting point.[8] To use my language, would this be a helpful anticipatory fore-structure or interpretive category that would enable us get hold of Scripture's teaching?

Christopher Wright believes it is. In his book on the mission of God, perhaps a book that has taken us further down the road of a missional hermeneutics than any other to date, Wright speaks of God's mission as the long-term purpose or goal of God to renew the creation.

---

6. Green, "Rediscovering Mission-Church."
7. J. A. Andrew, quoted by Hutchison, *Errand to the World*, 60.
8. Westfall, "Hebrew Mission," 187–88.

Our mission is to participate in God's redemptive purposes for the sake of the world. Wright puts it this way: *"Fundamentally, our mission (if it is biblically informed and validated) means our committed participation as God's people, at God's invitation and command, in God's own mission, within the history of God's world for the redemption of God's creation."*[9] So it is playing our part in the purpose of God narrated in the biblical story that gives us our identity as God's people.

Wright draws on a shift that has taken place in the latter part of the twentieth century in missiology toward understanding mission as the mission of the *Triune God*. The emphasis is on what God is doing for the redemption of the world. Thereafter, consideration is given to how the church participates in God's redeeming mission. Karl Barth was the first modern theologian to connect mission with the intra-Trinitarian sending of God—the Father sends the Son, the Father and Son send the Spirit, Jesus sends the church to continue his mission in the power of the Spirit. This sending of God was an old theological theme that went back to Augustine. Now it was connected to the church's mission. It became popular in mission circles after the Willingen Ecumenical Missionary Conference in 1952. Its most famous statement reflects this: "There is no participation in Christ without participation in his mission to the world. That by which the church receives its existence is that by which it is also given its world mission. 'As the Father hath sent me, even so send I you.'"[10] Following that conference Karl Hartenstein coined the term *missio Dei* to refer to this connection of mission to the Trinity. Its use, while understood in different ways, has become widespread in missiology throughout all the confessional traditions of the church.

Michael Knowles builds his paper on mission in Matthew and Mark on the notion of the *missio Dei*. The burden of Knowles's paper is to emphasize that mission is first of all *God's* activity, and to relativize the church's role in the spread of the gospel by highlighting the failure and weakness of the disciples: ". . . the 'gospel' of God's kingdom flourishes and bears fruit in spite of them."[11] This is an important insight in view of the anthropocentric and triumphalist way mission has been understood and practiced for the last two centuries, shaped as it has been by the Enlightenment. In fact, this is the primary reason the language of *missio*

---

9. Wright, *The Mission of God*, 22–23. His emphasis.
10. Goodall, ed., *Missions under the Cross*, 190.
11. Knowles, "Mark, Matthew, and Mission," 76.

Dei has emerged.[12] I believe Knowles's emphasis is correct, although I would want to make sure that emphasizing the failure of the disciples does not provide an excuse for the church today to fail in its call to be a living embodiment of God's salvation. In fact, it is in Matthew where the theme of faithful obedience finds its strongest expressions.

I want to flag, however, important insights in Knowles's paper that may not be the main burden of his argument but are integral to his discussion, and are important themes in current missiology surrounding God's mission, Jesus' mission, and the disciples' mission in the Gospels.

- To understand our ecclesial and missional identity, it is essential to return to the historical origins of the disciple community in Jesus' mission. The story told in the Gospels is our story; the disciple community formed in the Gospels is the nucleus of the church.

- The first sending is the sending of Jesus by the Father to make known the kingdom of God in word, deed, and life to Israel. Jesus' mission is rooted in God's mission.[13]

- In the context of this kingdom mission, Jesus calls and forms a disciple community. That disciple community is first the *object* of God's missionary concern and only after that do the disciples participate as *instruments* of his mission.[14]

- From the beginning, calling, discipleship, and mission belong together. This community is called to participate in Jesus' mission by imitating and continuing the mission of Jesus. Thus mission is central to the identity of this community from the start.[15]

- This mission to make known the gospel of the kingdom of God is thus broader than evangelism. Their mission is to follow Jesus

---

12. "To understand this new develoment [of the *missio Dei*], it is necessary to go back to the Enlightenment which, for the first time in history, did not regard mission as God's very own work but as a purely human endeavour. Thereafter, a very anthropocentric theology emerged, which intentionally severed the . . . strong link between mission . . . and the doctrine of the Trinity" (Jongeneel, *Philosophy, Science, and Theology of Mission*, 60).

13. Cf. Knowles, "Mark, Matthew, and Mission," 65.

14. Cf. ibid., 66–67.

15. Cf. ibid., 66.

in the breadth of his mission. It involves witness to the salvation of God's kingdom in word, in deed, and in communal and individual life.[16] It is to "merely live out a new identity as companions of the Messiah, witnesses of God's in-breaking reign, those who learn by following, watching, and receiving for themselves all that they will later offer to others."[17]

- The Gospels are not bare or neutral historical narratives but crafted to equip the church years after Jesus' life and work to carry out its missional calling. They are products of the church's mission that aim at missional faithfulness.

MISSIONARY DIMENSION AND INTENTION

The *missio Dei* (God's mission) offers us a perspective to understand the *missio ecclesiae* (church's mission). Our identity is shaped by our participation in God's redemptive purposes. Three further distinctions may also be helpful in negotiating the tricky terrain of the nature of mission. We begin by noting what, at first blush, appears to be a tension between Stanley Porter's and Cynthia Westfall's understandings of mission. Westfall points out that much discussion of Christian mission begins with a more narrow definition. She takes Köstenberger and O'Brien to task for defining mission too narrowly as a "conscious, deliberate, organized, and extensive effort to convert others to one's religion by way of evangelization or proselytization."[18] Porter, on the other hand, defines mission (quoting Plummer approvingly) as "the attempt to convert non-Christians to the Christian faith, regardless of any geographical or cultural considerations."[19] Porter's definition sounds much like Köstenberger and O'Brien's, which Westfall finds too narrow.

This is not mere wrangling over terms; our understandings have consequences. On the one hand, Porter points out that a definition reduced to cross-cultural mission may eclipse missionary endeavor at home, and a too broad understanding may justify business-as-usual in non-missional, non-evangelistic, ingrown churches. On the other hand,

16. Cf. ibid., 68–69.
17. Ibid., 69.
18. Westfall, "Hebrew Mission," 188, quoting Köstenberger and O'Brien, *Salvation to the Ends of the Earth*, 254.
19. Porter, "Content and Message," 135, quoting Plummer, *Paul's Understanding*, 1.

Westfall notes that reducing mission to evangelism may mean that other dimensions of the church's mission to make known the good news, especially the suffering that comes from a missionary encounter in public life, might be missed. Indeed, our pre-understandings will affect the way we read Scripture and what we understand to be obedient practice. Do Westfall's and Porter's concerns stand in irreconcilable tension?

Perhaps the distinction between missionary dimension and missionary intention is helpful here. Lesslie Newbigin made this distinction in 1958 in an important booklet entitled *One Body, One Gospel, One World,* and it has never left missiological discussion. The background of this distinction was a growing consensus in ecumenical circles that mission is as broad as the Christian life—all of life is mission. The trouble was, for Newbigin, that this had the potential of marginalizing the intentional evangelistic and missionary task of the church. Yet he acknowledged the importance of the insight that the whole life of the church is the visible means through which the Holy Spirit carries on his mission to the world, and that therefore the whole of the church's life partakes of the character of witness or mission. Thus there is justification in using the word "mission" in a broad way. He says: "The whole life of the church has a missionary *dimension,* though not all of it has mission as its primary *intention.*"[20]

The church's missionary dimension will evoke specific, intentional acts and words that directly engage the unbelieving world with the gospel. "While all the activities of the Church have a missionary *dimension,* there are needed specific activities which have the *intention* of crossing the frontier between faith and unbelief—and that frontier is no longer the old geographical one, but runs through every land."[21] He presses further saying that (and I hear Porter echoing this concern) "unless there is in the life of the Church a point of concentration for the missionary intention, the missionary dimension which is proper to the whole life of the Church will be lost."[22] This distinction enables us to affirm the validity of evangelism and intentional missionary activities as an essential and yet distinct activity within the total mission of the church.

---

20. Newbigin, *One Body,* 21.
21. Newbigin, *Unfinished Agenda,* 155.
22. Newbigin, *One Body,* 43.

MISSION AND EVANGELISM

A second distinction, common in mission studies, is between mission and evangelism. This distinction has been a special concern of David Bosch for years.[23] For Bosch, mission is wider than evangelism: "Mission denotes the total task God has set the church for the salvation of the world"[24] and "embraces all activities that serve to liberate man from his slavery in the presence of the coming God."[25] Evangelism is a central and indispensable dimension of the church's mission that involves a (verbal)[26] witness to what God has done, is doing, and will do in Jesus Christ. It aims at a response, inviting people to respond to the gospel. Yet there is more to the church's mission than evangelism. To simply note three of Bosch's observations:

- Evangelism cannot be separated from the corporate witness of the church's life: "*Evangelism is only possible when the community that evangelizes—the church—is a radiant manifestation of the Christian faith and exhibits an attractive lifestyle.*"[27] This emphasis on a communal embodiment of salvation as the most powerful witness is an increasingly frequent theme in missiology today. The announcement: "Good news: The kingdom of God has come" may evoke the question "where?" That announcement carries power only as the life of the church substantiates those words. In fact, Newbigin suggests (on the basis of his understanding of Acts) that the reason Paul does not exhort his churches to evangelism is that their attractive life provoked questions about its source. Evangelistic proclamation was the response to their questions.

- Evangelism cannot be separated from the calling of the church in the public life of culture to pursue mercy, justice, and recon-

---

23. Bosch, *Transforming Mission*, 411–20.
24. Ibid., 412.
25. Moltmann, *Church in the Power of the Spirit*, 10.
26. Newbigin narrows evangelism to verbal witness while Bosch includes the witness of word and deed. See Bosch, *Transforming Mission*, 420. For Lesslie Newbigin's view of evangelism see Goheen, *As the Father Has Sent Me*, 278–91.
27. Bosch, *Transforming Mission*, 414. Emphasis his.

ciliation: "... *evangelism cannot be divorced from the preaching and practice of justice*."[28]

- And finally, evangelism as verbal proclamation cannot be separated from deeds that authenticate that announcement: "The deed without the word is dumb; the word without the deed is empty. Words interpret deeds and deeds validate words..."[29]

Defined this way, Porter's primary concern is for evangelism, and his chapter offers helpful insight into Paul's evangelistic message. One set of questions that Bosch might pose to Porter is this: Is reconciliation the only image for interpreting what God has done in Jesus that is appropriate to Paul's evangelistic proclamation? If this is the heart of Paul's evangelistic proclamation, and he instructs his congregations to proclaim it as well, is he privileging only this image in evangelism? It would seem that reconciliation would be one powerful image to speak to the Corinthian church. But are other images that interpret God's work in Christ equally valid in other contextual settings? Would Paul instruct the church in the twenty-first century to use this image or to find another that interprets the fullness of salvation that has come in Christ that would speak in fresh and powerful ways today? How do we contextualize Paul's message today? All these questions are concerned with the issue of how to relate Porter's meticulous exegesis of Paul's message in 2 Cor 5:20 to our evangelistic task today.

MISSION AND MISSIONS

A final distinction, again made by Newbigin, is between mission and missions. This distinction is tied to the concern mentioned previously, that is, the broadening of mission and the eclipse of intentional missionary endeavor. Newbigin was editor of the leading missionary journal of the time, the *International Review of Missions*. There was strong pressure to remove the 's' from missions in the title of that journal since, it was believed, everything the church did was mission. He steadfastly refused, insisting that maintaining the "s" would distinguish the task of missions from the more comprehensive mission of the church.[30] Mission is the

---

28. Ibid., 418. Emphasis his.
29. Ibid., 420.
30. I am reminded here of the difference one letter made in another debate in church history with much more at stake. The Nicene Council, led by the youthful Athanasius,

all-embracing term which refers to "the entire task for which the Church is sent into the world"[31] while the plural or adjectival form, missions, refers to the more specific task of making Christ known where he is not yet known. Newbigin believed it important "to identify and distinguish the specific foreign missionary task within the total mission of the church."[32] He defines missions as follows: "Missions [are] particular enterprises within the total mission which have the primary intention of bringing into existence a Christian presence in a milieu where previously there was no such presence or where such presence was ineffective."[33]

This understanding of mission in Acts is supported by Porter and Westfall's paper on Acts especially as they consider the strategy of Paul's missionary journeys. The scattering of believers from the Jerusalem church under heavy persecution produced an enormous missionary expansion. There was, however, no missionary intention on the part of the church. In Acts 13:2–3 we find something different. The church in Antioch laid hands on Saul and Barnabas and "sent them off" to preach the gospel among the Gentiles. Here the missionary intention is fundamental. In Antioch, there is for the first time a "concerted and planned act of outreach."[34] So this text constitutes "the central New Testament paradigm for missions."[35] The Spirit moved the church to set aside some men for a specific purpose of taking the gospel to places where it was not yet known. The continuing story of Acts shows that when Paul established an authentic witness in a place, he moved on and, as it were, said to the church "Now you are the mission in this place." (This, in fact, is what a missionary bishop in India used to do. He would have the whole church put their hands on their heads and say "Woe to me if I do not

---

confessed that Jesus was *homoousios* (of the same substance or essence) as the Father over against the Arians who used the term *homoiousios* (of similar substance or essence). The Roman historian Gibbon mocked at the spectacle of Christians fighting over a diphthong! Yet one letter (in Greek)—an iota no less—protected the confession that Jesus was God and not just very much like God. I wish, incidentally, that some professor during my seminary days had told me that this Nicene formulation was the product of a missionary encounter with neo-Platonic culture, a classic example of faithful contextualization in making the gospel known in a culture very different from Jewish culture.

31. Newbigin, *Gospel in a Pluralist Society*, 121.
32. Newbigin, "Mission and Missions," 911.
33. Newbigin, "Crosscurrents," 149.
34. Porter and Westfall, "A Cord of Three Strands," 120.
35. Newbigin, "Crosscurrents," 150.

preach the gospel of Christ." Then the bishop would say, "Now you are the mission in this place.")

In terms of the distinction between mission and missions, Eckhard Schnabel's chapter offers insightful perspectives on missions from Paul's missionary strategy. Schnabel reflects on Paul's words in Rom 15:15–21: "Paul describes himself as a pioneer missionary: 'I make it my ambition to proclaim the good news, not where Christ has already been named, so that I do not build on someone else's foundation' (15:20–21). As an *architektōn* moved from city to city working on major building projects, Paul travels to regions in which the gospel had not been preached and to cities in which no church had yet been established."[36] Schnabel notes again: "Paul understands his task to be that of a missionary called by God to 'plant' ([1 Cor] 3:6) and to 'lay the foundation' as a 'skilled master builder' (. . . *sophos architektōn,* 3:10), i.e., to establish new congregations. In other words, Paul is a pioneer missionary who travels from city to city proclaiming the message of Jesus Messiah, Savior, and Lord, before audiences who had never heard that message before." As they respond to the gospel they are gathered into "a new community of people who meet regularly, representing God's presence in the world as his 'temple' (3:16)."[37] Note the progression Schnabel recounts: Paul as a pioneer church planter forms a church in a new place; then that church represents God's presence to the people in that place.[38] I believe this perspective can also help us to understand the missional concern of Paul in his letters.[39] He is concerned to nurture churches to carry out their calling

---

36. Schnabel, "Paul's Missionary Strategy," 161–62.

37. Ibid.," 157.

38. In *The Spontaneous Expansion of the Church,* Roland Allen analyzes the success of the church's mission in the book of Acts. First, churches were planted and witnessing communities established in places of importance. It was then the attractive life of the community and spontaneous evangelism of common members that led to "the spontaneous expansion of the church." He summarizes: "This then is what I mean by spontaneous expansion. I mean the expansion which follows the unexhorted and unorganized activity of individual members of the Church explaining to others the Gospel which they have found for themselves; I mean the expansion which follows the irresistible attraction of the Christian Church for men who see its ordered life, and are drawn to it by desire to discover the secret of a life which they instinctively desire to share; I mean also the expansion of the Church by the addition of new churches" (Allen, *The Spontaneous Expansion of the Church,* 7).

39. See, e.g., Ridderbos's discussion in *Paul: An Outline of His Theology,* 432–35. He says: "This grand vision of the world-encompassing significance of the gospel and of the expansion of the church causes him furthermore to involve the church that has already

of representing the good news to their contemporaries.[40] Paul is both a pioneer missionary and a missionary pastor.

Similarly, Porter and Westfall's chapter on the book of Acts offers helpful insight into missions by tracing the strategy, approach, and content of Paul's missionary journeys. For example, consideration of Paul's evangelistic speeches continues to be helpful for missionary communication today.[41] Where there is knowledge of Scripture, evangelism tells the story of Jesus as the fulfillment of that bigger Old Testament story. Where there is no knowledge of Scripture, as is usually the case in missions, Paul carefully proclaims the gospel building on their common humanity and religious experience, with both continuity and discontinuity, fulfillment and challenge. Hendrik Kraemer has called this way of proclaiming the gospel "subversive fulfillment,"[42] while Lesslie Newbigin, following A. G. Hogg, has termed it "challenging relevance,"[43] and J. H. Bavinck "possessio."[44] What each is doing with differing terminology is noting the way in which missionary communication today, as was the case with Paul in Lystra and Athens in his day, proclaims the gospel as the fulfillment of common human aspirations and religious longings, while at the same time, with a demand for repentance and conversion, challenging the idolatry that twists those aspirations and longings.

Many questions remain about how to use Schnabel's and Porter and Westfall's thorough analyses today. How does Paul function as a model

---

been brought to salvation in this missionary work in a great many ways, and to awaken the church itself to a missionary attitude" (433). He notes at least three ways the church became involved in this mission: in its enablement of Paul's missionary work; in a more indirect way by manifesting the gospel in its life, commending it to outsiders; in more direct, deliberate evangelistic endeavors. Ridderbos comments on the second of these: "This motif recurs throughout all the epistles of Paul in various nuances and elaborations: the life of the church must be a recommendation of its faith, in conformity with, 'worthy of' the Lord (Col.1:10) and the gospel of Christ (Phil. 1:27). In this last point the missionary element is very clear" (434). He goes on to tie in the upbuilding of the church for this expressly missional calling.

40. See, e.g., Allen, *Missionary Methods*, 107, 132.

41. Porter and Westfall, "A Cord of Three Strands," 128–31.

42. Kraemer, "Continuity and Discontinuity, 2–4; Kraemer, *The Christian Message*, 351–52.

43. Hogg, *Christian Message to the Hindu*, 9–20; Newbigin, "Christ and the Cultures," 11–12; Newbigin, "Mission in the 1980's," 155. Cf. Goheen, *As the Father Has Sent Me*, 356–61.

44. Bavinck, *Science of Missions*, 121–90. This term is used and explained on pages 178–79.

for a church living in very different settings? To take one example: Can advocates of urban mission today simply embrace his strategy? Schnabel is not so certain, as my old professor Harvie Conn was, that today's urban missionary strategy can be drawn from Paul's example. How does Paul's strategy to go first to the Jews and then to the Gentiles relate to today's missions? What parts of Paul's mission remain normative? How can we appropriate and continue Paul's missionary concern in imaginative and creative ways in new contexts and cultural settings?

These questions, like the ones earlier posed to Porter, probe the contemporary relevance of ancient biblical texts. It is interesting to note that some missiologists trained in biblical studies, like Bosch[45] and Johannes Nissen[46] among others, believe a problem exists in the dialogue between mission and biblical scholars. To put it (perhaps too) starkly: biblical scholars, oriented to the original meaning of the text in a very different setting, are reticent to draw any kind of direct connection between the text and our situation. Thus they "frequently fail to show whether, and, if so, how, the Bible can be of significance to the church-in-mission and how, if at all, a connection between the biblical evidence and the contemporary missionary scene can be made."[47] By contrast missiologists, seeking contemporary relevance, frequently fail to respect the cultural distance between text and context, and thus read their own concerns back into the biblical text. Sometimes they are guilty of simplistic or obvious moves from the New Testament to our missionary setting in an attempt to make a direct application of Scripture to the present situation. The problem is how to merge the horizons of the ancient text and the contemporary setting with integrity, or to co-ordinate the concern of missiologists to be relevant today with the concern of biblical scholars to be faithful to the divine authority of yesterday.

But, at the very least, the affirmation of pioneer missions is important today. In some ecumenical parts of the church, embarrassment about the colonial missionary enterprise of the past two centuries, coupled with a loss of confidence in the truth and universal validity of the gospel, has led many to the abandonment of missions. Conversely

---

45. Bosch, "Mission in Biblical Perspective," 531–38; and Bosch, "Toward a Hermeneutic."

46. Nissen, *New Testament and Mission*, 13–15.

47. Bosch, "Mission in Biblical Perspective," 532; Bosch, "Toward a Hermeneutic," 66.

in some evangelical parts of the church, it is business as usual: missions continues to be defined simply as cross-cultural work. Any money that is given for people who are "overseas" is missions. Bryant Myers notes the serious problem with this: "Christians are allocating only 1.2% of their mission funding and their foreign missionaries to the 1.1 billion people who live in the unevangelized world."[48] He calls the disproportionate allocation of monetary and human resources a "scandal." In this situation a distinction between mission and missions, with the insistence on taking the gospel to places where there is no witnessing community, remains important.

But the importance of Paul's pioneer missions work goes beyond simply maintaining the task of taking the gospel to people who have not yet heard it. Missions expresses also the ultimate horizon of God's and, therefore, the church's mission—the ends of the earth. All nations and the ends of the earth is the horizon of God's mission through Israel. As Mark Boda has pointed out on the Psalms and Craig Evans on the servant songs of Isaiah, in the Old Testament, since there is one God, his rule is to be recognized by all peoples "to the ends of the earth."[49] This horizon remains in the New Testament. Jesus says, "And this gospel of the kingdom will be preached in the whole world as a testimony to all nations, and then the end will come" (Matt 24:14). This theme is explicit in the structure of the book of Acts, as Westfall and Porter point out in their chapter.[50] The risen Christ says to the apostles that they will be his witnesses beginning in Jerusalem to Judaea and Samaria and on to the ends of the earth (Acts 1:8). Explained in this way, missions is not just another part of mission that stands alongside of others but is the ultimate horizon of the whole missionary task of the church. Mission without missions is an emaciated and distorted concept. As Newbigin puts it: "The Church's mission is concerned with the ends of the earth. When that dimension is forgotten, the heart goes out of the whole business."[51]

---

48. Myers, *New Context*, 48.
49. Cf., e.g., "the ends of the earth" in Ps 72:8; Zech 9:10; Mic 5:4; Ps 2:8; Isa 49:6.
50. Porter and Westfall, "A Cord of Three Strands," 131–32.
51. Newbigin, *One Body*, 27.

THE CENTRALITY OF MISSION TO THE BIBLICAL STORY

We have discussed the mission of the New Testament church as it continues to the ends of the earth. This mission is rooted in the Old Testament. While there is a growing recognition among many in mission studies of the importance of the Old Testament,[52] study of the Old Testament material still remains relatively underdeveloped.[53] Mark Boda's chapter is an excellent addition. Boda's summarizing sentence at the end of his first section is a good place to start: "The 'meaning' of Israel's existence is the mission to the peoples."[54] This is clear, Boda points out, especially in Psalm 67: "May God be gracious to us and bless us and make his face shine upon us—*so that* your ways may be known on earth, your salvation among all nations. . . . May God bless us still, *so that* all the ends of the earth will fear him" (Ps 67:1, 6).[55] I have often used the language we find here and elsewhere in the Old Testament to describe the community God chooses as a "so that people." That is, we exist *so that* the nations might come to be blessed. At the end of his essay, Boda notes that the Psalms are part of a greater narrative. He notes among the high points Gen 12:1–3, Exod 19:4–6, and the prophets' vision for the nations.[56] Taking only those texts we see the thread of the Old Testament missional narrative.

Against the dark spread of sin along with its terrible consequences as narrated in Genesis 3–11, God chooses Abraham. He promises to make him into a great nation and bless him. But the blessing on Abraham is *so*

---

52. A couple of classic older books on the Old Testament and mission include Rowley, *Missionary Message of the Old Testament*, and Blauw, *Missionary Nature of the Church*. A couple of helpful recent books are Filbeck, *Yes, the God of the Gentiles Too* and Kaiser, *Mission in the Old Testament*. Other books treat the Old Testament along with the New Testament: Köstenberger and O'Brien, *Salvation to the Ends of the Earth*, 25–71; Senior and Stuhlmueller, *Biblical Foundations for Mission*, 9–138. See also Wright's book *The Mission of God*.

53. In *Transforming Mission*, Bosch devotes about 184 pages to developing a biblical foundation for mission. Only four pages are devoted to the Old Testament, and his approach is to elaborate themes important for mission to the nations. Bosch quotes Rzepkowski approvingly when he says: "The decisive difference between the Old Testament and the New Testament is mission. The New Testament is essentially a book about mission" (17). Chris Wright counters this in his *The Mission of God*.

54. Boda, "Declare His Glory among the Nations," 27. Boda is quoting Kraus, *Theology of the Psalms*, 59.

55. Boda, "Declare His Glory among the Nations," 23.

56. Ibid., 37.

that all the peoples on earth will be blessed through him (Gen 12:1–3; cf. Gen 18:18–19). William Dumbrell comments on this verse: "What is being offered in these few verses is a theological blueprint for the redemptive history of the world..."[57] How that blessing would flow to others is articulated in God's call to Israel in Exod 19:4–6.[58] Israel is called to be a priestly nation, that is, to play a priestly role among the nations. John Durham relates the purpose of this call in Exodus 19 when he comments that Israel was to be "a display-people, a showcase to the world of how being in covenant with Yahweh changes a people."[59] In the later language of Isaiah, Israel is to be a light to the world. Georg Vicedom notes a consensus among a number of mission scholars on Israel's election. He says: "Israel's election was a call to service. She was to impress the world so that, by the example of Israel, the rule of God would become evident to the nations."[60] Dumbrell notes the significance of this call for the rest of the Old Testament: "The history of Israel from this point on is in reality merely a commentary upon the degree of fidelity with which Israel adhered to this Sinai-given vocation."[61]

We see this theme strongly in the Psalms, as Boda has noted well, because the Psalms, as the hymnbook of Israel, nourished Israel in her missional calling. But, alas, Israel failed. Israel's failure did not mean God's redemptive purposes for the world failed. The prophets looked to the future and promised that one day he would restore Israel to her missional role among the nations. We might describe the importance of the prophetic message with Lucien LeGrand as an "eschatological, centripetal universalism" that is "brought to complete expression in the New Testament."[62]

One of those prophets, of course, was Isaiah. Craig Evans's chapter helps to see how Luke makes extensive use of Isaiah 40–66 throughout his books to interpret both the mission of Jesus and the mission of the church. Perhaps one of the most helpful images that shows us the thread of mission in the biblical story is taken from the phrase from Isa 42:6, the

---

57. Dumbrell, *Covenant and Creation*, 66.

58. We note in passing that this missional role of Israel has been transferred to the New Testament church. Cf. 1 Pet 2:9. See Westfall, "Hebrew Mission," 199.

59. Durham, *Exodus*, 263.

60. Vicedom, *The Mission of God*, 94.

61. Ibid., 90.

62. LeGrand, *Unity and Plurality*, 3.

title and theme of Evans's chapter, "a light to the nations." These words are spoken of the Lord's servant. Who is that servant? Evans shows us that Luke depicts Jesus as the one who comes to fulfil the calling of the servant in Isaiah.[63] Further, we see that Luke also formulates his version of the concluding missionary commission to the apostles (Luke 24:44–49) with the servant of Isaiah in mind. Paul is not hesitant to apply the words to the missionary ministry of himself and his colleagues (Acts 13:47).[64] In this way the mission of Jesus is connected to the mission of the church: both discharge the ministry of the Isaianic servant to be a light to the nations and to bring salvation to the ends of the earth. Thus, in the words of Thomas Moore, Luke "used the Servant concept not only for his Christology, but also for his missiology." Consequently, as "followers of Christ, believers today are privileged to be commissioned by Him to take up the mission of the Servant."[65]

But the connection can be made not only forward from Jesus' mission to the church's mission, but also back from Jesus' mission to Israel's mission. Not only does the church continue Jesus' mission, Jesus fulfills Israel's mission. The servant songs of Isaiah must be placed in the broader Old Testament story of a people called to incarnate as a community the redemptive purposes of God in the midst of the world for the sake of the nations. Isaiah's promise comes in the midst of Israel's failure to be the faithful servant and looks forward to one who will arise out of Israel to fulfill her mission to be a light to the nations. Jesus comes as "one who fulfills Israel's destiny." When "Israel's role of world mission ... was forfeited through disobedience" that role pictured in the servant is "transferred in the Gospels to Jesus."[66] The Servant will also gather a renewed Israel who will continue the Servant's mission. Thus, we see a missional connection between the roles of Israel, Jesus, and the church as each participates in the missional purpose of God.[67]

63. Cf. Moore, "Lucan Great Commission."
64. Ibid., 51–58.
65. Ibid., 60.
66. Köstenberger and O'Brien, *Salvation to the Ends of the Earth*, 49–50. The role is not only transferred in the Gospels but already in Isaiah. Commenting on Isa 49:1–6, Brevard Childs speaks of a servant that arises within Israel "as a faithful embodiment of the nation Israel who has not performed its chosen role (48:1–2)." See Childs, *Isaiah*, 385.
67. It is important, of course, to note both the continuity and the discontinuity between Israel's and the church's mission. But it is not true that the "decisive difference between the Old Testament and the New Testament is mission. The New Testament is

Porter and Westfall add an important distinction. The burden of their argument on mission in the book of Acts is that there is a connection between the mission of Jesus, the Jewish mission, and Paul's Gentile mission. They point out further that in Paul's mission his strategy was to proclaim the gospel first to the Jew and then to the Gentile.[68] In his brief biblical theology of mission, J. H. Bavinck points out that the Old Testament prophets promised that when God ushered in the new age, the "first condition for the fulfillment of this promise is the genuine conversion of Israel itself."[69] God would transform Israel first to fulfill its missionary calling. This condition could only be fulfilled in connection with the work of the Messiah. It is only then that the salvation of the nations could take place. Israel's mission and failure in the Old Testament, the mission of the Messiah, Israel's renewal to take up her mission again, the salvation of the Gentiles and incorporation into the new Israel and her mission—this is the redemptive-historical sequence of the prophets and the missional thread that runs from Israel to the nations.

It is this overarching missional purpose of God that must be grasped for a consistent missional hermeneutic. Wright puts it strongly,

> To read the whole Bible in the light of this overarching perspective of the mission of God, then, is to read 'with the grain' of this whole collection of texts that constitute our canon of Scripture. In my view this is the key assumption of a missional hermeneutic of the Bible. It is nothing more than to accept that the biblical worldview locates us in the midst of a narrative of the universe behind which stands the mission of the living God.[70]

MISSIONARY ENCOUNTER WITH CULTURE

Faithfulness to our mission to make known the good news of the kingdom in life, word, and deed will mean a missionary encounter with our culture. In his well-known and important book, *The Mission of God*, written in 1957, Georg Vicedom ends with a section entitled "The Church of Suffering."[71] He argues that suffering is the normal experience of a

---

essentially a book about mission" (Rzepkowski, "Theology of Mission," 80).
68. Porter and Westfall, "A Cord of Three Strands," 123–24.
69. Bavinck, *Science of Missions*, 19.
70. Wright, "Mission as a Matrix," 134–35.
71. Vicedom, *The Mission of God*, 136–42.

faithful church as it carries out its mission among powers that oppose the Lordship of Christ. He finds it "peculiar" that the theology of missions hardly enters the discussion of the missional significance of suffering.[72] Since that time the topic is much more present in missiological literature.

An incident that occurred less than ten years before Vicedom penned these words impressed on Newbigin the close connection between a faithful missionary church and suffering. After independence the government of India required all elementary schools to switch to the Ghandian model of education. Hindu syncretism was built into the program. The teachers were to be tightly knit communities that engaged in daily acts of worship that acknowledged all religions to be equally valid paths to God. A village boy who took up a teaching position in Madurai lost his teaching certificate rather than participate in syncretistic worship. Newbigin reports the result: "The costly witness of a village boy who was willing to lose his teaching certificate rather than compromise his faith so shook the whole institution that I was soon baptizing students within the college campus."[73] This event—and others like it—convinced Newbigin of three things: the incompatibility of the gospel with the dominant doctrine shaping public institutions, the cost of faithful witness to the gospel, and the power of suffering to draw others to Christ. Suffering comes in a missionary encounter with the idolatrous powers at work in a culture. Newbigin explains:

> No human societies cohere except on the basis of some kind of common beliefs and customs. No society can permit these beliefs and practices to be threatened beyond a certain point without reacting in self-defense. The idea that we ought to be able to expect some kind of neutral secular political order, which presupposes no religious or ideological beliefs, and which holds the ring impartially for a plurality of religions to compete with one another, has no adequate foundation. The New Testament makes it plain that Christ's followers must expect suffering as the normal badge of their discipleship, and also as one of the characteristic forms of their witness.[74]

---

72. Ibid., 139.
73. Newbigin, *Unfinished Agenda*, 120.
74. Newbigin, *Trinitarian Faith*, 42.

Cynthia Westfall, in her chapter on the Hebrew mission, calls attention to this theme in a number of books including Hebrews, 1 Peter, and Revelation, and links it with their missional calling.[75] Westfall finds herself in company with others considering this theme.[76] The book of Revelation, for example, places the church's mission in the context of a cosmic battle. Dean Flemming comments: "John is convinced that when the church prophetically testifies to God's truth against the idolatry and injustice of Rome, against its claims to ultimate allegiance, the result may be the shedding of the blood of the saints."[77] He continues: "But Revelation also gives its readers the confidence that the saints' faithful testimony even to the point of death will have the magnetic effect of drawing people from the world's nations to worship the one true God (Rev 11:3-13; 15:1-4; cf. 5:9; 7:9; 14:6; 21:3, 24, 26). Courageous witness is a powerful instrument of mission."[78] Richard Bauckham treats this theme in his volume on Revelation. In his book *Bible and Mission* he employs this theme again to urge the church in the West today to take up its missional call to embody the good news of the kingdom and to resist the idolatrous power of the story of global capitalism.[79]

Bauckham's prophetic call takes us to the heart of Brian Irwin's chapter. Our discussion of missionary encounter thus far has highlight-

---

75. There is a difference in how 1 Peter is treated. Both Nissen and Senior and Stuhlmueller contrast 1 Peter and Revelation in their approaches to culture. "It is interesting to compare the book of Revelation with 1 Peter on the issue of mission. These two works are radically different in form and tone, but both share a concern with witness in face of the Greco-Roman world" (Senior and Stuhlmueller, *Biblical Foundations for Mission*, 302). Nissen summarizes this difference: "Common to 1 Peter and the Book of Revelation is the call for witness. In the case of 1 Peter it meant the active participation in the structures of society, in the case of Revelation it meant the active withdrawal" (*New Testament and Mission*, 151). Conversely, both Westfall, and Köstenberger and O'Brien call attention to the fact that both of these books view mission in terms of suffering in the midst of a hostile world (Westfall, "Hebrew Mission," 202-3; Köstenberger and O'Brien, *Salvation to the Ends of the Earth*, 232-33). Perhaps the difference can be explained in terms of the fact that 1 Peter views mission in terms of suffering, but it is suffering as one participates in the public life of culture, while in Revelation, the opposition of a hostile state precludes this.

76. For example, Nissen, *New Testament and Mission*, 143-56; Bauckham, *Theology of Revelation*; Bauckham, *Bible and Mission*, 83-112; Flemming, *Contextualization*, 266-95.

77. Flemming, *Contextualization*, 281-82.

78. Ibid., 283.

79. Bauckham, *Bible and Mission*, 83-112.

ed the *negative* side of the church's relationship with its cultural context. That is, because the whole seamless texture of culture is stained by rebellious idolatry, the gospel speaks a "no," a word of judgment on the sinful twisting of all cultural customs, symbols, institutions, and systems. The church, then, finds itself in a stance of opposition to its culture, and in the process sometimes suffers. Yet, the church's relation to the dominant culture is not only to "resist the idolatry of the pagan state and pagan society."[80] In the New Testament, "good citizenship was also a missionary strategy which commended the gospel to those of good will."[81] There is thus a *positive* side to the church's mission to its culture. Judgment and opposition are not the only words. The gospel also speaks a "yes," a word of affirmation on cultural development as a good part of God's creation. The church, then, finds itself also in solidarity with its culture, participating fully in the unfolding of culture in keeping with God's creational intentions.

From the 1950s on, the emphasis on the calling of the layperson in the world of public life as central to the church's mission has made a resolution to this issue urgent. On the one hand, how can the church live in solidarity with its culture without falling into syncretistic accommodation or uncritical domestication, taking the form of a chameleon? On the other hand, how can the church stand in opposition to the idolatrous twisting of its culture without falling into a repellent sectarianism or polemical confrontation, taking the form of a ghetto? Both must be avoided if the church is to mediate good news. Wrestling with this question has become important in contextualization studies in missiology.

Irwin begins his paper with a reference to Douglas John Hall. Hall has taken a certain stance on this issue that has become common among some in the missiological tradition who have occupied themselves with a missionary encounter with Western culture. Stephen Bevans, in his well-known book on contextualization models, terms this the "countercultural model."[82] Hall believes that because of a long Christendom arrangement between the church, the gospel, and culture in the West, the church has lost its critical, prophetic stance in culture. He is in fundamental agreement with Newbigin who said that the Western church

---

80. Bauckham, *Theology of Revelation*, 92.
81. Dunn, *Theology of Paul*, 679–80.
82. Bevans, *Models of Contextual Theology*, 117–37.

is in "an advanced state of syncretism."[83] Therefore, it is the side of opposition to culture, the gospel's word of judgment on idolatry that must be stressed.

There is a range of positions, however, within this counter-cultural model. Some, like Hall, stress the negative side of the church's engagement with culture to the degree that the positive side is almost eclipsed. To illustrate: About the same time Newbigin delivered the paper *Can a Modern Society Be Christian?*,[84] offering his agenda for the pursuit of this goal, Hall made the comment at a 1996 Gospel and Culture Conference that it is wicked to seek a Christian society.[85] For Hall, cultural formative power for the Christian community was the problem of Christendom. For Newbigin, cultural formative power is good and part of our mission; the problem comes when we lose the prophetic, critical dimension.

I believe the emphasis on the critical side of the church's calling in culture is a much needed emphasis today for the church in the West. But I share Irwin's concern with Hall's over-emphasis on the church's negative stance for a number of reasons: it offers no help for a church that must participate in society's cultural development; it does not recognize the great gains of the Christendom period that we are still enjoying because of the gospel-salted Western culture; it takes a cultural strategy or emphasis appropriate at one point in history and makes it normative for all situations.

It is this last concern that motivates Irwin's chapter. He rightly notes that to "apply the wrong model may lead to ineffectiveness in engaging culture or an unwarranted pessimism when imagining the church's future."[86] His analysis of Daniel rightly shows that there are different ways that the church engages society. Sometimes a faithful missionary stance enables the church to participate in structures in a transforming way; other times believers will be opposed by a hostile state and their witness will be one of suffering martyrdom.[87]

83. Newbigin, *A Word in Season*, 67.
84. Newbigin, "Can a Modern Society Be Christian?"
85. See Hall, "Metamorphosis," 73.
86. Irwin, "Old Testament Apocalyptic," 62.

87. Irwin notes that "there is nothing to say that the available models should be limited to the two that have been outlined here" (62). In fact, if we look at the church in the former Soviet Union and Eastern Europe, we can see that the church there has engaged society in at least three models. Before communism the church was in a Christendom situation where the state was relatively friendly, and the church was able to participate

CONCLUSION

When theologian Nicholas Lash addressed members of a New Testament seminar, he commented that, while biblical scholars attend the meetings with their festal robes of professional exegesis, he felt a little naked, unable to suitably attire himself in such garments. As one trained in theology and not biblical studies, he wondered what he was doing there.[88] I feel a little bit like Lash; my work is not in the area of biblical scholarship, but worldview and missiology. I cannot adorn myself with a fitting wedding garment at the feast of biblical scholarship. Yet Lash's further hermeneutical reflections encouraged me to accept the invitation to contribute to this volume.

According to Lash's model, the relationship that exists between biblical scholarship and missiology is often conceived in terms of what he refers to as the "relay-race" model. It is a relationship of one-way dependence: the biblical scholar determines what the text originally meant and then passes along the complete package of original meanings to the missiologist, who, in turn, transposes those meanings into the contemporary situation, rendering the text relevant to the missionary task of the church in the present. Contrariwise, Lash believes there needs to be a two-way dialogue. The biblical scholar Marion Soards agrees. He notes four themes in current New Testament scholarship that are important

---

freely in the structures of society. After Lenin the church faced a hostile state in which the costly witness of Revelation was more appropriate. With the fall of communism, and the incursion of liberalism, the church is now ignored or simply relegated to the private realm. Each of these situations presents different challenges. See Goheen, "Building for the Future," for a brief description of these three models in the church of the former Soviet Union and Eastern Europe. See also the insightful discussion by Flemming of two differing models of mission in Romans 13 and Revelation 13. He affirms that "different contexts call for different responses" to the Roman Empire. While the contexts differ, the key is that in both situations the church is called to witness to God's kingdom: "Both, in fact, engage their public worlds with a missional goal, but they do so from alternative angles." The book of Romans seems "to encourage Christians to positively participate in the life of society in redemptive ways." On the other hand, Revelation takes a more sectarian stance because of the demonic depths idolatry has reached. Thus Revelation "launches a countercultural critique" and calls the church to a "prophetic and costly witness." In Romans and Revelation "we discover two different but complementary theological visions. Each spotlights one side of the church's relationship to the Empire; each shows sensitivity to the particular needs of the communities they address" (Flemming, *Contextualization*, 288–91).

88. Lash, "What Might Martyrdom Mean," 14.

for mission today.[89] He recognizes that biblical studies can help to bring the light of Scripture to bear on our current mission practices. But he also believes that it is not only missiology that needs biblical scholarship; it works the other way as well. He says: "Mission studies should remind biblical scholars that many of the writings that we study (often in painstaking and even painful detail) came to be because of the reality of mission. An awareness of, and a concern with, the key issues of mission studies may well help biblical studies find foci that will bring deeper appreciation of the meaning of the Bible."[90] For the sake of faithfulness to our call to participate in God's mission in a changing time, I hope that at least something of that dialogue between biblical studies and missiology has taken place in this volume.

---

89. The four issues are first-century Judaism, the life of Jesus, Pauline theology, and the character of the early church.

90. Soards, "Key Issues," 107. Chris Wright notes similarly: "So a missional reading of such texts is very definitely not a matter of (1) finding the 'real' meaning by objective exegesis, (2) cranking up some 'missiological implications' as a homiletic supplement to the text itself. Rather, it is to see how a text often has its *origin* in some issue, need, controversy, or threat that the people of God needed to address in the context of their mission. The text in itself is a product of mission in action" (Wright, *Mission of God*, 49).

BIBLIOGRAPHY

Allen, Roland. *Missionary Methods: St Paul's or Ours?* Grand Rapids: Eerdmans, 1962.

———. *The Spontaneous Expansion of the Church.* Grand Rapids: Eerdmans, 1962.

Bauckham, Richard. *The Bible and Mission: Christian Witness in a Postmodern Age.* Grand Rapids: Baker, 2003.

———. *The Theology of the Book of Revelation.* Cambridge: Cambridge University Press, 1993.

Bavinck, J. H. *An Introduction to the Science of Missions.* Translated by David H. Freeman. Phillipsburg, NJ: Presbyterian and Reformed, 1960.

Bevans, Stephen. *Models of Contextual Theology.* Revised and expanded ed. Maryknoll, NY: Orbis, 2002.

Blauw, Johannes. *The Missionary Nature of the Church: A Survey of the Biblical Theology of Mission.* New York: McGraw–Hill, 1962.

Boda, Mark. "'Declare His Glory among the Nations': The Psalter as Missional Collection." In *Christian Mission: Old Testament Foundations and New Testament Developments,* edited by Stanley E. Porter and Cynthia Long Westfall, 13–41. Eugene, OR: Wipf & Stock, 2010.

Bosch, David. "Mission in Biblical Perspective." *International Review of Mission* (October 1985) 531–38.

———. "Reflections on Biblical Models of Mission." In *Toward the 21st Century in Christian Mission,* edited by James Phillips and Robert Coote, 175–92. Grand Rapids: Eerdmans, 1992.

———. "Toward a Hermeneutic for 'Biblical Studies and Mission.'" *Mission Studies* 3.2 (1986) 65–79.

———. *Transforming Mission: Paradigm Shifts in the Theology of Mission.* American Society of Missiology Series 16. Maryknoll, NY: Orbis, 1991.

Childs, Brevard. *Isaiah.* Louisville: Westminster John Knox, 2001.

Dumbrell, William. *Covenant and Creation: A Theology of Old Testament Covenants.* Nashville: Nelson, 1984.

Dunn, James G. D. *The Theology of Paul the Apostle.* Grand Rapids: Eerdmans, 1998.

Durham, John I. *Exodus.* WBC 3. Waco, TX: Word, 1987.

Filbeck, David. *Yes, the God of the Gentiles Too: The Missionary Message of the Old Testament.* Wheaton, IL: Billy Graham Center, 1994.

Flemming, Dean. *Contextualization in the New Testament: Patterns for Theology and Mission.* Downers Grove, IL: InterVarsity, 2005.

Goheen, Michael W. *"As the Father Has Sent Me, I Am Sending You": J. E. Lesslie Newbigin's Missionary Ecclesiology.* Zoetermeer: Boekencentrum, 2000.

———. "Building for the Future: Worldview Foundations of Sand and Rock." *Religion in Eastern Europe* 20.5 (October 2000) 30–41.

Goodall, Norman, ed. *Missions under the Cross: Addresses Delivered at the Enlarged Meeting of the Committee of the International Missionary Council at Willingen, in Germany, 1952; with Statements Issued by the Meeting.* London: Edinburgh House, 1953.

Green, Joel. "Recovering Mission-Church: Reframing Ecclesiology in Luke–Acts." Unpublished lecture, given at the Epworth Institute, 2003, n.p.

Hall, Douglas John. "Metamorphosis: From Christendom to Diaspora." In *Confident Witness—Changing World: Rediscovering the Gospel in North America,* edited by Craig Van Gelder, 67–79. Grand Rapids: Eerdmans, 1999.

Hogg, A. G. *The Christian Message to the Hindu*. London: SCM, 1945.

Hutchison, William R. *Errand to the World: American Protestant Missionary Thought and Foreign Missions*. Chicago: University of Chicago Press, 1987.

Irwin, Brian. "Old Testament Apocalyptic and the Roots of New Testament Mission." In *Christian Mission: Old Testament Foundations and New Testament Developments*, edited by Stanley E. Porter and Cynthia Long Westfall, 42–63. Eugene, OR: Wipf & Stock, 2010.

Jongeneel, Jan. *Philosophy, Science, and Theology of Mission in the 19th and 20th Centuries, Part II*. Frankfurt: Lang, 1997.

Kaiser, Walter C. *Mission in the Old Testament: Israel as a Light to the Nations*. Grand Rapids: Baker, 2000.

Knowles, Michael. "Mark, Matthew, and Mission: Faith, Failure, and the Fidelity of Jesus." In *Christian Mission: Old Testament Foundations and New Testament Developments*, edited by Stanley E. Porter and Cynthia Long Westfall, 64–92. Eugene, OR: Wipf & Stock, 2010.

Köstenberger, A. J., and P. T. O'Brien. *Salvation to the Ends of the Earth: A Biblical Theology of Mission*. NSBT 11. Downers Grove, IL: InterVarsity, 2001.

Kraemer, Hendrik. *The Christian Message in a Non-Christian World*. London: The Edinburgh House, 1938.

———. "Continuity and Discontinuity." In *The Authority of the Faith: The Madras Series*. Vol. 1:1–21. New York and London: International Missionary Council, 1939.

Kraus, H.-J. *Theology of the Psalms*. Translated by K. R. Krim. Continental Commentaries. Minneapolis: Augsburg, 1986.

Lash, Nicholas. "What Might Martyrdom Mean?" *Ex Auditu* 1 (1985) 14–24.

LeGrand, Lucien. *Unity and Plurality: Mission in the Bible*. Translated by Robert R. Barr. Maryknoll, NY: Orbis, 1990.

Moltmann, Jürgen. *The Church in the Power of the Spirit: A Contribution to Messianic Ecclesiology*. Minneapolis: Fortress, 1977.

Moore, Thomas S. "The Lucan Great Commission and the Isaianic Servant." *BibSac* 154 (1997) 47–60.

Myers, Bryant L. *The New Context of World Mission*. Monrovia, CA: World Vision/MARC, 1996.

Newbigin, Lesslie. "Can a Modern Society Be Christian?" Unpublished address given at King's College, London, 1 December 1995, as the Second Annual Gospel and Culture Lecture.

———. "Christ and the Cultures." *SJT* 31 (1978) 1–21.

———. "Crosscurrents in Ecumenical and Evangelical Understandings of Mission." *International Bulletin of Missionary Research* 6.4 (1982) 146–51.

———. *The Gospel in a Pluralist Society*. Grand Rapids: Eerdmans, 1989.

———. "Mission and Missions." *Christianity Today* 4.22 (1 August 1960) 911.

———. "Mission in the 1980s." *Occasional Bulletin of Missionary Research* 4.4 (October 1980) 154–55.

———. *One Body, One Gospel, One World: The Christian Mission Today*. London and New York: International Missionary Council, 1958.

———. *Trinitarian Faith and Today's Mission*. Richmond: John Knox, 1963.

———. *Unfinished Agenda: An Autobiography*. Revised and expanded ed. Grand Rapids: Eerdmans, 1993.

———. *A Word in Season: Perspectives on Christian World Missions.* Grand Rapids: Eerdmans, 1994.

Nissen, Johannes. *New Testament and Mission: Historical and Hermeneutical Perspectives.* Frankfurt: Lang, 2006.

Plummer, R. L. *Paul's Understanding of the Church's Mission: Did the Apostle Paul Expect the Early Christian Communities to Evangelize?* PBM. Carlisle: Paternoster, 2006.

Porter, Stanley E. "The Content and Message of Paul's Missionary Preaching." In *Christian Mission: Old Testament Foundations and New Testament Developments*, edited by Stanley E. Porter and Cynthia Long Westfall, 135–54. Eugene, OR: Wipf & Stock, 2010.

Porter, Stanley E., and Cynthia Long Westfall. "A Cord of Three Strands: Mission in Acts." In *Christian Mission: Old Testament Foundations and New Testament Developments*, edited by Stanley E. Porter and Cynthia Long Westfall, 108–34. Eugene, OR: Wipf & Stock, 2010.

Ridderbos, Herman. *Paul: An Outline of His Theology.* Trans. John Richard de Witt. Grand Rapids: Eerdmans, 1975.

Rowley, H. H. *The Missionary Message of the Old Testament.* London: Carey, 1944.

Rzepkowski, H. "The Theology of Mission." *Verbum SVD* 15 (1974) 79–91.

Schnabel, Eckhard J. "Paul's Missionary Strategy: Goals, Methods, and Realities." In *Christian Mission: Old Testament Foundations and New Testament Developments*, edited by Stanley E. Porter and Cynthia Long Westfall, 155–86. Eugene, OR: Wipf & Stock, 2010.

Schüssler Fiorenza, Elisabeth. "Miracles, Mission, and Apologetics: An Introduction." In *Aspects of Religious Propaganda in Judaism and Early Christianity*, edited by Elisabeth Schüssler Fiorenza, 1–25. Notre Dame, IN: University of Notre Dame Press, 1976.

Senior, Donald, and Carroll Stuhlmueller. *The Biblical Foundations for Mission.* Maryknoll, NY: Orbis, 1983.

Soards, Marion. "Key Issues in Biblical Studies and Their Bearing on Mission Studies." *Missiology* 24 (1996) 93–109.

Vicedom, Georg. *The Mission of God: An Introduction to a Theology of Mission.* Translated by Gilbert A. Thiele and Dennis Hilgendorf. Saint Louis: Concordia, 1965.

Westfall, Cynthia Long. "The Hebrew Mission: Voices from the Margins?" In *Christian Mission: Old Testament Foundations and New Testament Developments*, edited by Stanley E. Porter and Cynthia Long Westfall, 187–207. Eugene, OR: Wipf & Stock, 2010.

Wright, Christopher J. H. "Mission as a Matrix for Hermeneutics and Biblical Theology." In *Out of Egypt: Biblical Theology and Biblical Interpretation*, edited by Craig Bartholomew, Mary Healy, Karl Möller, and Robin Parry, 102–43. Grand Rapids: Zondervan, 2004.

———. *The Mission of God: Unlocking the Bible's Grand Narrative.* Downers Grove, IL: InterVarsity, 2006.

Modern Authors Index

Abbott, T. K., 164
Aland, K., 48
Alexander, P. S., 193, 203
Allen, R., 166, 219, 220
Allison, D. C., Jr., 50, 83, 85
Allmen, D. von, 148
Anderson, A. A., 28
Anderson, R. D., 27
Andrew, J. A., 211

Barclay, J. M. G., 144
Bardtke, H., 33
Barnett, P., 144–46
Barrett, C. K., 144, 176
Barth, K., 212
Barth, M., 151, 164
Bartholomew, C. D., 43, 44
Bash, A., 143–46
Bauckham, R., 228, 229
Baur, F. C., 109
Bavinck, J. H., 37, 220, 226
Beale, G. K., 56, 57
Beare, F. W., 84
Becker, J., 171
Belleville, L. L., 144, 146
Bevans, S., 229
Bienert, W. A., 109
Blanke, H., 164
Blauw, J., 223
Bock, D. L., 43
Boda, M., 222–24
Booij, T., 19, 24, 25
Bosch, D. J., 65–68, 203, 204, 208, 216, 217, 221, 223

Botermann, H., 156
Bowers, W. P., 139, 141, 142, 144
Brawley, R. L., 110
Breytenbach, C., 168
Briggs, C. A., 28, 29
Briggs, E. G., 28, 29
Brownlee, W. H., 32, 33
Bruce, F. F., 43, 55, 110, 115, 116
Brueggemann, W., 30, 31
Bultmann, R., 145, 197
Burgoon, M., 175

Carrez, M., 142, 145
Carter, W., 81
Cavanaugh, J., 61
Chester, A., 189, 198, 205
Chester, S. J., 183
Childs, B., 225
Clarke, A. D., 155
Clavier, H., 164
Colbert, D., 61
Collange, J.-F., 143
Collins, J. J., 53
Conn, H. M., 166, 221
Cranfield, C. E. B., 142, 170
Creach, J. F. D., 32, 33

Dahood, M. J., 28
Danby, H., 83
Das, A. A., 196, 204
Daube, D., 71
Davies, W. D., 50, 83, 85
deClaissé-Walford, N. L., 27, 35
Derret, J. D. M., 162

deSilva, D. A., 114
Dick, K., 142
Dickson, J. P., 188, 189
Donaldson, T. L., 50
Drury, J., 73
Duchesne, L., 115
Dumbrell, W., 224
Dunn, J. D. G., 164, 170, 190, 191, 193-98, 205, 229
Dupont, J., 110
Durham, J., 224

Eaton, J. H., 21, 22
Elliger, K., 48
Ellis, E. E., 165
Evans, C. A., 66, 222, 224, 225

Filbeck, D., 223
Finn, T., 195
Fitzmyer, J. A., 43, 117
Flemming, D., 228, 231
Forseth, P., 61
Fox, R. L., 167
Furnish, V. P., 144, 145

Gehring, R. W., 171
Gese, H., 27, 29
Gill, D. W., 167, 175
Gnilka, J., 164
Goheen, M. W., 43, 44, 216, 220, 231
Goldingay, J., 55
Goodall, N., 212
Goodman, M., 193
Goppelt, L. A., 192
Goulder, M. D., 109, 195
Green, J. B., 43, 97, 209-11
Gundry, R. H., 85

Haenchen, E., 110
Hagner, D. A., 60
Hahn, F., 139
Halfmann, H., 167
Hall, D. J., 42, 62, 229, 230
Hamel, G. H., 75, 83

Hanson, P. D., 53
Harris, G. R., 66, 71
Hartenstein, K., 212
Hawthorne, G. F., 183
Hays, R. B., 177
Hemer, C. J., 155
Hengel, M., 175, 177
Herford, R. T., 193, 204
Hofius, O., 175
Hogg, A. G., 220
Holtz, T., 141
Howard, J. D. M., 27
Hübner, H., 164
Hughes, P. E., 145, 146
Hurtado, L. W., 175
Hutchison, W. R., 211

Irwin, B., 228, 230

Jacquet, L., 27
Jeremias, J., 75
Jervell, J., 129
Jewett, R., 150
Johnson, L. T., 43
Jongeneel, J., 213

Käsemann, E., 170
Kaiser, W. C., 23, 26, 223
Kammler, H.-C., 174
Kee, H. C., 129
Keener, C. S., 85
Kidner, D., 28
Kijne, J. J., 145
Kim, S., 143
Kim, T. H., 66
Kissane, E. J., 28
Knowles, M., 212-14
Köstenberger, A. K., 110, 140, 188, 203, 214, 223, 225, 228
Kraemer, H., 220
Kraus, H. J., 15, 20, 26-28, 37, 38, 223
Kreitzer, L. J., 175
Kreml, P. B., 61

Kruse, C. G., 181
Kupp, D. D., 78, 85

Lane, W. L., 192
Langevin, P.-E., 141
Lash, N., 210, 231
LeGrand, L., 210, 224
Lieu, J. M., 191, 195, 202
Lightfoot, J. B., 164
Lipinski, E., 33
Litfin, D., 156
Lohfink, N., 27
Lohse, E., 164
Longman, T., 36
Luz, U., 84

MacLean, M. S., 175
Manson, T. W., 83
Marcus, J., 67, 71, 72, 75
Marshall, I. H., 43, 144, 147, 192, 196, 198, 199
Martin, R., 141, 144
Martin-Achard, R., 26
Martín-Asensio, G., 128, 129
Mays, J. L., 27, 32
McCann, J. C., 26, 27, 32
McCann, N. R., 26, 27, 32
McDonald, L. M., 108, 121, 124, 191, 192
McGinn, A., 17
McHugh, J., 194
McIver, R. K., 75
McKay, J. W., 28
Mealand, D. L., 70, 83
Mendenhall, G. E., 44
Menken, M. J. J., 14
Meyer, H. A. W., 146
Michel, O., 183
Miller, P. D., 27, 31
Mitchell, S., 167, 169
Moessner, D. P., 129
Moltmann, J., 216
Moore, T. S., 225
Morgenstern, J., 17

Mowery, R. L., 66
Mowinckel, S., 28, 29
Moyise, S., 14
Mullen, E. T., 17
Murphy-O'Connor, J., 148
Myers, B. L., 222

Nasuti, H. P., 27
Newbigin, L., 215–18, 220, 222, 227, 230
Nissen, J., 221, 228
Nobbs, A., 167

Oakman, D. E., 75
O'Brien, P. T., 110, 140, 164, 188, 203, 214, 223, 225, 228

Padberg, L. E. von, 170
Pao, D. W., 93
Patzia, A. G., 204
Peterson, J. C., 83
Plummer, A., 144
Plummer, R. L., 135–37, 139–41, 214
Pogoloff, S. M., 156
Pokorný, P., 164
Porter, S. E., 108, 121, 124, 126–30, 136, 142, 143, 145–47, 150, 151, 191, 192, 214, 215, 217, 218, 220–22, 226
Powell, M. A., 108
Puech, É., 106

Rackham, R. B., 129
Rahlfs, A., 48
Rajak, T., 195
Ramsay, W., 123, 168
Rapske, B. M., 177
Reck, R., 175, 176
Reinbold, W., 169, 170
Reynolds, J., 195
Ridderbos, H., 219, 220
Riedel, L. T. W., 28–30
Riesner, R., 162, 167, 177
Robinson, J. M., 72, 89

Rogerson, J. W., 28
Roloff, J., 128
Rowland, C., 200
Rowley, H. H., 223
Rudolph, W., 48
Ryken, L., 36
Rzepkowski, H., 223, 225, 226

Sahlin, H., 110
Sanders, J. A., 93
Sanders, J. T., 110
Schnabel, E. J., 68, 84, 109, 114, 115, 139, 140, 155, 158, 177, 179, 190, 219, 221
Schneider, G., 128
Schrage, W., 158
Schreiber, S., 177
Schüssler Fiorenza, E., 209
Schweizer, E., 83, 164
Schwemer, A. M., 177
Scott, J. M., 163
Seccombe, D. P., 93
Senior, D., 223, 228
Setzer, C. J., 179
Shannon, C. E., 175
Shanor, J., 157
Sheppard, G. T., 32
Smith, D. M., 198
Smith, M. S., 27
Soards, M., 231, 232
Squires, J. T., 128
Stanley, C. D., 177
Stenschke, C. W., 181
Stuhlmacher, P., 182
Stuhlmueller, C., 223, 228

Tannehill, R. C., 113
Tannenbaum, R., 195
Tate, M. E., 17
Taylor, V., 83
Thornton, C.-J., 108, 155
Thrall, M., 144–46, 160, 176
Tiede, D. L., 93
Tolbert, M., 73, 75

Twelftree, G. H., 177
Tyson, J. B., 179

Vallée, G., 205
van der Horst, P. W., 130
van Unnik, W. C., 110
VanGemeren, W. A., 17
Vicedom, G., 224, 226, 227
Voss, F., 174

Wagner, J. R., 161
Walters, S. D., 45
Watts, R. E., 71
Weaver, W., 175
Webster, J., 65, 66
Weinfeld, M., 44
Weiser, A., 28
Westermann, C., 28, 30
Westfall, C. L., 192, 197, 199, 200, 211, 214, 215, 218, 220–22, 224, 226, 228
Westley, B. H., 175
Whybray, R. N., 27
Wilckens, U., 169
Wilcox, M., 126
Wilhoit, J. C., 36
Willis, J. T., 32, 33
Wilson, G. H., 27, 31-33, 44
Windisch, H., 146
Winter, B. W., 130, 155, 156, 172
Witherington, B. III, 131
Wolff, C., 144, 146
Wolter, M., 150, 164
Wright, C. J. H., 211, 212, 223, 226, 232
Wright, N. T., 66, 85
Wuellner, W., 67

Zenger, E., 17, 18, 24, 25, 27, 29, 33, 34

Ancient Sources Index

OLD TESTAMENT

Genesis

1–11	37
3–11	223
10:22	164
12:1–3	24, 37, 223, 224
17:19	97
18:18–19	224

Exodus

12:11	71
15	16
15:3	16
15:18	16
18:21	72
18:25	72
19:4–6	37, 223, 224
19:6	44
25:3	84
31:4	84
35:5	84
35:32	84

Numbers

6:1–3	97
6:24–26	23
31:22	84

Deuteronomy

1:15	72
8:2–4	71
17:14–20	33
19:15	83
25:4	89
29:5–6	71
32:8	19

Joshua

1:3	83
6:19	84
6:24	84

Judges

13:2–21	97

2 Samuel

7:12–16	97
8:15	16
12:5–6	16
14:4–20	16

1 Kings

3:28	16
17:1–16	100

2 Kings

5:1–14	100
8:10	84

1 Chronicles

1:1	37
22:14–16	84
29:2	84

2 Chronicles

2:6	84
2:14	84

Job

36:1	86

Psalms

1–89	34
1–41	27
1–2	32–36
1	31, 33
1:1	32, 33
1:2	32
1:6	32
2–89	33
2	15, 16, 18, 20, 31, 33, 35, 38
2:1–6	31
2:1	18, 32
2:3	18
2:4	32
2:7	18, 32, 129
2:8	31
2:9	31
2:10–12	24, 31
2:10	33
2:11–12	18
2:12	20, 32
2:12b	31, 33
7	20
7:6–11	17
7:6–8	20
7:7–8	16, 17
7:11	20
8	18
8:1	18
8:6	18
8:9	18
9–10	32
9	20, 21, 32
9:8	38
9:11	21, 22
9:17	21
9:19–20	17
10	20, 32
10:16	16
10:17–18	16
14:1ff.	38
16:8–11	102
17:10	129
18	20, 21
18:43–44	18, 20
18:47–49	18, 21
18:49	38
19:4	38
19:5	161
22	24
22:27–29	24
22:27	14
22:28	15
32–33	32
32	32
33	18, 32
33:6–7	18
33:8	18, 24
33:9	18
33:10–11	20
33:10	18
33:13–15	18, 19
33:15	19
36:1	38
41	32, 33, 36
41:13	28, 29
42–72	27
44:11	25
44:17	25
45:5	18, 20
45:17	18
46	16, 20, 21, 23
46:4	19
46:9	15
46:10	21
47	24
47:1	22
47:2	15, 22
47:3	24
47:5	15
47:7	15
47:8–9	24
47:9	24
48	16, 20, 23

Psalms (cont.)

50:1–2	15
50:12	15
53:2	19
56	20
56:7	20
57:9	21
59	20
59:5	20
59:8	20
59:9	38
59:13	22
65:7	19
65:8	19
65:10	86
66:1–2	22
66:4	22
66:7	19, 20
67	22, 223
67:1	23, 223
67:2	22, 38
67:3–5	22, 23
67:6	23, 223
67:7	24
68:12	20
68:14	20
68:29	16
68:30–31	16
68:32	22
72	29, 32–34, 36
72:8–11	18
72:8	15
72:11	15
72:17	18, 24
72:18–19	28
72:18	28
72:19	28, 30, 31
73–89	27
75:4–5	36
76:11	16
77:14–15	21
77:14	21
78:43	21
78:55	21
79:1	25
79:5	25
79:6	20, 21
79:8	25
79:10	22, 23
80:8	21
81:10	21
82:1	17
82:8	15, 17
83	20
86:9	19, 22, 24
87	24
87:4	25
87:6	25
89	29, 30, 32, 34, 36
89:10	21
89:17	36
89:27	18
89:50–51	29
89:50	34
89:51	34
89:52	28
90–150	33
90–106	27, 36
92:10	36
93–100	17, 19, 22, 34
93	19
93:1	19
93:2	19
93:3–4	19
93:4	19
94	2, 10, 17, 20
96	22
96:1	22
96:2–3	22
96:5	19
96:7–9	24
96:7–8	22
96:9–10	19, 22
96:13	17, 38
97:1	22
97:5	15
97:6	23
97:8	34

Psalms (cont.)		117	22, 23, 26
97:9	17	117:1	38
98:2	22, 23	118:10–12	20
98:3	38, 94	126:1–3	23
98:4–6	22	132:17	36
98:9	17, 38	135	29
99:1–3	15, 22	135:1–3	29
99:2	34	135:8–12	21
99:9	34	135:19–21	29, 30
100:1	22	136–150	29
101–103	34	136:10–22	21
101:2	34	136:25	86
101:8	34	137	16
102:13	34	138–145	35
102:15–17	34	138–143	36
102:15	23, 24	138:4–5	22
102:21–22	16, 22, 34	140:3	38
102:22	24	144–145	32, 35
103:7–12	34	144	31, 35, 36
103:19	15, 19, 34	144:2	18, 20, 31, 35
104–106	34	144:5–6	35
104:27	86	144:7	19, 20, 31
105:1	21, 22	144:10–11	31
105:38	21	144:10	20
105:44	21	144:15	31
106	25, 29, 32, 34	145	30, 31, 35, 36
106:26–27	26	145:15	86
106:41	25, 26	145:20	31
106:47	26, 29	145:21	29–31, 35
106:48	28	146–150	29, 30, 32, 35
107–150	27	146–148	35
107	34	146	35, 36
108:3–4	21	146:3–4	17
108:7	15	146:7–9	17
110	18, 20, 35, 36	146:7	86
110:2	18	146:10	17
110:4	18	147	35–37
110:5–6	20	147:9	86
110:5	20	147:20	35
111:5	86	148	35, 37
111:6	21	148:1–6	35
112:9	36	148:7–13	35
113:4	15, 19	148:11–12	35
115:2	23	148:11	22

Psalms (cont.)

148:14	36
149	20, 36, 37
149:2	20
149:6–7	20
149:9	20
150	29, 36, 37
150:6	22

Isaiah

2:2–3	102
6:1	97
7:14	97
9:1–2	95
9:6–7	97
9:7	16
11:1–5	16
14:28	97
16:5	16
32:1	16
35	60
35:5–6	60
40–66	224
40–55	71
40:1	95, 107
40:3	94, 98, 101
40:4	99
40:5	95, 98–101
40:10	99
41:8–9	94
42:1–7	16
42:6	96, 102, 224
43:10	102
43:12	102
44:3	102
44:8	102
46:13	96
48:1–2	225
49:1–6	225
49:6	96, 102–5, 162
49:9–11	39
49:13	95
50:2	39
51:5	39
51:9	39
52:7–10	39
52:7	39, 160, 161
52:9	96
52:10	95, 96
52:13—53:12	39
53:1	39, 161
53:7–8	101
55:3	129
56:7	189
58:6	99, 100
58:8	94, 100
59:8	95
59:21	102
60:1–2	94, 95
60:17	84
61:1–3	16
61:1–2	99
61:1–2a	100
61:2	100
62:10	39
66:19	162, 163

Jeremiah

1:1	97
1:2	97
6:10	98
16:16	67
23:5	16
33:15	16

Ezekiel

29:21	36

Daniel

1–7	58, 59
1–6	45
1	48
1:5–7	48
1:5–6	48
1:9–10	48
1:9	48
1:21	48
2–6	50
2	48, 53

Daniel (cont.)

2:11	48, 49
2:20–21	49
2:21	48, 49, 53, 54
2:27–45	49
2:31–35	53
2:32–45	84
2:34	54
2:35	50, 59
2:36–45	50
2:44–45	50
2:44	53, 58
2:45	54
2:46–47	49
2:46	59
2:47	49
2:48–49	49
3	50, 58
3:1–23	50
3:15	58
3:24–27	50
3:28	50
3:29	50
3:30	50
4	52, 59
4:3	51
4:10	59
4:12	59
4:15b–17	51
4:17	51, 59
4:20	59
4:21	59
4:22	59
4:23	59
4:26	59
4:34–35	51
4:34	51
4:36b	52
4:37	51
5	52
5:4	84
5:18–21	52
5:22–24	52
5:23	84
5:29	52
5:30	52
6:25–27	53
6:26	59
6:28	53
7/8–12	45, 56, 57, 61
7	53, 57, 58
7:2–14	53
7:3	57
7:4	57
7:5	57
7:6	57
7:8	57
7:13–14	58
7:14	53
7:21	57
7:22	57
7:25	53, 54
8–12	54
8	54
8:11–12	54
8:12	54
8:13	55
8:25	54
9:3–19	54
9:17	55
9:24–27	55
9:26–27	58
10:1	55
10:4	55
10:13	55
10:20	55
11:3	55
11:4	55
11:5–13	55
11:14–19	55
11:16	55
11:20	55
11:21–45	55
11:21	55
11:28	55
11:31	55, 58
11:33	55
12:11	58

Ancient Sources Index

Hosea

6:2	102

Joel

2:28–32	102

Amos

9:11–12	105

Micah

7:20	94

Habakkuk

1:5	129

Malachi

3:1	98
4:5–6	97

APOCRYPHA

1 Esdras

8:54–60	84

2 Esdras

8:24–30	84

Judith

2:23	163

2 Maccabees

1:5	148
7:33	148
8:29	148

Wisdom of Solomon

16:20	86

Pseudepigrapha

1 Enoch

1:6–9	98, 99
1:6	99
1:8	97
1:9	99

Psalms of Solomon

8:15	103, 104
18:10	97

Testament of Levi

5:1	97

NEW TESTAMENT

Matthew

1:22–23	77
3:1–3	44
3:2	43, 78
3:3	98
3:8	85
4:8	81
4:17	43, 78
4:18–22	78
4:23	60, 80
5:2	80
5:3–4	99
5:10–12	87
5:35	81
5:45	76
6:9–13	43
6:9	44, 85
6:10–11	44
6:12	44
6:25	86
6:33	86
7:14	87
7:21	44
7:28–29	80
8:4	60, 78
8:5–13	60
8:11–12	189
8:11	60
8:34	78
9:27	60
9:35	60, 80
10	79
10:1–14	78
10:1–4	78
10:5–20	60

Matthew (cont.)

10:5–6	81, 189
10:7–8	80
10:7	78
10:8	89
10:9–10	82
10:9	84
10:10	82, 83
10:10b	89
10:13	86
10:14	80, 84, 86
10:15	87
10:16–31	86
10:16–23	87
10:17–20	60
10:17–18	89
10:18	80
10:22	89
10:23	60, 189
10:34–36	86
10:34	86
10:37–38	85
10:40	83, 85
11:1	80
11:2–6	60
11:2	81
11:5	60, 81, 99
11:12	82
11:20–24	81
12:6	84
12:8	84
13:31–32	59
13:33	59
13:36–43	58
13:44–46	58
13:47–50	58
13:50	58
13:52	58
13:53–58	81
13:54	80
14:12	80
14:14	78
15:24	189
15:31	78
16:19	87
17:1–13	50
17:14–16	81
17:20	81
18:16	80
18:18	87
18:20	77, 83, 85
19:2	78
21:12–13	85
21:23	80
22:8	86
22:15–22	60
22:33	80
22:41	80
23:7–10	80
23:37–39	81
24	57
24:1	80
24:5–7	57
24:9–14	57
24:9	87
24:14	80, 222
24:15	57
24:30	57
24:31	57
26:13	80
26:65	80
28:18–20	43, 83
28:18	77
28:19–20	111
28:19	81
28:20	77, 80, 81, 85

Mark

1:1	64, 70
1:2–3	98
1:4–8	44
1:4	69
1:7	69
1:14–15	64, 67, 70
1:14	69
1:15	78
1:16–20	64, 78
1:16–17	66

Mark (cont.)

1:16–17a	67
1:17b	67
1:18	68
1:20	68
1:21–22	80
1:38	69
1:39	69
1:45	69, 70, 78
2:2	73
2:13	78
2:14	68
3:12	70
3:13–19	64, 68, 78
3:14–15	68, 70
3:14	77, 78
3:15	69
3:31–35	68
4:1–2	78
4:13–19	78
4:14–15	73
4:17	74
4:19	74
4:20	74
4:26–29	75
4:27	76
4:31–32	76
4:33	73
4:40	76
5:18	68, 77
5:20	69, 70, 78
5:34	76
5:36	76
6	79
6:1–6	81, 99
6:2	80
6:6	80
6:7–13	64, 70
6:7–8	82
6:7	69, 70, 83
6:8–11	70, 78
6:8–9	71
6:8	84
6:9	70
6:10–11	72
6:11	80, 84
6:12–13	73
6:12	70, 78
6:13	69, 80
6:30	70, 73, 80
6:31	72
6:34	78
6:35–44	72
6:37	72
6:40	72
7:36	69, 70, 78
8:1–10	72
8:2	68
8:4	72
8:14–21	72
8:22–26	73
8:27—10:45	75
8:27—9:29	73
8:27	64
8:31	73, 78
8:32–33	73
8:34–35	76
8:38	74
9:2–13	50
9:2	68, 77
9:14–29	69, 74
9:14–17	81
9:23–24	76
9:29	81
9:30–10:31	73
9:31	73, 78
10:1	78
10:21–22	74
10:23–25	74
10:28	74
10:30	74
10:32–45	73
10:33–34	73
10:46–52	73
10:52	76
11:15–17	85
11:17	78, 189
11:22–24	76

Mark (cont.)

11:27	80
12:13–37	71
12:27	80
12:35	78, 80
12:41–44	74
13:9	89
13:10	70
13:19	74
13:24	74
14:6–9	69
14:9	70
14:10–11	74
14:18–20	68
14:33	77
14:36	74
14:38	74
14:49	80
14:50	74
14:66–72	74
14:67	68

Luke

1–2	97
1:1–4	111
1:1	111
1:4–8	109
1:4	115
1:14–17	96, 97
1:32–33	96, 97
1:35	96, 97
1:46–55	94
1:54–55	94
1:67–79	94
1:76	94, 101
1:78–79	94, 100, 105
1:78	94
1:79	95
1:80	98
2:14	96, 97
2:25	95
2:26	100
2:29–32	94
2:30–32	105
2:30–31	95, 98
2:30	100
2:32	96, 98, 102–104
2:34–35	94
2:38	96
3:1–2	97
3:3–6	44
3:4–6	98
3:6	98, 101
3:8	85
4:16–30	99
4:18–19	99
4:25–26	100
4:27	100
4:28	100
6:12–16	111
6:20	99
7:22	99
9:1–2	109, 111
9:2	60
9:3	82
9:11	60
9:28–36	50
9:52–55	87
10:1–9	87
10:1	111
10:7	89
10:9	60
10:10–12	87
10:13–15	87
11:2–4	43
13:29	189
14:21	86
14:26–27	86
17:20–21	44
19:1	43
19:11–27	43
19:11	43
24	101
24:25–27	101
24:26	14
24:27	14
24:44–49	14, 101, 225
24:44–47	105

Luke (cont.)

24:44	13, 14
24:46–48	101, 46–48, 111
24:46–47	14, 38
24:47	103
24:48–49	109
24:48	102, 111
24:49	113

John

1:14	85
1:31	44
3:16	196
3:19–21	196
3:36	196
4:1–42	194
5:17	76
5:24	196
8:12	196
9:4–5	196
10:16	199
11:9–10	196
12:35–36	196
12:46	196
13:1–20	85
13:34–35	199
15:12–13	199
15:17	199
16:8–11	203
18:36	82

Acts

1	101
1:1–2	108, 111
1:1	70
1:4–5	113
1:4	113
1:8	102–4, 110, 111, 113, 119, 121, 222
1:21–22	111
2	114, 194
2:4	113
2:5–12	114, 116
2:5	114
2:16–21	102
2:22	128
2:27	102
2:29–32	102
2:38–39	113
3–5	194
3:12	128
4:25–26	38
5:35	128
6	112
6:9	112
7	115, 119
7:2–50	128
7:58	120
7:59—8:8	189
8	113, 120
8:1–31	117
8:1–4	116
8:1	115, 116, 119, 120
8:3	120
8:4–8	116, 189
8:4	116, 194
8:14	114
8:20	89
8:25	114
8:26–40	116, 189
8:32—11:18	117
8:32–33	101
9–11	117, 119, 124
9	120
9:1–31	118
9:1–19	112
9:1–9	120
9:3	103
9:15–16	118
9:15	104
9:17	113
9:28–30	118
9:31–32	114
9:32—10:48	114, 190
10:1—11:18	114
10	113, 120, 189
10:1–48	117
10:1–47	118

Acts (cont.)

10:2	126, 195
10:22	126, 195
10:35	126, 195
10:44–45	113
10:45	104
10:47	113
11:1–3	118
11:1	104
11:4–17	117
11:15–17	113
11:18	104, 119
11:19–30	189
11:19–29	117
11:19–24	114
11:19	116
11:20–21	116
11:22–24	116
11:22	120
11:25–26	116
11:25	120
11:30	120
12	115
12:3–17	190
12:17	114, 115
12:25	120
13:2–3	218
13:2	120, 121
13:4—14:28	121
13:5	124
13:6–12	166
13:7	125, 180
13:8–11	125
13:12	167, 177, 180
13:14–15	172
13:15	124
13:16–41	124, 128, 136, 140
13:16	126, 128, 195
13:23	131
13:26	126, 128, 195
13:30	131
13:32	129, 131
13:33	32, 129, 131
13:34	129, 131
13:35	102, 129, 131
13:38	128, 182
13:41	131
13:42	121
13:43	121, 126, 180
13:46–47	104
13:46	103, 125
13:47	103, 225
13:48–49	166
13:48	104, 125, 180
13:49	125, 166, 180
13:50	125, 167, 168
13:51	89
13:52	180
14:1	124, 180
14:2	125
14:4	109
14:8	126
14:11–13	180
14:12	126
14:14	109, 121
14:15–17	129, 136
14:15	131
14:17	131
14:19	126
14:21	180
14:27	104
15	113, 114, 119, 190, 204
15:5	194
15:7–11	117
15:12	104
15:14–21	109
15:15–18	105
15:19–20	118
15:19	104
15:29	118
15:36—18:22	121
15:36–41	108
16:6	164
16:7–8	165
16:8–10	194
16:9	165
16:12–40	122
16:13	124, 172

Acts (cont.)		18:19	124
16:14	126, 179, 180	18:23—21:17	122
16:16–19	180	18:31	167
16:17	125	19	113, 164
16:18	125	19:1–41	122
16:19–34	60	19:1–7	196
16:20–21	180	19:6	113
16:22–23	180	19:8	124
16:23	125	19:9	125
16:32	125	19:12	177
16:33–34	180	19:17	180
16:34	180	19:18	180
16:37–38	177	19:23–27	180
17:1	124	19:29–34	180
17:2	124, 172	19:35–40	180
17:4	126, 167, 180	20:1–2	122
17:5	125	20:2–3	122
17:7	172	20:3–6	122
17:10	124	20:7	172
17:12	124, 167, 180	20:13–38	122
17:13	125	20:18–35	127
17:15–34	122	20:21	182
17:16–33	196	20:33	89
17:17	124, 126, 169	21	204
17:18–20	180	21:17	105
17:22–31	136	21:18	109
17:24–29	131	21:19	105
17:27	131	21:20	114
17:30–32	131	21:25	118
17:30	182	21:28	128
17:31	37, 131	22:1–21	127
17:32	180	22:3–16	112
17:34	180	22:3	177
18:1–18	122	22:6	103
18:2	157	22:9	103
18:4	124, 172, 180	22:11	104
18:6	89, 125	22:15	112
18:7	125, 126, 180	22:21	104
18:8	180	22:25–29	177
18:11	157	23:27	177
18:12	157	24:10–21	127
18:14–25	190	24:24	180
18:14–16	180	24:25	180
18:19–21	121	24:27	167

Acts (cont.)

25:9	167
25:10–11	177
25:25	180
25:31	180
26:2–23	127
26:12–18	112
26:13	104
26:16	112
26:17–18	104
26:18	182
26:20	182
26:22–23	105
26:28	182
27:1—28:15	123
28:14	103, 123
28:17–20	127
28:19	177
28:28	38, 103
28:30–31	123

Romans

1	140
1:1–2	140
1:1	140
1:3–4	140
1:5	140
1:14	156, 168
1:15	122
1:15–16	140
1:15	137
1:16–17	140
1:16	123, 124
1:18–32	131
1:18	150
2:9	124
2:10	124
2:22	170
3	140
3:7–8	181
3:10–18	38
3:18	38
3:21–26	140
5:1	150
5:9–11	150
5:9	151
5:11	150
5:21	150
8:18	183
8:22	183
8:31–39	183
9–11	124
10:9	182
10:14–21	156, 160
10:14–17	176
10:14–15	160
10:15	38, 137
10:16	161
10:17	161, 176
10:18	38, 161
13	231
13:48	183
14:52	183
15:9	38
15:11	38
15:14–21	164
15:15–21	156, 161, 219
15:17	162
15:18	162
15:19–23	139
15:19	123, 163
15:20–21	162, 177, 219
15:20	137, 162
15:22–24	163
15:23–28	123, 165
15:23	117
15:24	123
15:28–29	163
16:34	183

1 Corinthians

1:17	138
1:18—2:5	157, 172
1:18–23	181
1:23	157, 174, 180–82
1:26ff.	169
1:26–30	182
2:1–5	173, 176

1 Corinthians (cont.)

2:1–2	171
2:1	172, 174
2:2	157, 175, 177
2:4	173, 174, 182
2:5	173, 174
2:14	181
2:17	178
3:5	156
3:6–9	156
3:6	157, 219
3:7	157
3:7a	157
3:8	157
3:8b	158
3:9b	158
3:10–15	156
3:10	157, 219
3:11	157
3:12–15	158
3:16	157, 219
3:19	181
4:11–12	177
4:16	138
5	178
6:9–11	183
7:12–16	138
8–10	159
9:3–12	89
9:5	114, 190
9:6–18	177
9:9	89
9:13–23	156
9:14	89
9:16	138
9:18	89, 138
9:19–23	158
9:19	158
9:20	159
9:20a	159
9:20b	159
9:21	159
9:22	159
9:23	159
9:24	158
11:1	138
14:23–25	139
15:1–11	156
15:1	138
15:2	138
15:9–10	90
16:8–9	171

2 Corinthians

2:12	171
2:14–16	156
2:14	145
3:1–3	177
3:16	182
4:7–15	156, 160
4:7b	160
4:10	160
4:15	160
5:1–10	142
5:11–21	142
5:11	142
5:14–15	142
5:17	142, 149
5:18—6:2	141
5:18–21	188
5:18–20	148, 176
5:18–19	145
5:18	142, 144–46, 148, 149
5:18b	145
5:19	142, 144–46, 148, 149
5:19b	145
5:20–21	142, 145
5:20	141, 143–45, 147, 148, 176
5:20a	143
5:20b	143, 145
5:20cd	143
5:20c	146
5:20d	146
5:21	143, 146, 147
6:1	142
6:3–10	203
6:5	177

2 Corinthians (cont.)

10:16	138
11:7–10	177
11:7	138
11:23–29	177
11:24	169, 181
11:26	181
11:30–33	181
11:32	164
12:11–12	115, 177

Galatians

1:6–9	194
1:8–9	138
1:11	138
1:13–24	181
1:16	123, 138
1:17	164
1:19	190
1:23	138
2:2	123, 195
2:6–9	195
2:7–8	109
2:7	118, 164, 189, 194, 196
2:9	190
2:11–14	194
2:11	114
2:12	191
2:15–21	181
2:16	182
3:8	123
4:9	182
4:13	138, 168
4:14	171
4:29	181
5:11	181
6:15	149

Ephesians

2:14	151
2:16	151
2:17	138
3:8	138
6:15	138

Philippians

1:12–18	138
1:27	220
3:4–8	181
3:10	203
3:15	203

Colossians

1:7	164
1:10	220
1:20	150, 151
1:22	150, 151
1:24–29	156
1:24	203
4:3	171

1 Thessalonians

1:4—3:10	177
1:5–6	183
1:5	182
1:9–10	141, 177
1:9	171, 182
2:2	178
2:9	177
2:13	176
2:15–16	181

1 Timothy

1:3	123
1:5	123
5:18	89

2 Timothy

4:6–8	115
4:8	158
4:13	123
4:16	115
4:19	123

Titus

1:5	165
3:12	123

Hebrews

2:14–15	192
3–4	200
4:1	200
4:11	200
6:1–12	200
6:1–2	200
8–10	200
10:24–25	200
10:26–39	200
10:32–35	192
11	192, 199, 200, 205
12	199
12:1–17	200
12:1–4	192
12:18–29	200
13:3	192
13:11–13	192
13:12	205

James

2:1–17	191
2:14–26	191, 197
2:18–19	201
5:1–6	191
5:7–11	191

1 Peter

1:1	190
1:6	191
1:14	195
1:15–16	201
1:18	195
2:1–10	199
2:9–10	195
2:9	199, 224
2:25	195
3:1–2	201, 202
3:6	195
3:9	203
3:13–18	202
3:13–17	191
3:15–16	202
3:15	202
3:18	202, 203
4:3–4	195
4:3	195
4:6	202
4:12–19	192
4:12	203
4:13	202
4:17	199
5:2–4	199
5:9	192

2 Peter

3:9	196

1 John

1:1–3	192
1:5–10	201
2:18–28	192
2:18–19	192
2:22	199
3:4–10	201
3:10–24	199
3:23	199
4:2–3	192
4:2	199
4:7–21	199
4:15	199
5:1	199
5:5	199
5:6	192
5:10	199
5:12	199

2 John

7	192, 199

Jude

4	201

Revelation

1:3	201, 202
1:9	56
1:12–13	202
2–3	201
2:3	202

Revelation (cont.)

2:9–10	202
2:9	192
2:10	193
2:13	193, 202
5:9	228
6:9–11	202
6:9	193
7:1–8	196
7:9–17	202
7:9–16	196
7:9	228
7:10	203
11:3–13	228
11:3–12	202
11:7–12	202
11:15	188
13	57, 231
13:1	57
13:2	57
13:4	192
13:5–10	202
13:5	57
13:7	57
13:15–16	193
14:1–5	202
14:6	228
14:9–11	193
15:1–4	228
15:2	193
15:3–4	203
16:2	193
17:6	193
18:24	193
19:2	193
19:20	193
20:4	193, 202
21:3	228
21:24	197, 228
21:26	228
22:6–19	202
22:15	201
22:17	201, 203

DEAD SEA SCROLLS

4Q246	97
11Q13	100

RABBINIC WRITINGS

b. Berakot

62b	83

m. Baba Mezia

7.1	86

m. Berakot

9.5	83, 84

m. Shabbat

6.4	83
24.1	83

t. Berakot

7.19	83

y. Berakot

9.8	83

JOSEPHUS

Jewish War

2.1–100	43
2.124–125	85
7.47–62	81

GRECO-ROMAN WRITINGS

Aratus, *Phaenomena*

5	131

Aristides, *Oration*

51.29–34	173

Aristotle, *Rhetoric*

1.1.1356a	173

Homer, *Odyssey*

1.23	116

MAMA
(Monumenta Asiae Minoris Antiqua)

II 321	167
VII 319	167
VII 486	167

Sophocles, *Ajax*

743–744	148

Thucydides

1.22.1	127

EARLY CHRISTIAN WRITINGS

1 Clement

5:5–7	165
5:7	123

Acts of Peter

1	165

Didache

11:6	89
13:1–2	89

Eusebius, *Ecclesiastical History*

2.14.6	115

Irenaeus, *Against Heresies*

3.12.10	116

Justin, *Dialogue with Trypho*

47.4	195

Martyrdom of Polycarp

10:2	202
16:1	202

Muratorian Canon

35–39	165

Protevangelium of James

23:1–3	106
23:3	106

Lightning Source UK Ltd.
Milton Keynes UK
UKHW021834280121
377862UK00003B/192